DA
670
.C9
L8

THE WORTHIES OF CUMBERLAND.

THE HOWARDS.

REV. R. MATTHEWS,
JOHN ROOKE,
CAPTAIN JOSEPH HUDDART.

BY

HENRY LONSDALE, M.D.

ο. ε. μ.

LONDON:
GEORGE ROUTLEDGE AND SONS,
THE BROADWAY, LUDGATE.
1872.

PRINTED BY BALLANTYNE AND COMPANY
EDINBURGH AND LONDON

To

PHILIP HENRY HOWARD, Esq.,

of

CORBY CASTLE,

The worthy Son of a most worthy Sire,

This Volume

is inscribed

with the sincere good wishes

of the

AUTHOR.

PREFACE.

THE regular issue of the "Cumberland Worthies" has been interrupted for a time, owing to my being engaged on the scientific biographies of John Goodsir, the eminent Edinburgh Professor, and my no less eminent teacher and colleague, Robert Knox, the anatomist.

The Life of Dr John Heysham, published upwards of a year ago, would have formed part of the present series, had not his "Bills of Mortality," and other historical tables bearing upon Life Assurance, necessitated a *quarto* volume similar to that adopted for the illustrated biography of Musgrave Lewthwaite Watson.

In the present volume will be found a brief sketch of some of the Howard family whose lives and associations have been endeared to the people of Cumberland; also the Rev. R. Matthews of Wigton Hall; Mr John Rooke of Akehead; and Captain Joseph Huddart of Allonby.

Fresh research into the history of Lord William

Howard (*Belted Will* of Naworth) has elicited but few data in addition to those set forth in the "Memorials of the Howard Family," by the late Mr Henry Howard of Corby Castle; and perhaps there is little more for the reader to expect than a newer interpretation of the times and surroundings of the famed Border chieftain.

The "old Duke" of Norfolk ranked among the popular men of his day; and his timely political aid in the years 1780 and 1784, that rescued Carlisle from the hands of the feudal tyrant of the North, deserves honourable mention in these pages.

The estimate I have formed of Mr Henry Howard's qualities of mind is derived from his published writings, and a few letters and memoranda in the Corby archives, for the perusal of which I owe my cordial thanks to his son, my ever obliging and amiable friend, Mr P. H. Howard.

An entire volume would have been worthily occupied with the biography of George, the seventh Earl of Carlisle. He was the type of what an English Minister should be. He was graciously honoured by the Queen, and no less honoured by all men for his many excellent qualities of both head and heart.

The Rev. Richard Matthews cheered my early medical career, and oft conversed with me on subjects of public as well as personal interest. He was a rare type of a country gentleman, whom society, as well as intimate friends, would be disposed to designate nearly perfect in all things.

I had the opportunity of long walks, and equally long talks, with Mr Rooke after he had passed his meridian. Such experiences have enabled me to sketch his portraiture and proclivities. In reviewing his published works I have endeavoured to show the variety and breadth of the studies which so long engaged this remarkably self-taught man. His history should be considered along with that of Sir James Graham in a previous volume of this series—the able Minister's correspondence with Rooke throwing much light on the political economy and disquisitions of the Cumberland yeoman.

A memoir of the late Captain Huddart, published by his son Joseph in 1821, has furnished the principal facts of my narrative of the renowned Allonby sailor.

ROSE HILL, CARLISLE,
February 10th, 1872.

CONTENTS.

	PAGE
THE HOWARDS (INTRODUCTORY),	1
LORD WILLIAM HOWARD ("BELTED WILL" OF NAWORTH),	15
CHARLES, ELEVENTH DUKE OF NORFOLK,	57
HENRY HOWARD OF CORBY CASTLE,	65
MRS HOWARD,	122
GEORGE, SEVENTH EARL OF CARLISLE,	125
REV. RICHARD MATTHEWS, M.A.,	189
JOHN ROOKE,	201
CAPTAIN JOSEPH HUDDART,	293

THE HOWARDS.

"A theme of honour and renown,
A spur to valiant and magnanimous deeds."
—SHAKESPEARE.

THE noble House of Howard has stood for many centuries at the head of the English nobility. The initiative to this exalted position was ably commenced during the reign of the Great Plantagenet, and has been healthily sustained by succeeding generations to the present times; moreover, the English aristocracy, fondly cherishing a long ancestral line, and ever solicitous as to its purity, have, in the spirit of their order, been ready to recognize the claims of the Howards to the highest functions of the state.

Our national archives abundantly testify to the ability and action of the Howards, the record of whose lives forms no small constituent portion of the general history of living and modern England. For, great as have been their attainments, and high as is their nobility, they do not seem to have come with the marauding Normans; nay, it is quite as probable that they aided their Saxon brethren in repelling the aggressions of the Conqueror. In their earlier steps to fame and distinction, they were less prone than most men of their epoch to court the chivalry so exclusively attached to deeds of arms, but fought their way in the world as honourably and well under the banners of justice, enlightenment, and freedom. Their promotion among the patrician blood of England was not owing to the possession of feminine blandishments in their ranks—so apt to awaken the favouritism of courts; nor was it the result of any personal subserviency or successful political intrigue finding reward in the fitful bestowal of imperial patronage. Their rise in the world had nothing adventitious in its development and growth, nothing fortuitous in its advance and maturity. Large intrinsic merit and mental superiority brought them into favour; a thorough patriotism and magnanimity upheld them amid the contentions of political parties and the many vicissitudes of dynasties. Of the Howards it may be justly said, that six centuries of prominent official service have in nowise impaired either their excellence or their worth. Those who have studied history, and reflected on the contingencies and temptations besetting public men during the growth of England's greatness, may well be disposed to dwell upon the virtues of a family so little prone to personal aggrandisement, and ever so loyal and faithful to the best interests of the nation.

The Howards can be very distinctly traced to the transitional period that marked the dismemberment, if not the decadence and fall, of the social and political institutions of the Middle Ages, and the happy dawn of modern thought and a nobler civilization. The true founder of the family grew almost *pari passu* with the creative age of the thirteenth century—a century that rendered mighty service to public liberty in England, by casting off much that was worthless and effete, and giving birth to so much that was wholesome and new. Teutonic forms, Witenagemóts, and Great Councils, had no doubt helped to mould the plastic materials of a growing nationality; but these had had their day, and were getting antiquated and unfit instruments for the governance of the England of the future. New powers and fundamental principles were wanting to the State; a veritable parliament of the Simon de Montfort order, English statutes, English courts, and upright English officials. To aid in securing these great reforms in our constitution, Justice Sir William Howard came to the front—a man of learning, probity, and perseverance, whose legal attributes, and eminent co-operation with John de Mettingham and Ranulph de Heningham, under the direction of the famous Earl of Lincoln and Lord Chancellor Burnell, gave a halo to the reign of the Great Plantagenet. The time had come to put aside, and for ever, the domain of antiquaries and ecclesiastics, seeing that the professional corruptions and extortions, pictured in the chronicles of Henry III. as the result of judicial offices being held by bishops, deans, and other unscrupulous clericals, had well-nigh upset the workings of our *Magna Charta*, and destroyed all the nobler instincts of our national life.

In the modelling of our laws and institutions, and in the administration of justice by holding assizes * throughout the realm—a truly great legal reform—Sir William Howard took a fair share of work, and thus lent willing service to Edward I., the English Justinian, from whose reign the liberties of Englishmen may be said ostensibly to date. Thus the name of Howard is interwoven with the most promising period in our annals—the building up of the monarchy, and the framing of a constitutional government on a solid and popular basis. Sir William showed the promise of his family: his sons and grandsons followed in the wake of their honourable sire.† The *pur sang* of Justice Howard, allied with equal nobility of mind, continues to flow in the veins of his descendants to this day, as evidenced by their love of freedom, their loyal support to the crown, and their meritorious endeavours to uphold the principles of civil and religious liberty.

* There were ancient justices in eyre, *justicia rei in itinere*, previous to the establishment of the regular assizes of Edward the First; and to this class, or more probably the baronial judges, Robert de Vaux of Cumberland may have belonged in 1176—he who is traditionally said to have treacherously slain the rival Lord of Gillesland, and afterwards founded the Abbey of Lanercost in expiation of his crime.

† Sir John Howard, the grandson of the above-mentioned judge, was not only Admiral and Captain of the King's navy in the North of England, but Sheriff of Norfolk, in which county he held extensive property, which was subsequently increased by the marriage of his grandson, Sir Robert, with the co-heiress of the ancient and noble House of Mowbray, Dukes of Norfolk. Of the many honours conferred on various branches of the ducal House of Norfolk, it may suffice to say, that the "Howards either have enjoyed within the last three centuries, or still enjoy, the Earldoms of Carlisle, Suffolk, Berkshire, Northampton, Arundel, Wicklow, Norwich, and Effingham, and the Baronies of Bindon, Howard de Walden, Howard of Castle Rising, and Howard de Effingham."—*Chambers's Encyclop.*, vol. v. p. 442.

History recalls, in clear and unfeigned lines, the many grand achievements of the Howards. In times past, the chieftains of the race oft formed the theme, and as oft obtained the lofty praise, of the Western courts of Europe. In these latter days, they live, as of yore, to win golden opinions from all sorts and conditions of men. The patrician holds them in esteem for their honourable deeds and high graciousness; the plebeian speaks of them with reverence, and in a language only due to men of superior caste; and everywhere they are laudably instanced as representative leaders of a free and safe government. They enjoy the popularity due to public men for their consistency and integrity; in private life they are loved for their homely virtues, their high breeding, courtesy, and philanthropy.

Whence the name and the family of the Howards? Opinion is divided as to the time when our Saxon ancestors first assumed names. Perhaps they borrowed the mode of the Norman invaders, and that was varied enough. He who gained a holding of land thereby got a name; indeed, names and possessions were oft convertible terms, and are so to this day in the rural districts of Scotland. If habitations determined the landowner's name, the personal traits, physical or moral, afforded epithets to other members of society; so that, in eliciting the meaning of some English surnames, much is necessarily left to surmise and speculation. It was only when families had been founded or obtained fame that ancestors and archives claimed consideration, for with a vast majority the struggle for existence would be paramount to the question of birth and lineage.

There does not seem to be anything conclusively established as to the origin of the name Howard. It was variously spelt, as all names were in the olden times—Howard, Haward, Haeward, Howord, and occasionally with an *e* final, as in Belted Will Howard's signature— Howarde. In reference to genealogical matters, it is right to state that a very large quantity of coins (6500) were found at Beaworth, in Hampshire, in June 1833, of the reign of William the Conqueror and his successor, with the names of the monetarii, or mint-masters, on the reverses, in Saxon letters. Some of these mint-masters are the same persons that held office in the time of Edward the Confessor and of Harold. Among those struck at Norwich there are thirty-five with the monetarius of the name of Howord. This is the county in which the family resided, and though the individual cannot be pointed out, yet this may prove that they were Saxons. Coins and inscriptions may perhaps stand in lieu of chronicles and charters. The late Mr Howard of Corby, from whose "Memorials" this notice of the coins is borrowed, was disposed to look for the habitation of the Howards among the marshy parts of Norfolk and Lincolnshire, where Saxon families resorted for safety from the Normans. Similar opinions have been entertained as to the Howards being private gentlemen of small estate and Saxon origin, residing on the east coasts of England. This is further strengthened by a reference to "Domesday Book," where it is set forth that persons of the name of Hauuard and Hauuart held lands in Yorkshire as far back as the times of Edward the Confessor. Probably their residence along

Speculations as to their Origin.

the coast enabled the Howards to acquire their famed skill in nautical and military service. Be the explanation what it may, the Howards never failed to prove their valour both on sea and land, and on fitting occasions have rivalled the steady prowess of the Blakes and the Nelsons, and the bolder dash and daring of the Cochranes.

In this brief sketch of the Howards,* meant simply as an introduction to special members of the family, in whose history Cumberland takes sincere pleasure, much discussion would be entirely out of place. Speaking of the family generally, it may be said that neither names nor titles, nor many-century ancestral

---

* More than one speculation exists as to the historic Howards who lived antecedently to Sir William Howard, the great constitutional judge. *First*, That they sprang from the Earl of Passy in Normandy, who came to England with the Conqueror, and became Earl of Gloucester, and was slain at Cardiff. His kinsman, Roger Fitz-Valerine, wishing to revenge his death, took up arms against the Welsh, and possessed himself of the Castle of Howard, in Flintshire, where he so often secreted himself that it was named his "Denne, and to this day is called Howarden." [Is this the country residence, "Hawarden," of Mr W. E. Gladstone, the Prime Minister of England?] His son, born in the Welsh castle, got the name of William de Howard, from whom sprang Sir William Howard, the famous judge of the reign of Edward the First. *Secondly*, According to Mr Edmondson's tables, the patriarch of the illustrious House of Howard was Fulco, father of Galfridus, who had two sons, Alan and Humphrey. Alan was father of Sir William Howard of Wiggenhall, who had three sons; the oldest, John, succeeded to the estate of Wiggenhall, and by his wife Lucia, daughter to Germondi, was father of Sir William Howard above mentioned ("The Peerage of England," &c., by Arthur Collins, 4th ed. vol. i. pp. 48, 49, pub. in 1748). In confirmation of this origin, in a Deed preserved among the Norfolk House records, without date or arms, and, as Mr Howard considers, antecedent to the age of either, an ancestor of the Judge's styles himself Andreas Howard, but his seal is "Sigillum Andreæ de Wiggenhall," showing that names and possessions were at that time used convertibly.

lines, can measure with the broader aspects of honest worth, and the nobler aspirations that have guided the Howards in all stations of life.

A Saxon parentage is generally attributed to them; and as physical features are properly viewed as a characteristic guide to ethnological distinction, it is fair to presume that the Saxon element is stamped upon their bodily and mental constitution.* They have a fair complexion generally, blue eyes, and more or less florid aspect; the men, who are frequently tall and handsome, show a fine front and honest meaning; the women, cast in the finest mould of form, please by their beauteous expression of good-nature and gracious refinement, whilst they reflect the highest breeding of the *blonde* race. Be they Saxon, Scandinavian, Danish, or Teutonic in descent, the Howards of to-day are true Englishmen; they indicate the best blood; they exhibit the highest moral equivalent; and, happily for the entity of our aristocracy, have been productive of a long succession of high-minded men and nobly virtuous women. They are oft instanced as types of our grand nobility, and their family alliances are eagerly sought for by the highest of the land. They are spoken of everywhere—at home, in our colonies, and in the United States—as steady props of the old country, and Englishmen with blood of the true blue sort. That

* Though the Saxon blood be strong, and the characteristics mainly as stated in the text, some of the family, like Shakespeare's Jockey of Norfolk, show an Italian cast of countenance. Of this Howard, so well known in history, and so true to the loyalty of his lineage, it was said that he regarded more than his oath, his honour and promise made to King Richard, that "as he faithfully lived under him, so he manfully died with him."

blood has retained its purity through successive generations; it is fibrinous and rich, tenacious of life and health, yielding nerve and bone and muscle proportionately; it has also amalgamated freely with other families, to the genetic advantage of the Commonwealth.

Whether the pre-historic Howards were cultivators of their own land, sea-rovers, or military champions, at no time had they been wanting in that laudable self-esteem that covets distinction and eminence in the scale of social life. With a strong Saxon affinity, they aimed at a meritorious independence, and gained it honestly and well. Guided by their natural instincts, they uphold the representative principle, and abide by the people's privileges. Visible among the great men of the time, the Howards were no small factors in the political calculations of every Ministry. They had their stand by the side of the rulers of England, and naturally came under the influencing fortunes of the country at large. In season and out of season, they have ever been consistent advocates of national rights; they have also held by the true Conservative principle of respecting our time-honoured institutions. Having for centuries helped to build up the fabric of England's greatness, they wish it to stand like the gnarled oak of which English hearts are metaphorically said to be composed; and like good foresters, whilst lopping off the decaying branches, seek to nourish the roots in accordance with the dicta of healthful husbandry.

The mental proclivities of the family are good; they are also attractive and diversified. The resources of their moral power are great and lovingly exhibited. They have large hearts and broad sympathies; they are complacent, gracious, and winning; kind to the stranger, and much given to hospitality. Society is part of their being; and this very notable feature in English life they adorn by their classical and æsthetic culture, their unaffected good manners and polished conversation. Whilst holding in due respect their social status, a modest reserve guides all their opinions and actions. They show a thoughtfulness for others, a large generosity, and willingness to serve the interests of every class. Inspired by a genuine piety and the love that cherishes our neighbour's well-doing, and daily eschews every attitude of bigotry, both the Protestant and Catholic Howards have practised an exemplary Christian life. Their philanthropic labours are well known in both hemispheres, and their private charity, though little heard of in public prints, is largely bestowed.

In the administration of home affairs, in the venturesome paths of diplomacy abroad, in the capacity of heralds of war or glorious peace, or special representatives of English chivalry at foreign courts, the Howards have taken a creditable part; indeed, the Government of this country is seldom without one of their members; and if not always in the first rank of State direction, they have ever been the most reliable and trustworthy of counsellors. In the sterner paths of politics, they have, for one reign at least, been too diffident and vastly too amiable to brave the position their prudence and sagacity entitled them to. The coming generation, it is to be hoped, will show a fresh impetus of life, and prove a higher indoctrination of " all the blood of all the Howards."

The Howards have fought on many a battle-field, and in many naval encounters dear to English memories. They took the side of York in the Wars of the Roses. In the bitter conflicts which England waged with France and Spain, and in various parts of the globe, they fought like true Britons, and—

> "Ne'er called a halt nor made a stand,
> But cried—'St George for Merry England.'"

Ever in the van or thick of the fight, they have proved themselves thorough soldiers and sailors. In the days of the Plantagenets they occasionally fought a losing game, as at Bosworth Field;* but under all circumstances of victory or defeat, they were loyal to the cause they espoused. Their loyalty was often unrequited, and sometimes dishonoured, by tyrannical kings and revengeful queens. Brave, public-spirited, and devoted, their word of honour was their bond of service at all times, even when oaths were lightly

---

* Sir J. Howard, perhaps the most illustrious subject under three successive monarchs, was Duke of Norfolk, and created Earl Marshal of England by Richard the Third. He fell at Bosworth Field in the King's service. The opposing party, commanded by Henry, so esteemed Howard, that it is said they conveyed the following warning to him in his tent:—

> "Jockey of Norfolk, be not too bold,
> For Dickon, thy master, is bought and sold."

Sir John Beaumont, in his poem on Bosworth Field, makes the valiant Oxford, who had fought with Lord Howard in the early part of the day, thus deplore his antagonist's fate:—

> "Farewell, true knight, to whom no costly grave
> Can give due honour. Would my fear might save
> Those streams of blood, deserving to be spilt
> In better service. Had not Richard's guilt
> Such heavy weight upon his fortune laid,
> *Thy glorious virtues had his sinnes outweighed.*"

made, and too often lightly broken, by public men of the Tudor period. They have stood manfully by the helm amidst the dangers of the deep, as ready single-handed to meet a score of Spanish galleons as a solitary French or Dutch frigate. Wherever the Howard bent his course with topsails unfurled to the wind, he had but one thought, and that was to honour his flag and to serve his king and country.

In speaking of Thomas Howard, Earl of Surrey, the victorious general at Flodden Field, and created Duke of Norfolk by Henry the Eighth (February 1514), and endowed with various manors and privileges for his many and lasting services to the crown, the able and learned editors of the "Great Governing Families of England" thus express their estimate of the Howards up to that period:—

"The Howards had finally won the game. It had taken two generations of them to secure the position won originally by a marriage; and in the whole history of the English peerage there is no passage more brilliant than that struggle of seventy years. In an age of universal treachery, and with a stake at issue enough to crush any ordinary virtue, the two Howards deliberately preferred their honour as gentlemen to their position as nobles, flung titles and estates away rather than submit to a 'transaction' sanctioned by the example of a Stanley, and won back with the sword while defending England all they had lost by their fidelity to the house of York. Strangely enough, it was given to their house once more to play for the Tudors the part they had played for the Yorkists; and a Howard repaid the grace of Henry the Eighth by securing to his daughter her tottering throne. It was a Howard who won Flodden, a Howard who defeated the Armada; and to such services the blood of the Bohuns, the Mowbrays, or the Plantagenets can add nothing."

Lord Edmund Howard, the son of the famous Flodden Field Howard, and himself a prominent actor in the fight, was father of the unfortunate Queen Catherine Howard, whilst his sister Elizabeth, by marrying Sir Thomas Boleyn, became the mother of another of King Henry the Eighth's wives— Queen Anne Boleyn—and grandmother of Queen Elizabeth.

In art, in literature, and in scholarly attributes, the Howards have shone far above their compeers; and history points with high regard to one of its poetical chiefs—

> "Who has not heard of Surrey's fame?
> His was the hero's soul of fire,
> And his the bard's immortal name."

Not the less regretting his untimely end, the victim of a brutal tyranny, at the hands of one whom Sir Walter Raleigh aptly designated "the most merciless of princes in history."

However tempting the theme that treats of valiant and magnanimous deeds, the writer must adhere to his lines of brevity. Those who wish to study the Howards *in extenso*, may, in addition to the general works on English History, consult with advantage the "Peerage" by Arthur Collins, 1748; the grand folio volume, "The Memorials of the Howard Family," by the late Henry Howard of Corby Castle; and the modern and clever work, "The Great Governing Families of England," by Messrs Sandford and Townsend (Blackwood & Sons, 1865). These works, and more particularly the valuable folio of Mr Howard, have afforded the chief data of the historical sketch imperfectly rendered in the foregoing pages. The opinions hazarded by the writer on the family characteristics are derived from a careful study of the Howards personally as well as historically.

Keeping in view the title of this volume, the following names have been selected for special treatment and in chronological sequence:—Lord William Howard, the founder of the Cumberland family of Howards, and "Civiliser of the Borders;" Charles Howard of Greystoke, the jovial Duke of Norfolk and political reformer; Henry Howard of Corby Castle, "the fine old English gentleman;" and George William Frederick Howard, seventh Earl of Carlisle, the amiable scholar and high-minded and patriotic statesman of Victoria's reign.

for each other as well in point of numbers as in regard to sex: the Howard had three sons and one daughter; the Dacre had three daughters and one son.

Only a few words can be offered here relative to the noble house of Dacre, whose alliances with the families of De Vaux, De Multon, and others, belong to history. Dacre Castle, their original residence, was a place of note in early times, as Malmesbury records that King Athelstane there received the peace-making homage of Eugenius, King of Cumberland, and of Constantine, King of Scotland. This statement seems corroborated by there being in the castle, now a ruin, a room, called to this day the room of the three kings. After the Conquest, however, if not before, Dacre was a mesne manor, held of the Barons of Greystoke by military suit and service. The arms of the Dacres, the pilgrim's scallop, would seem to imply that they had taken part in the Crusades. "That they were men of high spirit and enterprise, and favourites of the ladies, there exists convincing evidence. Matilda, the great heiress of Gillesland, was by Randolph Dacre carried off from Warwick Castle, in the night-time, whilst she was Edward the Third's ward, and under the custody and care of Thomas de Beauchamp, a stout Earl of Warwick. Thomas Lord Dacre dashingly followed the example of his ancestor one hundred and seventy years afterwards by carrying off, also in the night-time, from Brougham Castle, Elizabeth of Greystoke, the heiress of his superior lord, who was also the King's (Henry VII.) ward, and in the custody of Henry Clifford, Earl of Cumberland, who probably intended to marry her.

None but the brave deserve the fair. These bold champions of love got well requited for their valour in securing "heiresses" of high degree, with the baronies of Gillesland, Greystoke, and Burgh, and numerous demesnes, constituting the largest holding of one family in Cumberland.

Thomas, the last Lord Dacre of the North, and grandson to the gallant Dacre who ran off with the Baroness of Greystoke, married Elizabeth, daughter of Sir James Leiburne of Cunswick, in Westmoreland, and died in 1566, leaving a widow and four infants—George, Ann, Mary, and Elizabeth. This son George, three years after his father's death, came to an untimely end by the fall of a "vaulting wooden horse" upon his head, and Mary died in her infancy; so the great inheritance of the Dacres came to be divided between the sisters Ann and Elizabeth.*

---

* Leonard Dacre, brother to Thomas Lord Dacre, and uncle to the two ladies Ann and Elizabeth mentioned in the text, being discontented at the inheritance of his family going to females, and having no hopes of success in disputing it by law with his nieces, forcibly possessed himself of the castles of Naworth and Greystoke, and fortified them; and there, under colour of defending his own and the Queen's interests, he gathered together a force of three thousand Borderers and others. His rebellious character being ascertained, Lord Hunsdon brought the Queen's garrison from Berwick-on-Tweed, and attacked Dacre about three miles distant from Naworth Castle, on a moor between Middle Gelt and Talkin, by the side of Helbeck, and defeated him. Considering his superior force, and the aid of a great number of ferocious women in the ranks, the Dacre made a poor stand. He fled into Scotland, and was soon afterwards attainted. The high repute of the Dacres caused Leonard's arming to be much dreaded by Lord Scrope, who, in writing to Lord Cecil on the danger to the Queen's interests on the Border, said—"Verie fewe will be founde to execute their forces against a *Dacre*." This Leonard had something wrong with his back, as Mary Queen of Scots used to call him, "Dacres with the croked bake."

Thomas, fourth Duke of Norfolk, was married in 1556 to the Lady Mary Fitzalan, who, having given birth to a son—Philip Earl of Arundel—on June 28, 1557, did not recover from her puerperal state. She died a few weeks afterwards—August 25, 1557. For his second wife, the Duke took the Lady Margaret Audley, by whom he had Lord Thomas Howard, created Earl of Suffolk; Lord William Howard, afterwards of Naworth; and Lady Margaret Howard, married to Robert Sackville, second Earl of Dorset. The Duke becoming a widower for the second time, and wishing to strengthen the family compact with the Dacres in his own person *immediately* as well as by his sons *prospectively*, married the widow of his friend Lord Thomas Dacre. The children of the two families were now brought up together under the same roof, and, it may be inferred, were made fully alive to the parts assigned them. The mother's care of her daughters and intended sons-in-law was of short duration, as the Duchess died the following year; but her sister, the Lady Monteagle, took charge of her nieces immediately after the Duchess's death, and lived in the Duke's house. This lady was a zealous Catholic, as well as all the Dacres.

The uxorious vein of Norfolk bled anew, and to conquer fresh worlds of love required but the wooing of a gallant Howard. His heart sympathised, as did the nation generally, with Mary, Scotland's "bonnie Queen;" moreover, a higher step than that of premier peer in a Tudor Court may have pleasantly loomed in the distance. But, whether moved by pity or ambition, he negotiated for the hand of Mary Queen of Scots. Now, of all the English aspirants to that hand, the Howard showed the most merit and the highest claim. He was next in rank to the Queen of England, and the most popular man in the kingdom, a person of unblemished honour and of unspotted loyalty. On May 1, 1565, after "long deliberation and argument" in the English Council of Queen Elizabeth, the Duke of Norfolk was one of the three candidates selected for Queen Mary's acceptance as a husband, "who would maintain the amity between the two nations." Had he caught the tide of his affairs at its flow, and joined his friends in the North of England, to whom Elizabeth's reign had become intolerable, the result of the rebellion of 1569 might have been productive of the most lasting and momentous effects on the destiny of the empire. Instead of responding to the injunctions of Queen Elizabeth, whose jealousy of her rival queen knew no bounds, he should have raised the Howard standard, around which the best blood of England would speedily have rallied. Backed as he was by the "most able, powerful, and influential of the nobility and gentry," he would have carried his project, saved Queen Mary's life and his own, and probably have married her with advantage to the country. With a Howard as King, and Queen Mary for consort—the Saxon gravity to counterpoise the overflowing Celtic warmth—the discords of the two countries might have been healed by the cementing of the national interests under one sceptre. But it is idle to speculate. Norfolk hesitated, lost his game, was committed to the Tower, and suffered the fate of being a servant of the bloody Tudors!*

* The Duke of Norfolk gave his parting advice to his son, the Earl of Arundel—meant also for Lord William, his brother—in the follow-

Philip Earl of Arundel, born in 1557, was betrothed to Ann, eldest daughter of the Lord Dacre, in 1559, and the marriage ceremony took place as early as 1571—probably hastened by the threatened doom of his father, the Duke of Norfolk. Though so young, the Earl, as head of the Norfolk house, was intrusted with the care of his brothers and sister.

Lord William Howard, the subject of this memoir, and known as "Belted Will Howard" of Naworth, was the third son of Thomas, fourth Duke of Nor-

ing terms:—" When God shall send you to those years as that it shall be fit for you to company with your wife, then I would wish you to withdraw yourself into some private dwelling of your own; and if your hap may be so good as you may so live without being called to higher degree, then shall you enjoy that blessed life which your woful father would fain have done, and never could be so happy. Beware of high degree! To a vainglorious, proud stomach it seemeth at the first sweet. Look into all chronicles, and you shall find that in the end it brings heaps of cares, toils in the state, and most commonly in the end utter overthrow. Look into the whole state of the nobility in times past, and into their state now, and then judge whether my letters be true or no. You may, by the grace of God, be a great deal richer and quieter in your low degree, wherein, once again, I wish you to continue. They may, that shall wish you the contrary, have a good meaning; but believe your father, who of love wishes you best, and with the mind that he is fully armed to God, who sees both states, both high and low, as it were even before his eyes. Beware of the Court, except it be to do your Prince service, and that as near as you can in the meanest degree; for that place hath no certainty. Either a man by following thereof hath too much worldly pomp, which in the end throws him down headlong, or else he liveth there unsatisfied, sith that he cannot attain to himself what he would, or else that he cannot do for his friends as his heart desireth. Remember these notes, and follow them; and then you, by God's help, shall reap the commodity of them in your last years," &c. As if forgetful of his own precepts of mightily forgiving his enemies, he commended his children to Lord Burleigh, to whom he mainly owed his iniquitous condemnation, and Lord Leicester, and others, which was but recommending the lambs to the care of the ravenous wolves.

folk, by the Lady Margaret Audley. He was born on December 19, 1563, and died at Naward (Naworth Castle) October 9 (?), 1640. His mother, Lady Margaret, as already stated, only survived his birth by twenty-one days. When he was nine years of age, he had to witness the horrid spectacle of the public execution of his father, who was beheaded on Tower Hill, August 25, 1572, for his unfortunate attachment to Mary Queen of Scots. This sad event deprived him of his title, dignity, and estate, and reduced him to the condition described by his father when placing him, before his death, under the care of his elder brother, Philip Earl of Arundel, as "having nothing to feed the cormorants withal." At an early age Lord William was betrothed to Lady Elizabeth Dacre, third daughter of Thomas Lord Dacre, and it was well for him "that on the death of the Duke of Norfolk, who was her guardian, she was not placed by the Queen as a ward to some other person, who would, according to the ungenerous usage of the times, have disposed of her hand to some relative. She appears to have been left to the care of her married sister, Ann Countess of Arundel, though she herself was scarce fifteen." The ceremony of their marriage took place on October 28, 1577, at Audley End, near Saffron Walden, in Essex (which belonged to his brother Thomas), when the bridegroom had not attained his fourteenth birthday, and the bride fell short of her thirteenth; so that their united ages would only make twenty-five years. For a time, however, they lived apart as infantiles.* Four years

* "A portrait of Lady Elizabeth, inscribed 1578, ætatis 14, shows the ring on her wedding-finger put down to the middle joint only, supposed

elapsed between their marriage and the birth of their first-born, Philip. Subsequently they had a large family of sons and daughters.

Lord William studied at Cambridge for a time, and there, probably, he imbibed those studious habits that never forsook him; there also, it is likely, he got indoctrinated with Roman Catholicism through one of his teachers, Mr Martin. England was more Catholic than Protestant at the time, but men's minds were selfishly influenced by the Court. A sincere piety, more or less seclusion, and much reading of "The Fathers," were almost sure to influence such a temperament as Lord William's in favour of the old religion.

The brothers Howard and their wives, the sisters Dacre, seemed to bid fair for the world's enjoyment, and restoration to the lands of their inheritance, if not the Queen's confidence, when, unfortunately, the religious element then disturbing England crossed the threshold of the Earl of Arundel and changed all. The Howards had been brought up as Protestants, nay, had John Foxe ("Book of Martyrs") for their religious adviser in their early days; and the Protestant faith guided the Earl of Arundel till he reached the age of twenty-seven years, when circumstances induced him to go over to the Catholics. This

---

to mean that she and her husband did not yet live together. She is dressed in a brown *just-au-corps*, embroidered wide-puffed sleeves, and petticoat, also braided, of a deeper nuance, laced handkerchief, and cap of lace put on in the fashion of Mary Queen of Scots, with a long double pearl necklace and brooch. On the ear-ring is the god of love in enamel; on her forehead, the letters D.G., referring probably to Dacre and Greystoke, to which she was heiress, and not then subdivided with her sister Ann, the Countess of Arundel."

change of opinion he confided to his brother, Lord William, who seemed (at twenty-one years) ripe to follow the same persuasion. History does not enlighten us as to the influence exercised by their Catholic wives. It was a bold step on the part of the brothers Howard, as the profession of Catholicism was truly hazardous during Elizabeth's reign. For men of high station to hoist the Papal standard was to hoist a broad target for the aim of every enemy's shaft, and to subject them to the charge of high treason: it was not like playing a game of probabilities in the political world, but a positive renouncement of all expectation of honour or glory in the State. They must necessarily lose the countenance of the Court, then so arbitrary and vile, and possibly bring their heads to the same block as their father's. Like their noble ancestors in blood, they were faithful men to whatever cause they espoused, and having cast their fortunes with the Catholics, they would hold by them throughout. Policy dictated their going abroad for a time, and Arundel would start first. The Queen got to hear of this; and as the Earl was about to take ship from a creek on the Sussex shore, upon which Littlehampton now stands, he was seized and conveyed to the Tower of London. Lord William soon afterwards shared the same fate. In less than a year, however, he was liberated; but the Earl, to obtain the same privilege of freedom, had to pay a fine of £10,000 to the Star Chamber! As Elizabeth's coffers were benefited by these Star Chamber fines, no wonder she was tempted to further persecutions and exactions from this nobleman, in a manner as tyrannical as it was unlawful. .

As troubles never come single-handed to poor mortals, a claimant to the Dacre estates, in Francis, uncle to the ladies Ann and Elizabeth, appeared in the courts of law in opposition to the Howards. The aspiring pretender took advantage of the adversity under which the husbands of the Lady Dacres were suffering, and circumstances also point to the hand of the Queen in the matter. The law's delays were bad; possibly the intrigues of the regal Court were worse, seeing that the Chancellor and Judges always decided in favour of the Lady Dacres and their husbands, but without any real benefit to the rightful heirs till the lapse of several years.

Lord William relates that the title of the Dacre inheritance was awarded to be tried on the right of presentation to a living—*de jure patronatus*. "Mr Fr. Dacre, not omitting his advantage of tyme, prosecuted his cause with great violence when both his adversaries wear close prisoners, in danger of their lives, and in so deep disgrace of the tyme, as scarce any friend or servant durst adventure to show themselves in their cause; nay, the counsellors at law refused to plead their title when they hadd been formerly reteyned. Frinds were made, and letters were written in favour of Mr Fr. Dacre; jurors chosen of his near kindred and professed frindes: *Sed magna est veritas*—for even that tryall passed for the co-heires."

After Lord William had been "enlarged out of the Tower," and his brother released, after having been fined £10,000 by the Star Chamber, they presented a petition to Lord Burleigh, claiming that the trials might proceed without delay. On St Peter's Day,

28 Eliz. (June 30, 1586), the cause being considered by the Lord Chancellor, Judges, and Queen's learned counsel, it was absolutely decided in favour of the co-heirs.

In his narrative, Lord William gave a minute account of the *chicanes* and pretexts for withholding their lands. It appears that before 1585, the estates had actually been divided between the two sisters, but of this partition they then got the shells only, whilst the oyster was kept by the Government. In 1588, the Earl of Arundel was again arrested, tried for his life in 1589, and condemned; and "Lord William again, upon a quarrel purposely pickt unto him, was kept close prisoner; but as soon as the office was found and returned, he was presently sett at libertye, soe as thearby the worlde may easily gesse the cause of his close imprisonment: thus was the Dacres lands gotten from them, and the Queen colorably possessed thereof."

During the confinement of the Earl of Arundel in the Tower, from 1589 till he died there in October 1595, as half the Dacre estate was forfeited during his life, it appears that this served as a plea for not restoring the other part to Lord William! Petitions for the right and title to his land were in vain; indeed, after the Earl of Arundel's death, his widow had to join with Lord William in this suit to recover her own estates and *her jointure*, and they were eventually compelled to purchase their own lands by letters-patent, dated December 19, anno 44, Eliz. R. (1601), for which they, according to Lady Arundel's Memoirs, paid £10,000.

" Thus it was that Lady Elizabeth Dacre, an orphan

and co-heiress to estates of great magnitude, before she was seven years of age, was kept out of possession till she had attained her thirty-seventh year. How she and her husband managed to subsist, and pay the high charges of such suits, does not clearly appear; but his accounts from the year 1619 to 1628 inclusive, show that he was still in debt, and paid 10 per cent. interest for it."*

Lord William and Lady Elizabeth lived for many years in a house in Enfield Chase, called Mount Pleasant, Middlesex, and there their children were born. He was restored in blood in 1603, and was in Cumberland the same year to meet King James on his entry into the kingdom.

Soon after the year 1604, it seems that the Lord Dacres of the South pulled down the castle of Kirkoswald and disposed of the materials, as Lord William Howard (who, according to Camden, began the repairs of Naward Castle in 1607) purchased the oak ceilings and wainscot work of the ancient hall and chapel of Kirkoswald, and applied them to the same uses at Naward; and as there are remains of the paintings of the window at Corby and elsewhere, it is probable that he also bought what remained of them. He seems to have effected considerable changes at Naworth by heightening the hall, enlarging its win-

---

* If the two Lady Dacres had a cruel uncle in Francis Dacre, their husbands had very malicious enemies in the Lowthers of Westmoreland, whose grasping covetousness knew no bounds. Lord W. Howard conquered them in a costly and most provoking litigation; he also exposed their baseness in good set terms; and exhorted his family for ever to avoid the race of Lowther. But this historical matter can be better discussed in the volume of "*Un*worthies," to be headed by Jerrard and Jemmy Lowther of well-known repute.

dows, repairing the Warden's Gallery, and converting dingy apartments into dwelling rooms. He applied the south-eastern angle of the fortress to his own special use—library, oratory, and bedrooms; and to-day this portion of the castle bears the name of "Belted Will's Tower." Whilst these reparations were being made in the old Border castle, Lord William and his lady and children lived at Thornthwaite, a favourite hunting-seat in Westmoreland, which he had bought from Sir Henry Curwen. In a few years he had gathered around him at Naworth his sons and daughters, and their wives and husbands —tradition says that the two generations made fifty-two in family! From that year Naworth got a name in history, due entirely to the bold energies of "Belted Will Howard," the founder of the family of Cumberland Howards.

If Ralph de Dacre, or the Lord Dacre, who married the heiress of Multon, selected Naworth for the erection of his stronghold or castle of defence, he showed due ingenuity, and a correct interpretation of the disturbed times along the Border. At Irthington, on the 27th July 1335, Edward III., who, on his way against the Scots, stayed at this famed castle, authorized his host, the Lord Dacre, to fortify and castellate "his mansion of Naward with walls of stone and lime, and to hold the same so fortified to himself and his heirs for ever." Irthington Castle was in those days an important stronghold; and under its towers King John, as well as the Edwards, his royal successors, had been hospitably entertained by the Dacres. When Naworth was receiving its crenellated or embattled mouldings, the more ancient

Irthington furnished some of the building materials for that purpose.

Naworth Castle is of quadrangular form, enclosing an extensive courtyard, and occupies a triangular piece of ground, bounded by deep ravines and rivulets, except on the south; and this, the only side on which it was accessible, is said to have been protected by a double moat and a barbican guarding the drawbridge, so that the external defences were everywhere made complete. At the angles of the south front, he raised lofty battlemented towers, from which, it may be supposed, the red beacon-fire oft blazed as a signal to the neighbouring hills. The castle well fulfilled the description—

> "When English lords and Scottish chiefs were foes,
> Stern on the angry confines Naworth rose;
> In dark woods islanded, its towers looked forth,
> And frowned defiance on the growling North."

Its interior arrangements were no less stern; its long warder's gallery, its many staircases, its few and narrow windows on the outer wall, and its dark dungeons, proclaimed the martial manners and barbaric usages that prevailed on the Border, when—

> "Lord Dacre's bill-men were at hand:
> A hardy race, on Irthing bred,
> With kirtles white and crosses red,
> Arrayed beneath the banner tall
> That streamed o'er Acre's conquered wall."

Ralph Dacre might well change his quarters from Irthington Castle for the forest slopes and rocky dells on the southern bank of the Irthing, a position commanding the grey pile and sombre cloisters of Lanercost Abbey, standing in peaceful solitude amid the fresh verdure of St Mary's Holme, and, at the same time, in sufficient proximity to the lawless districts of the Border-land. The wild chase might be another inducement to the Baron of Gillesland, for around Naworth portions of the primeval forest still remained, sheltering wolves and wild boars and red deer; nay, three centuries later, after the civilizing hand of Belted Will had been exercised, as in 1675, Sandford tells us there were at Naworth "pleasant woods and gardens; ground full of fallow dear, feed on all somer tyme; brave venison pasties, and great store of reed dear on the mountains, and white wild cattel with black ears only on the moores, and black heath-cockes, and brone more-cockes and their pootes."

On approaching Naworth from the town of Brampton, from which it is little more than two miles distant, you enter the park by the side of a deep dell, the banks of whose murmuring stream are well wooded; and on attaining the rising ground, you see the venerable Abbey of Lanercost below; the direction of the Roman wall, extending on the northern slopes of Irthing; and much of the broad barony of Gillesland, long held by the hardiest and most warlike houses of the Border. The road to the castle from "the Naworth Gates Station" leads you into the highest part of the park, commanding a large extent of pastoral and woodland scenery, the rich valley of Irthing, the elevated Bewcastle district, "the Debateable Land," stretching westwards to the Solway Frith, and the Border counties, backed by the Scottish hills. Southwards is the majestic range of Crossfell, and more westward the Lake mountains.

Over this expanse of country, to the north, where waste, dilapidation, and turbulence prevailed before the stern rule of "Belted Will," you now survey neat farmsteads, enjoying peace and homely plenty, and herds of cattle browsing and thriving unmolested. The knolled eminences, the undulating lines and surface of green, with dark masses of plantations, and all as varied as Nature herself, having a setting in the distant purple hills, affect the observer with an air of wildness and freedom. Moreover, from this

> "Land of brown heath and shaggy wood,
> Land of the mountain and the flood,"

the atmosphere rushes along fresh and free and fully oxygenised. Whilst enjoying the soul-and-body invigoration proceeding from an instinctive admiration of the scenery, your eye comes to rest upon Naworth and its "wood-environed towers."

The men of Cumberland point with pride to Naworth Castle, the most characteristic specimen of a feudal stronghold to be met with in England. The Castle of Naworth, built

> "In the antique age of bow and spear,
> And feudal rapine clothed in iron mail,"

stands unrivalled as a Border fortress. As a homestead, it testifies to the greatness of the Barons of old; its construction reflects the dynamic pith of its builders; its architectural lines are bold and grandly severe. The grey massive walls, the embrasured battlements, and lofty square towers breathe defence and defiance all round. The natural environs of the castle are no less apposite and impressive in character. Outside the safeguards which art has developed on level greensward, on declivitous steeps, in solitary grandeur, or in avenued lines, stand noble oaks as ancient as the days of Norman rule, beeches and other forest trees in full and lofty maturity. Then there are the deep dells shaded in the gloom of foliaged masses, echoing the sounds of falling waters, or the soughing of the winds so wild and dreary.

It is easy to fancy the Naworth of the past—

> " When, as the portals wide were flung,
> With stamping hoofs the pavement rung;
> And glistening through the hawthorn green
> Shone helm, and shield, and spear."

Before entering the castle, you pass along the road that covers the ancient moat,* under an embattled gateway, and recognise above its arch, amid mouldering armorial bearings, the motto, *Forte en loyaltie.* These words, "strong in loyalty," to whomsoever applied in days gone by, find a fitting response in the hearts of the present representatives of Naworth. From the courtyard you ascend to the grand hall, which in the olden time witnessed many a glorious meeting of the Dacres and the Howards, their kinsmen and guests.

> " And in the lofty arched hall
> Was spread the gorgeous festival.
> . . . . .
> Round go the flasks of ruddy wine
> From Bordeaux, Orleans, or the Rhine.
> Their tasks the busy servers ply,
> And all is mirth and revelry."

---

* The only vestige of the ancient moat, in close proximity to the curtain wall defending the southern front of the castle, that is now visible, forms part of the garden, and during the summer months is rich n the growth of strawberries and gay flowers.

The poetic mind, looking upon the family portraits, the quarterings, and other emblems of the historic Howards, will hardly fail to picture the festive scenes that used to grace this noble hall, where ladies fair of high degree and chivalrous lords and knights enjoyed the music and the dance; or, under the cover of shows and masques, told their little nothings, or gossiped askance, or, with more intent, breathed a clear articulate meaning in the language of love.

The rooms of "Belted Will," his study and oratory, the staircase that led him to the turret's watch above, or supposed to give him access to the dungeons below, divide the visitor's attention with the pictures, heraldic insignia, tapestry, armoury, and articles of vertu in the long gallery. No attempt is made in these pages to describe the old castle, nor would any description of the writer at all convey its topographical and majestic feudal character.

"It is remarkable," writes Sydney Gibson,[*] "that by an heiress, the heiress of De Vaux, Naworth passed to the family of De Multon; that by the heiress of Thomas de Multon, it came to the family of Dacre; and that by another heiress, the co-heiress of Thomas Lord Dacre, it was carried to Lord William Howard."

The castle that Lord William had rendered impregnable to the Scottish foe before 1640 remained as he left it for two centuries, till May 18, 1844, when a fire destroyed part of the baronial hall and chapel and gallery and domestic offices, &c.—a calamity felt far beyond the Howard circle, who suffered

[*] "Descriptive and Historical Notices of Northumbrian Castles, Churches, and Antiquities," p. 16.

this great loss; for did not the men of Cumberland look upon the ancient fortress as a portion of the historical honour of the county, obtained through the lasting achievements of the famous "Belted Will." Under the direction of George, seventh Earl of Carlisle, Naworth was restored, and pretty faithfully, on the old model of the castle. The Carlisle family make Naworth their summer residence.

Storm and strife had reigned along the Borders from the middle of the thirteenth century to the end of the seventeenth; nay, indications were not wanting of the old leaven at the advent of George the Third's reign.* The Plantagenets knew it well; the Tudors fought against it; yet there was no peace for the Stuarts in what James I. of England called the *middle* of his kingdom. A national, if not a blood or racial antagonism, existed among the Borderers; and that which times of bloody war might have sanctioned became a daily practice, in times of professed peace, among the denizens of a wild country ranging along both sides of the Roman Wall, that extends from the Tyne on the east, to the Solway Frith on the west coast. There was a general disregard of the rights of persons and of property; and robbery, violence, and encroachments constituted the social life of an extensive district. These Borderers levied *black mail,* or protection and forbearance money, in the unre-

---

* Having in a previous volume ("Life of Sir James Graham") described the character and doings of the sojourners on the Debateable Land, and given trite examples of their lawless lives, the writer must be careful not to trespass further on the patience of his Cumberland readers than the present requirements of this sketch of Lord William Howard demand.

lenting spirit of Spanish brigands; they plundered homesteads, and carried off cattle and sheep, showing as much rapacity as a merciless enemy spoiling a vanquished foe. Nothing portable escaped them, and all seizures were held valid that could be made to turn a spit, fill the kail-pot, or get shaped into bannocks and brose. The Laird of Gilnockie's (Johnnie Armstrong) argument with James V., when he sought to excuse his reiving habit, that it was only practised at the expense of the enemy on the southern side of the Esk, is fairly expressed in the ballad :—

> "Save a fat horse and a fair woman,
>   Twa bonny dogs to kill a deir;
> But England suld have found me meal and mault,
>   Gif I had lived this hundred yeir!
>
> "She suld have found me meal and mault,
>   And beef and mutton in a' plentie."

No wonder the canny lairds and farmers of Cumberland cried out for redress against the Gilnockie tribes o'er the Border, and often cried in vain. These Scottish miscreants cared nothing for the statutes of the Tudor or the windy proclamations of the Stuarts; they recognised no moral obligation; and only practised one religious form, that of counting their beads on their way to effect devil's work. What adepts they were in carrying off English beeves, and what a fine instinct they showed in ransacking the bishop's palace at "Rose," where sherries, venison pasties, and home-brewed were cellared in abundance!

These cattle-lifters knew every public and private road, crooked turning, and bridle-path; the fords and shallow places of the Eden and Irthing, Esk and

Liddel; the available sands in the estuary of the Solway Frith; the lone dales and mountain passes, and every channel of escape from Cumberland to the north. Hundreds of persons were employed as night-watchers of these miscreants; all the river waths had two watchers at least; Linstock had three, when the bishop lived at the castle close to the ford. Seen in daylight, these men wore a quiet, demure look, almost simplicity itself; at night they raised their eyebrows, and acted as if in league with the powers of darkness. As ordinary modes of pursuit failed, sleugh dogs, or bloodhounds, were kept in numerous parishes to hunt out these fellows in their resorts amid bog and morass, or other inaccessible lurking-places. Something more, however, was wanted — a ruler with a strong arm—to place these Borderers in subjection to the laws.

It is probable that Lord William Howard was first invested with the office of King's Lieutenant and Warden of the Western Marches on the death of George Earl of Cumberland, in 1605. Being so appointed, he, as a martial chieftain and political ruler, gave himself up to the diligent discharge of his official work. Aided by a commanding presence and lofty stature, he proved himself fit to lead and to make others follow; moreover, a noted vigilance secured obedience to his orders. Many nobles and knights had served as Wardens of these Marches, but none obtained such signal success as "Belted Will."[*] He held a firm and bold front, and never

[*] The Lord William Dacre, the son of Thomas Lord Dacre, who commanded the right wing of the English forces at Flodden Field (9th September 1514), was appointed Warden of the Western Marches by

swerved from his path of duty as a guardian of the interests of the Crown. With the characteristic allegiance of his race, he was determined to uphold the loyal, and to reform or crush the disloyal denizens of the district; to protect both life and property, and to make the standard of England the emblem of peace and order paramount over the whole of the Western Marches. Unlike the pedantic King James, for whom he acted, he was a man of deeds, active, earnest, and uncompromising. Where rascality was so prominent as along the Debateable Land, nothing less than the strong arm availed. It would, however, be wrong to suppose that martial law was his only practice; his rule was tempered by a judicial calmness becoming his authority and responsibility.

Nothing could more clearly indicate the need of a man of thorough capacity to put down the turbulent and offensive spirit prevailing on the Borders than the instance about to be cited. Lord William Howard, it is believed, met James V. of Scotland on his way to take possession of the English throne in 1603; and whilst the nobles of the land were welcoming their liege lord, intelligence was brought of grievous robberies and riots committed by a body of two or three hundred banditti of the West Marches, who had spread their ravages as far as Penrith, thirty miles south of the Scottish Borders.

Henry VIII., on 2d December 1527, and his name was unquestionably a name of terror to the outlaws and marauders of the Border lands. This Lord W. Dacre is said to have been buried at Lanercost, and it is possible that as a Lord William, he has been confounded with Lord William Howard. The Earl of Surrey, to whom Henry VI. confided the Middle and Eastern Marches, as his Lieutenant-General, also did right good service on the Borders.

Belted Will went the right way to work; he strengthened the approaches and ramparts of his castle, made his gates and dungeons secure, whilst he kept watch and ward from his high towers. He enrolled a hundred and forty good men and true in his service,* and with such a force he could scour the country around, ferret out the worst criminals, and waylay the night-foraging parties. Every unknown person had to give an account of himself; the roadside lounger was admonished to be up and doing, or risk a whipping; the thief was marched off to Carlisle; whilst those assembled in groups, who were bold enough to resist his rule, shared the fate due to rebels in the field—the point of the blade, the dungeons of Naworth, or the gibbet at Carlisle. At that period of our history, it may be observed criminals were subjected to a more decisive tribunal than the hap-hazard verdicts of the Cumberland juries of these latter days. It is well at all times that punishment should not lag far behind the commission of crime; and in those days of outlawry on the Borders, it was essential to make the punishment not only peremptory and severe, but often final. Imprisonment hardly touched the skin of these hardened wretches. The gallows was the only effective instrument; and however paradoxical it may appear, a

---

* His Naworth tenants probably held by suit and service to the Lord. A sword picked up years ago on the Naworth estate, and in the possession of Joseph Parker, of Brampton, has on its blade I * 4 ** which is supposed to imply that the owner of it held his land on condition of bringing one horseman and four foot-soldiers to the service of the Baron. On this matter, however, the writer can offer no satisfactory opinion. The sword is short, very handy, and with a slight curve in its blade.

timely use of the gallows saved hundreds of lives. The ringleaders and worst ruffians were the first to suffer from—

> "The cordis, baith grit and lang,
> Quhilk hangit Johnnie Armistrang."

And as their skulls were made to figure on the Scottish gates, less daring outlaws saw how their own fate portended, and that life and labour might be as desirable as the gibbet and a cranial exhibition after death. Soft methods and a doubtful jurisdiction were quite in vain. The whip, the chain, and the screw were the only reliable instruments for breaking in these Border harpies to decent behaviour and obedience to the laws.

"When at their greatest height," says Fuller, "the Mosstroopers had two enemies—the laws of the land, and Lord William Howard of Naworth. He sent many of them to Carlisle, that place where the officer always does his work by daylight." The probability is that the great Warden submitted his culprits to the laws; but the story is told, and not without some variation in the narrative, that Lord William was one day deeply engaged in his library, among his schoolmen or fathers, when a soldier, who had captured an unfortunate mosstrooper, burst into the apartment to acquaint his master with the fact, and inquire what should be done with the prisoner. "Hang him," or "Hang him, in the devil's name!" exclaimed Lord William; and the soldier obeyed his commands. The late Mr Henry Howard, of Corby, who carefully inquired into the jurisdiction and acts of his great ancestor, does not seem to have given much, if any, credit to this story, and further cites the fact of a list of prisoners, in the handwriting of Lord William Howard, entitled, "*Felons taken, and prosecuted by me, for felonies committed in Gilsland and elsewhere, since my abode here.* There are of them twenty-nine taken, and most of them executed, before 1612. From that time, the dates are added to their names, the last of which, making the sixty-eighth, is in the year 1632. But there is no such thing as any execution, otherwise than by convictions at the regular assizes at (mainly) Carlisle, Newcastle, Durham, or in the courts of justice in Scotland."

At a dinner at Greystoke Castle early in the century, Mr Milbourne, of Armthwaite Castle, during a pause in the conversation, accosted the late Mr Henry Howard, of Corby Castle, in a voice that attracted the notice of a very large party, asking him to drink a glass of wine with him, "For," said he, "you and I are connected." "I am happy to hear it," was the reply; "but am not aware how." "I'll tell you," said Mr Milbourne; "your ancestor, Lord William Howard, hung twenty-nine out of thirty-two of my ancestors." Mrs Howard, who relates this in her "Reminiscences," adds, "This unexpected denouement excited great laughter; for certainly, to say the least, it was quite a new sort of TIE." The Armthwaite squire was hardly fair to his ancestors, or had mistaken the Warden under whom they suffered so terribly, as there is only one Milbourne, whilst the Grahams, Armstrongs, and Bells occur frequently in the list of persons whom Belted Will caused to be hung.

There is a full-length portrait of Lord William Howard, by Cornelius Jansen, at Castle Howard, a copy of which is at Naworth Castle; also a second portrait, supposed to be painted by a less noted artist, at Corby Castle. In both of these pictures he is represented as a tall person, six feet high, and well proportioned. His forehead appears remarkably high, the more so, perhaps, from the want of hair on that part of the head above the temples. The elevation of the upper region would imply a sugar-loaf or conical formed head, the frontal part gradually receding from the eyebrows up to the vertex, the portrayal of which by Jansen is inconsistent with nature. Lord William's features are evenly formed, and pretty well marked. His eyes are full, and so are his waving eyebrows; his nose is pronounced in character; whilst the expression of his mouth and form of chin are hidden by moustache and beard. His physiognomy is not so easily read; there is gravity, decorum, and masculine thought, without any semblance of fierceness or the most remote tendency to sinister-mindedness. His dress in both the portraits is the same—a *juste-au-corps*, or close jacket of black figured thick silk, with rounded skirts to mid-thigh, varying in the pattern, a number of small buttons, the hose the same as the jacket, black silk stockings coming above the knee, tied with silk garters and bows, his shoes with rosettes, a plain falling shirt collar, with sleeves turned up at the wrist. His rapier or sword, with a gilt basket-hilt, hangs by a narrow belt of black velvet with gilt hooks.

Sir Walter Scott has added a portrait of the noble

chieftain's appearance, drawn from the poetical and chivalrous aspect, thus :—

> "Costly his garb; his Flemish ruff
> Fell o'er his doublet shaped, of buff,
>   With satin slashed and lined;
> Tawny his boot and gold his spur,
> His cloak was all of Poland fur,
>   His hose with silver twined;
> His Bilboa blade, by March-men felt,
> Hung in a broad and studded belt:
> Hence, in rude phrase, the Borderers still
> Call Noble Howard, *Belted Will.*"

A "broad and studded belt," consisting of leather three or four inches broad, and covered with a couplet in German, the letters on metal studs, used to be shown at Naworth; and from this, no doubt, Sir Walter derived the notion of calling Lord William Howard "Belted Will Howard," taking it for granted that his Lordship was in the habit of wearing the *baldrick*, or broad belt—a distinguishing badge of persons in high station. It so happens that Lord William's belts were particularly narrow. "But," as Mr Howard remarks, "the characteristic epithet with which his name has come down is *Bauld*, meaning Bold Willie (or William.) That of his lady is *Bessie with the Braid Apron*—not, I conceive, from any embroidery on that part of her dress, but using the word *broad*, which is often so pronounced, in allusion to the breadth and extent of her possessions."

Border feuds and fights have afforded lasting themes for both poet and historian; and among the great chiefs who earned a name for valour and chivalry during those eventful times, was our Belted Will Howard, whom the Border Minstrel describes in glowing colours on his way to the battle-field :—

> "But louder still the clamour grew,
> And louder still the minstrels blew,
> When, from beneath the greenwood tree,
> Rode forth Lord Howard's chivalry;
> His men-at-arms, with glaive and spear,
> Brought up the battle's glittering rear.
> There many a youthful knight, full keen
> To gain his spurs, in arms was seen;
> With favour in his crest or glove,
> Memorial of his ladye-love.
> So rode they forth in fair array,
> Till full their lengthened lines display;"

The Lord Dacre was a man of impetuosity and temper, and could brook no delay or hindrance to his fighting humour:—

> "And let them come! fierce Dacre cried;
>
> . . . . .
>
> Draw, merry archers, draw the bow;
> Up, bill-men, to the walls, and cry,
> 'Dacre for England, win or die!'"

Sir Walter Scott draws the distinction between the two English Lords by adding:—

> "Yet hear, quoth Howard, calmly hear,
> Nor deem my words the words of fear;
> For who, in field, or foray slack,
> Saw the blanche lion e'er fall back!"*

The Borders were far from settled at a later period. Lord William states, "That he had made known to His Majesty, at his being at Carlisle, the needless use of the commission and garrison, and the abuse in disposing of the paye allowed for many years by His Majesty, neer £1000 per annum; and that Sir William Hutton did then, in His Majesty's presence at Car-

---

* Sir Walter Scott remarks:—"This was the cognizance of the noble house of Howard in all its branches. The crest or bearing of a warrior was often used as a *nomme de guerre*. In the violent satire on Cardinal Wolsey written by Roy, the Duke of Norfolk, or Earl of Surrey, is called the *White Lion*."

The Judges of Assize Armed!

lisle, in August 1617, confess that there was not a *true man* on my Lord of Cumberland's boundes in Liddale to make a constable or officer to apprehend a malefactor." Lord William, in the same writing, gives numerous instances of collusion, and of the actual escape of felons passed over in silence by sheriffs and other officers of the counties of Cumberland and Northumberland, without any one being called to account for it. Sir Dudley North also relates that the gentlemen who formed the Grand Jury were then obliged to go armed to the assizes; and a custom long prevailed that each of the Judges, on their leaving Newcastle to cross the Borders, received a present from the Mayor of a *Jacobus* (a large gold coin of James the First) to procure a dagger for defence during their journey. Another custom, not dropped till the nineteenth century, it is said, was that the Sheriff of Cumberland, accompanied by the noblemen and gentry of the county, and by numbers of the yeomanry, with many mounted men bearing javelins, met the Judges as an escort, probably at Temonbridge, on the Newcastle road, where the Powtross-beck separates Northumberland from Cumberland, and where it may be supposed that the Sheriff of Northumberland would get rid of his responsibility. The story of the Sheriff meeting the Judges of Assize at the "Capon Tree," near Brampton, and there regaling the said Judges and his retinue with "fat capons," seems apocryphal. However, both tradition and history go to prove that Border depredations were long protracted after the accession of the Stuarts, and still lingered in the minds of men of authority till the reign of George the Third.

The stern public duties of Lord William Howard were softened by a pleasant social life that offered hearty welcome to all visitors of these northern parts. His well-known literary and archæological acquirements would probably tempt the historic Camden and the learned Spelman to join his hospitable hearth. The former, in his exploration of the Borders, only got as far as Carevorran Hills, above Thirlwall Castle, believing himself insecure if he ventured beyond the wholesome jurisdiction of the Great Warden. Lord William's position of King's Lieutenant in one of the most arduous posts in the realm, and where, if anywhere, danger to the throne was to be apprehended from the spirit of insubordination to the laws' either emanating from Scottish rebels or banded freebooters, proved the confidence of the Crown in his patriotism and valour. He was surely the man for the times, whether seen in the homely circle, surrounded, like the patriarch of old, with sons and daughters and their large progeny ; or in the character of mine host, entertaining men of ability ; or in his study, conning over the lore and legends of the past ; or in his public office, contending with a hydra-headed, lawless crew, only to be coerced by a rough-handed justice that admitted of no appeals. If a stern ruler, he was no less a zealous patriot. He was noted for his scholarly and thoughtful habits. He was prone to forgive his enemies, and zealous in his love of friends—glorious attributes in any man's character, and specially glorious in one who had suffered so much personally and publicly.

He meditated much on the doctrines of the Churches, and acted faithfully in the spirit of his religion. The martyrdom he suffered in his early days seems to have hallowed the proscribed creed of Catholicism; and as a sufferer at the hands of the unjust Tudors, he had learned to extol the merits and mercy of real justice. He sought to administer the laws conscientiously and equitably.

The history of this picturesque old chieftain gives a long and living interest to the grey towers of Naworth, adding the light of personal association to the kindred scenery which surrounds it. "Belted Will's" fame is of the true historical sort, resting not on adventitious claims, but on the sure basis of solid worth, energy, and capacity. He secured the peaceful interests of Cumberland beyond any of his predecessors of the Tudor and Stuart reigns, and advanced them almost a century nearer the better times of civilization and order. He made his name a dread to the evil-doer; he banished human savagery from the Borders; and by giving encouragement to industrial labour, reclaimed these frontier lands from their continuous wildness and waste. It is not too much to say, what others have said before to-day, and not less emphatically, that Lord William Howard was "The Civilizer of the English Borders."

It may interest the political economist to know that the cost of one of Lord William's journeys to London from Naworth, with from eighteen to twenty-four attendants and twelve horses, going and returning, amounted each way to from £15 to £21. In 1619 he allowed himself £1 for pocket-money each month; in 1627, he seems to have become extravagant, as this allowance rose from £12 to £36 per annum! About this time he began to buy plate and books and costly furniture, to plant trees, to purchase land and tythes, and to pay his daughters' marriage portions by instalments. Towards the close of 1622 he had a serious illness; the fee to his doctor is £10, and the bill of his apothecary four guineas. In 1623 he went to Spa for the benefit of his health, accompanied by Lady Elizabeth. The total cost of this journey was £212, 10s. 3d. Highly methodical in all his work, he made due record of every item of his expenditure.

By his steward's account, in 1625, the household charges for fourteen days at Naworth amounted to £16, 17s. 1d. This would include all his followers and domestics. There are several payments of five shillings to the barber for cutting hair and trimming my lord's beard. A pair of silk hose cost 35s.; a pair of gloves for my lord, 5s.; a pair of boots, 10s.; and a pair of spurs, 2s.; a silk belt for the sword, 4s.; and a scarf for my lord to wear in riding, 6s.; shirtbands (probably of lace) and handkerchief, £6, 8s.; and every year at least two pairs of spectacles: one pair is set down at the small figure of eighteenpence, a price implying poor manufacture, which may account for the need of so many purchases. He often made presents "to my lady." A watch for her in 1624 cost £4; a gown for my lady in somer, £6; a black fan with silver handle, 6s. 6d.; and two fine felt hats for my lady, 14s.

Of a studious and reflective mind, Lord William gave much of his time to literary pursuits, chiefly the history and antiquities of his own country, with heraldic researches relative to his own, his lady's, and other families. There are several letters of his on northern antiquities addressed to Sir Robert Cotton. Through the medium of Sir R. Spelman he was in correspondence with Olaus Wormius and other Danish archæologists. He edited the Chronicle of Florence of Worcester, the best of our Latin writers, and a translator, and famous monastic historian of England. According to the account of the Arundel Manuscripts, he collected many valuable historical documents, of which part remain in that collection; a few were at Naworth, and probably at Castle Howard. In Norfolk House there is a genealogy of the Howard family, with transcripts of many deeds, and sketches from some painted windows and monuments, which is written in 1596; and to the pedigree of the family, dated 1605, in the College of Arms, he has added notes and dates, as well as to Smith's "Baronagium Angliæ Recens." of 1597; and at Corby there are manuscript accounts of the owners of the barony of Gillesland and of Corby Castle, with copies of deeds from early times. His interest in the archæological remains to be found in Cumberland extended far beyond the immediate district of Naworth—namely, to Old Carlisle near Wigton. The inscription on a stone found in the remains of a hypocaust at Castlestead or Cambeckfort was sent by Lord William to Camden, and published by him in 1607 in the enlarged edition of his "Britannia." In the Chartulary of Lanercost Priory, in Lord William's own handwriting, is a description of a cross discovered in the green before the church. (*See* Lyson's "Magna Britannia," vol. iv. pp. clxxix., clxxxi., ccii., and the illustrations in that volume.) Like many others before and since his time, he studied the Bewcastle obelisk or monument, and examined the inscriptions on the rocks of Gelt. He furnished the antiquary with inscriptions of Roman stones and altars then gathered together at Naward and now at Rokeby. Camden spoke of him as "a singular lover of venerable antiquitie, and learned withall."

Considering the martial and stern character generally ascribed to Lord William Howard for several generations, it is pleasant to reveal another side of the picture of a man evidently born with higher aims than the mere militant ruler. Lying before the writer are some memoranda of the late Mr Henry Howard of Corby, copied from the "Literatura Runica" of Olaus Wormius, and various references to authors on the history of the Northern nations. These notes recall the names of those worthies whose historic studies and enlightenment gave consistency and breadth to archæological pursuits at the dawn of the seventeenth century. Cumberland is the more interested, that her own edificial structures and fragments brought such men as our "Belted Will Howard" in correspondence with the learned and philosophic Olaus Wormius, and the scholarly Sir Henry Spelman in personal relations with Palæma Rosicranta. In satisfying themselves as to the nature of the characters of the obelisk at Bewcastle, these renowned authors and others—to wit, Bishop Nicholson of Carlisle—displayed a vast amount of historic lore and research.

Mr H. Howard's part in similar inquiries will be discussed in a future page of this volume.

He showed considerable research in various departments of history and literature, and devoted himself to the study of the law and biblical and patristic theology. Among the leaves of an old black-letter folio, clasped and bound in oak, there was discovered on a sheet of paper—" A catalogue of my lord's books on the shelves next the fire," endorsed, also " A catalogue of my books at Narward." On these eight shelves he had nearly one hundred volumes—an extensive library for the period—and amongst them Shakespeare's Plays. He was in the habit of making remarks on the books he read; thus, in a book of Martin Luther's against the Romish Church, he wrote—"William Howarde, *Volo sed non valeo* (the motto of the Howards), *non possum quod desidero.*" On a copy of Calvin's "Institutes," date 1569, is " *Qui sibi videtur stare, videat ne cadat.*" On a copy of Galateo is, "For their glory is to change, and their liberty is to rainge." On another volume is the softer language—"*Merces amoris amore*. Mary Howarde, W. Howarde, 1582."

Lord William ranked with the *literati* of his day, a small band of worthies deserving of every praise. Camden had the highest opinion of his Naworth friend, and in his preface to "The Annales of Ireland" he wrote:—"Thus far forward was the printer's presse a going, when the Honourable Lord William Howard of Naworth, for the love that he beareth unto the studies of antiquity, willingly imparted unto me the manuscript Annales of Ireland, from the yeere of our salvation MCLII. unto the yeere MCCCLXX. Which I thought good to publish; considering that, after Giraldus Cambrensis, there is nothing to my knowledge extant better in this kind; and because so noble and worthy a person, whose they were by right in private before, permitted so much. Unto whom the very same thanks in manner are duly to be yeelded for bringing them to light that were to be given unto the author himselfe, who first recorded them in writing. And albeit they are penned in a stile somewhat rude and barrain (as those times required), yet much matter is therein contained that may illustrate the Irish historie, and would have given good light unto mee, if they had not come to my hands so late."

Lord William was most affectionately attached to his wife, and never seemed weary of proving it. Thus, in his accounts there are a number of presents to her, even to decorate her person at an advanced age; and he had her portrait taken by the best painter, Cornelius Jansen, when she was in her seventy-third year. He fired with indignation, almost amounting to implacability, at Sir W. Hutton's having insinuated that she, during his absence, when he was Warden of the Marches, had connived at the escape of a prisoner, and would scarce accept an ample apology. In every estate which he purchased, and destined for their sons, he also gave her a life interest; and other proofs testify to their union being "one of the truest affection, esteem, and friendship."

The land possessions of Lord William were great, and, as he declared in 1621, "his parks, liberties, and forests, in the compass of his own territories, were as great in quantity in one place as any nobleman in England possessed." His demesne lands at Naworth and Brampton are set down "in the lord's hand" as containing 2178 acres, and there were then remaining

His "Parks, Liberties, and Forests."

on them 1110 cattle of all sorts, and 3000 sheep—facts of significance in those days, when a large portion of the available wealth of owners was commonly invested in live stock. He had also estates in the counties of Middlesex, Hertford, York, Durham, Northumberland, and Westmoreland, as well as Cumberland. The yearly value of the domain of Castle Howard, then known by its ancient name of Hinderskelf, was set down (in 1611) at £420, 10s. 10½d.; the Morpeth property was valued at £741, 11s.; the Cumberland estates produced £1173, 13s. 2½d.; and the total income from all the counties is set down at £3884, 11s. 1½d. This was a large yearly income for that period, and it has been computed to have been on an average equivalent to £10,000 or £12,000 a year of the present day.

Nothing has come down to us of his relationship to the Naworth tenantry. The long interregnum of nearly fifty years between the active management of the Dacre estate by its liege lord and the security of Lady Elizabeth Dacre's interests on her husband, Lord William Howard, must necessarily have affected the prosperity and well-doing of all concerned—landowner and farmer. In addition, there was the lawless state of the country, forbidding exertion and enterprise in the cultivation of the soil. It is fair to presume that Lord William's spirit of order and considerate methods would be rightly exercised to give stability of tenure and hopefulness of action to his tenantry. Until he had somewhat civilized the district, and sheltered his tenants from Scottish exactions they would earn little more than meal and malt for family use, and have next to nothing to spare for rent to the laird. After a time, something more was rendered than suit and service, and thus the tangible result of rent went on increasing *pari passu* with the progress of the times.

A letter in the Lansdowne MSS. in the British Museum, entitled, "A Short Survey by a Captain, a Lieutenant, and an Ancient (Ensign) of the Military Company at Norwich, begun August 11, 1634," is worth quoting in part, were it only to show how correctly the poet had read the Border chieftain's character:—

> "Howard, than whom knight
> Was never dubbed more bold in fight;
> Nor, when from war and armour free,
> More famed for stately courtesy."

These officers visited the many parks and liberties and forests of Lord William Howard, but unhappily did not find his Lordship at Naworth. They met with lucky entertainment in a poor cottage in his liberties, and got a "cup of nappy ale and a peece of red-deer pye," and then proceeded to Carlisle, and stayed at the "Angel," in the Market Place. There they received "a curteous invitation" to dine the next day at Corby Castle (for there his Lordship then was), which "we accompted a favour from soe noble a person." They then describe their visit to Corby:—

"The next day wee went thither, and were by that generous brave lord curteously and nobly entertayn'd; and sorry he said he was that hee was not at Nawarth to give us there the like. His Lordship's commaunds made us to transgresse good manners, for neither would he suffer us to speake uncovered, nor to stand up (although our duty required another posture), but plac'd us by his Lordship himselfe to discourse with him untille dinner-time. Anon appeared a grave and vertuous matron, his honourable lady, who told us indeed we were heartily welcome. The noble twaine (as it pleased themselves to tell us themselves) could not make above 25 years both together, when first they marry'd, that now can make above 140 years, and are very hearty, well and merry, and long may they continue soe, for soe have they all just cause to pray that live neere them; for their hospitallity and free entertainments agrees with their generous and noble extraction, and their yeares retaines the memory of their honourable predecessor's bountiful house-keepinge. Amongst other dishes that came then to his Lordship's table, one there was served at the second course, which was not usual, a live roe [probably a whole roebuck]; and as there was store of venison, soe was there plenty of wine, and as freely these two noble persons commaunded it to be filled. I verily thinke his honour may commaund venison there as our southerne gentlemen doe sheepe here: for I hearde his Lordship say that his sones had then killed, out of his owne parkes, 120 bucks of this season. Soon after dinner we desired to take our leaves, and to that ende we presented ourselves, which his Lordship curteously graunted. After we had told him our designes, and commaunded one his gentlemen to accompany us over those dangerous fells, and to be our guide to Greystocke Castle, this noble nephew and himself vouchsafed to bring us through his gardens and walkes to the rivir side, and there committed us to a noble gentleman, his sonne, to passe in a boate with us over the sayd river."

Lord William had five sons and three daughters. His eldest son, Sir Philip, born in 1583, died in his lifetime, leaving a son and heir, Sir William, the ancestor of the Earls of Carlisle. Lord William's second son was Sir Francis Howard, for whom he purchased Corby Castle in 1624; and from this Sir Francis is derived the Corby line of Howards. Charles Howard, a great-grandson of Lord William's, who sided with the House of Stuart, and aided the restoration of Charles II., was created, in 1661, Earl of Carlisle, and received other titles borne by the family to this day.

The Border chieftain seems to have kept himself bravely up beyond the threescore and ten; and his lady was no less vigorous in years. Doubts exist as to the cause of their deaths; and it is supposed that the plague, introduced by a lady's dress, had cast its shadow over Naworth as well as other parts of Cumberland in 1639 and 1640.

By the *inquisitio post-mortem* held at Carlisle, April 22, 1641, it would appear that Lord William died at Naworth on the 9th of October 1640. Mr Howard of Corby assigns the 7th of the month for his death, and the 9th for his funeral. Lady Elizabeth's death, according to the Corby necrology, took place on the 9th of October 1639—twelve months previous to her husband's; and if owing to the plague, the remissness of the registers, and the tardiness in summoning an *inquisitio post-mortem*, may be accounted for.

Traditional history assigned Lord William Howard's last resting-place to Lanercost Abbey, where the family of De Vaux, and many of the great Barons of Gillesland, had been interred. There is, however,

His Death and Interment.

no record of his interment there,* nor of his wife and children; nor were the registers of the burials of the period (1640) kept at Brampton, Wetheral, or Greystoke.

At the desire of George, sixth Earl of Carlisle, and the late Mr Henry Howard of Corby Castle, search was made in the chancel of Greystoke Church, in March 1819, for the remains of Lord William Howard. Mr Howard was led to suggest this procedure by having seen at Corby Castle, in the handwriting of Mr William Milbourne of Armthwaite Castle, Cumberland (who was a barrister-at-law), a paper that unluckily got lost, purporting to be an abstract from the accompts of the steward of Lord William Howard, dated 1640, and which ran to this effect:—

"Given to a poor man by my Lord, .	£0 0	6
To taking up the great blue stone in Greystoke Church for the burial of my Lord,	2 0	0
To the servants at Greystoke Castle, .	6 0	0

* Owing to the strong supposition in favour of Lanercost, it is believed by some that the coffin which enclosed Lord W. Howard's remains was stolen about a hundred years ago by Johnstone, a parish clerk and glazier, in concert with R. Warwick, joiner of Chapelburn, and Coulson, an old pensioner, for the sake of the old lead, out of which, among other things, a glue-pot was constructed, that still retains the designation of "the Belted Will." Now it is true enough that, in May 1775, a leaden coffin was "feloniously taken from a ruinous part of Lanercost Church," and a reward of ten guineas was offered by the Naworth family for the conviction of the offenders; but the coffin was that of Lord William Dacre (see foot-note, p. 36 of this volume; and Hutchinson's "History of Cumberland," vol. i. p. 55).

On August 24, 1858, in digging a grave in Brampton old churchyard, a big stone, with heraldic carvings, was found, which Lord Carlisle, guided by the late Mr Bell of The Nook, looked upon as possibly the tombstone of "Belted Will."

If Lord W. Howard died of the plague, it is quite as probable that he would be buried in the grounds of Naworth, as the readiest mode.

The "great blue stone" in the chancel of Greystoke Church, it should be premised, was inscribed to the memory of "*William le bone Baron de Graystok*," who died July 10, 1344, and was buried with much funereal pomp at Greystoke. If the steward's accompts be reliable, it would seem that Lord William Howard wished to be buried near the famous Baron, of Graystok, described as the "most valiant, noble, and courteous" knight of his times. The excavation below the "blue stone" revealed a skeleton of large size, and a skull whose "sloping shape made it remarkable, the forehead receding much." On the north side of the stone, and only two feet from the surface, was "an entire skeleton, five feet two inches in length, apparently a female from the smallness of the skull." The steward's accompts, and the male and female skeletons, would appear to prove the case in favour of Greystoke Church as the interment of "my Lord" and his Lady. In a previous page the reader's attention was drawn to the portraiture of Belted Will's head, as showing a strikingly high yet necessarily receding one. The writer, before these details of the exploration at Greystoke had come into his hand, had expressed an opinion regarding the cranial formation of Lord William's as one probably somewhat conical, which portraiture, unless duly shadowed, could hardly represent correctly. With the few data before him, the writer would not be justified in expressing a decided opinion as to the place of interment of "my Lord."

CHARLES HOWARD

OF GREYSTOKE,

Eleventh Duke of Norfolk.

———◆———

"First Graystock we'll nwotish, the seat o' girt Norfolk,
A neame still to freemen and Englishmen dear;
Ye Cummerlan' fwok, may your sons and your grandsons
Sec rare honest statesmen for ever revere."
—ANDERSON'S *Ballads.*

CHARLES HOWARD of Greystoke, sixth child, by the death of Edward Duke of Norfolk, inherited, on the 20th September 1777, the titles of Duke of Norfolk, Earl of Arundel (with its baronies annexed), and the Earldom of Surrey, the Hereditary Earl Marshal's office, and the Chief Butlership of England. Whilst Mr Howard, he married Catherine, second daughter of John Brockholes of Clayton, in Lancashire, in 1741, and had a son, Charles Howard, born 15th March 1746, who inherited his father's dignities in 1786, and died December 16, 1815. Of this Charles Howard a few memoranda will here be given.

Brought up at Greystoke Castle, and fully imbued with the constitutional principles of his house, Mr

58 Charles, Eleventh Duke of Norfolk.

Howard could hardly fail to recognize the political contests of the county, the election of 1768 having drawn the attention of all England to Cumberland and the Lowthers. At the Carlisle election of 1774 (see Life of Curwen—"Cumberland Worthies," vol. i. p. 19) a spirited band of freemen did their best to check the Lowther encroachment, and this so pleased Mr Howard that he called them "plucky fellows, worth fighting for." The next election for Carlisle took place in 1780, and Mr Howard (now Earl of Surrey) was as good as his word, he offered himself to the electors, and won the day. He was also returned, in 1784, along with Mr Norton, a Tory, and remained in the position of a Carlisle representative till the death of his father (31st August 1786).

The political service he rendered to Carlisle was no less useful than opportune; and it is doubtful if any two men in Cumberland but himself and John Christian Curwen of Workington Hall, could have saved the city of Carlisle from the clawing political grasp of the Lowthers.* Earl Surrey's six years' parlia-

---

* The Lowthers complain of the severity of the writer's remarks on their political house; and Lady Elizabeth Lowther, who, in her last days at Orleans (France), read the "Cumberland Worthies," sent him a rather angry message for comparing the Curwens with the Lowthers, to the disadvantage of the latter. Now the lineage and chivalry of the Curwens, no less than the simian propensities and tyranny of "Jemmy the bad Earl" of Lonsdale, are matters of history, and not of invention. The writer could only reply to her Ladyship, in all courtesy and forgiveness of spirit, that he had in nowise overcharged the family picture of the Lowthers, as she admitted a great part of the censure to be true; that in his attempts to delineate the lives of public men, he had neither party purposes to serve, nor personal ambition to gratify; that though a humble follower of science, he hoped ever to maintain a spirit of honest independence; and finally, that his pen rejoiced in the condem-

mentary service naturally placed him in alliance with the heads of the "Blue" party, and led to an agreeable fraternisation with the social circles of Carlisle and its vicinity.

Carlisle, at this period of its history, was well favoured in its society, being composed of numbers of eminent men and not a few clever women. Now the Earl of Surrey's good fellowship was prized by the gentlemen, who rejoiced in hearty festivities; and his rank naturally made him no less prizeable to the ladies of a country town, where titles were so thinly sown that the presence of an heir to a dukedom must have fluttered the feminine heart exceedingly. The Earl visited his kinsman, Mr Philip Howard, grandfather of the present owner of Corby Castle, a gentleman given to scientific research and literature; he also

---

nation of arbitrary rule and injustice, and all forms of political sycophancy.

Lest it be supposed that any bias operates, the writer quotes the opinion of the *Quarterly Review*, vol. cxxii. p. 375, the well known Tory organ. Writing of Sir James Lowther, "Old Thunder," the reviewer says:—"He was the strangest, most overbearing, most unscrupulous of men. His habit of never paying his bills till lawyers were employed to demand payment; his fighting a duel with the officer who politely tried in James's Street to make him obey orders on a levée day; his passion for the girl whom he betrayed in life, and loved so well after death, that he kept her head in a glass case; such facts as these make up a character which is quite incredible."

Dr Carlyle, a learned and cautious Scottish writer, in his much-praised Autobiography, mentions the way in which "Jemmy Lowther" damaged the Duke of Portland; and then adds, that Lowther "went off conqueror, but more detested than any man alive, as a shameless political sharper, a domestic bashaw, and an intolerable tyrant over his tenants and dependants."

Surely this is enough, and more than the writer of the "Cumberland Worthies" has said of the Lowthers, though he is not without the power of deepening the shadows of even these pictures.

spent much time with his friends the Loshes of Woodside, where he always found a hearty welcome, and rejoiced to meet the best society of the neighbourhood. His habits of eating and drinking were studied so well by Mr and Mrs Losh, that he was as much at home by their fireside as within the Halls of Greystoke Castle. He was specially fond of a suet-dumpling, and this was daily presented at Woodside; he liked it cut with a knife, so that on one occasion, when a stranger to his wishes used a spoon in serving him, he startled the dinner guests of Mr Losh by crying out—"Who is mine enemy that hath done this?" at the same time holding up his plate of pudding for all beholders.

In explanation of a little episode that exactly fitted his humour, it is needful for a moment to revert to Carlisle as it presented itself to the mind of the Earl Surrey. Nothing in the Border city tickled his fancy so much as the hackneyed proceedings of the Corporation, and the display of their baubles and pomposity. Old Jeremiah Wherlings, who crowned the capital of sycophancy and other puppets of the Lowthers, was the theme and joke of every circle, and specially diverting to Surrey and his friend John Losh and the dinner-parties at Woodside. At one of these pleasant meetings, after the Earl had succeeded to the Dukedom of Norfolk, the gossip arising out of the Carlisle corporates gave such a zest to the walnuts and the wine, that it was agreed to dramatise the said municipal body. As cock-fighting was an annual sport at Wreay (a small village one mile from Woodside, and five miles south of Carlisle), why not vary the amusement by caricaturing "ye men, ye manners, and ye customs" of the long-stomached

Lowtherites of the Carlisle Town Hall. Accordingly, the Duke, Messrs Losh and Liddell, and others, met as *dramatis personæ* in the parlour of the "Plough Inn" at Wreay, and there developed a corporation for the governance of "the town," consisting of half-a-dozen houses. The Duke was elected Mayor, John Losh, Sword-bearer; his brother James Losh, Recorder; and Mr Liddell, Town-Clerk; and others, down to the official bellman, to cry "O-yez, O-yez," on the village green. The *posse comitatus* in their robes of office sallied forth to show their smart clothes, and to proclaim their worshipful dignities. The Mayor, in blue sash, was chaired, to the great joy of the assembled rustics, whose "hurrahs," if not echoed from Barrockfell, found a response in the loud crowing of the "Dalston black reds," spurred for the coming cock-fight. A jolly dinner and jollier talk concluded the evening. A fresh election of office-bearers took place annually, the appointments being made to depend on a letter quite *a la mode*, professedly directed from the great bashaw of Lowther Castle. Every spring the Carlisle newspapers announce "the Mayoralty of Wreay and the annual hunt;" and the question has often been asked—"What is the meaning of a Mayor for Wreay?" The preceding narrative explains the history of the Mayoralty. The institution, founded by Norfolk and and his friends of Woodside some seventy or eighty years ago, for the sake of a laugh at the Lowther sham, may have lost some of its racy features; but there is still a Mayor, annually appointed from the farming or publican ranks, and he is chaired shoulder-high; a hunt, foot-racing, and English jollification.

spared those misfortunes, would have been more regular. Though all that had intercourse with him could not avoid doing justice to his superior qualifications, yet there were not many who, like myself, had the same opportunity of appreciating the high value of his head and heart—of his command of temper, fairness, and indulgence to others. Too much warmth, even impetuosity, are the faults I have to lay to my own charge; but with him I could think aloud, and when I ventured to oppose his fancies, his wishes, his objects, and what he thought his personal interests, I was certain never to experience any coldness or alteration towards me.

"His active zeal for the rights and liberties of the country, and his eagerness for a reform in our representation, are well known; and though he, by much exertion and expense, sought for Parliamentary influence and weight, yet he constantly and unhesitatingly declared and proved that his object in this was to obtain the reform which we have now acquired."

There are several portraits of the Duke to be found at Arundel, Greystoke, and Corby Castle. He is represented as a hearty, good-natured, jolly Englishman. His popularity in Cumberland was great, and to-day he is still spoken of as "the Old Duke" about Greystoke and Penrith. After a protracted illness, he died on December 16, 1816, and was buried at Dorking.

HENRY HOWARD

Of Corby Castle.

"Of soul sincere,
In action faithful, and in honour clear;
Who broke no promise, served no private end,
Who gained no title, and who lost no friend."
—POPE.

IN purchasing Corby Castle and its fair demesnes (1610-24) Lord William Howard of Naworth showed his wonted sagacity, his appreciation of valuable land, and his love of the beautiful in nature. The Corby estates fell to the share of his second son, Sir Francis Howard, a brave Colonel in the army, who made large personal and still larger pecuniary sacrifices in the service of Charles the First, and contributed greatly to the victory obtained on Atherton Moor in 1643. Passing over his eldest son, whom Sandford described as "the brave Monsieur Francis Howard, a great house-keeper and horse-courser, and in all jovial gallantries expert, and beloved of all men," and William Howard, who died in 1708, this narrative reaches Thomas, the son of William, born 1677, married three times, and died August 20, 1740. This Thomas Howard was a man of poetical and classical tastes, and during his thirty-two years' holding of the estate effected great and lasting improvements at Corby. He specially devoted himself to the adornment of the grounds by making walks, planting forest trees, erecting statues and a temple of Peace, and sparing neither money nor thought in creating for himself an earthly paradise. He married Barbara, daughter of John Lowther, Viscount Lonsdale, but none of the sons of this marriage had issue. His second wife was also a Barbara, daughter of Sir Philip Musgrave of Eden Hall; and the only surviving son by this marriage was Philip, born September 3, 1730, who had eleven years of minority before he came into possession of Corby. Philip Howard is credited with being a person of high moral principle and religious feeling. He wrote an esteemed work on the scriptural history of the earth and of mankind, compared with the cosmogonies, chronologies, and original traditions of ancient nations, explaining philosophically the Mosaic account of the creation and deluge, and its consequences. He had correspondents in De Saussure, the distinguished Genevan, and M. de Luc, and other continental philosophers of his epoch.

Philip Howard deserves special mention in these pages for being the first person to cultivate the growth of turnips for the use of cattle in Cumberland; this was in the year 1755. Three years previous to the introduction of the turnip in open field, Mr P. Howard had sown a field with clover, and taught his countymen the use of artificial grasses. These were two mighty improvements, and may be said to have effected a marked revolution in the farming world of Cumberland. Mr Howard's successful effort and indoctrination of his neighbours sprang from scientific knowledge. His instance affords another proof of the value of that knowledge to the advancement of a practical art like agriculture.

Mr Philip Howard married an accomplished lady—Ann, the eldest daughter of Henry Witham, Esq., of Cliff, in Yorkshire, on November 11, 1754. From this marriage sprang Henry Howard, whose life will be briefly considered in the following pages.

Henry Howard was born at Corby Castle on July 2, 1757. He inherited a good name and a valuable property, and had the further advantage of being affectionately cared for by parents of refined character and estimable worth. The Howards would have been serenely happy in every way had not the penal laws against the Catholics been in full force, and these were necessarily felt under the roof-tree of Corby, suspected of Jacobite tendencies. The Scottish Rebellion of 1745, believed to have the approval of the great body of Catholics in the United Kingdom, was still a fresh wound in the side of the Government; and as long as the "Pretender" Prince Charles Stuart was alive—whom the Gaelic Scot specially looked upon as his liege lord—it was held to be safe policy to keep an eye upon all who were likely to favour his cause, and amongst these were the Howards of Corby. Late in the autumn of 1715, after the raising of the Stuart standard by the Earl of Mar in the Highlands, the Government took the strong precautionary measure of sending the more influential representatives of the English Jacobites to the Tower of London or provincial prisons. Mr Thomas Howard of Corby and Mr Curwen of Workington Hall, viewed as the most influential partisans of the Stuarts in the North of England, were arrested and confined in Carlisle Castle till the fate of the Earl of Derwentwater, Lord Lovat, and others was sealed.

Many interdictions were imposed on the Catholics. They had no civic rights; and though ready to fight for the national interests, they could only enlist and continue in the army as private soldiers—nay, could not rise even to the dignity of a corporal! Socially, also, the Catholics suffered in repute, and most of all the richer families, over whom a kind of mistrust lingered fatal to the peaceful enjoyment of citizenship. Young Howard would soon be made aware of these untoward facts, and the compulsorily isolated position of his family; but no teaching of what Catholics had suffered, or were likely to suffer, would be half so impressive upon his mind as his first visit to Carlisle, where he saw the bleached heads*

---

* The author of Waverley alludes to this "mummery of exposing the senseless head" in a speech which he puts into the mouth of Fergus MacIvor on the morning of his execution—"I hope they will set it on the Scotch gate, that I may look, even after death, to the blue hills of my own country, which I love so dearly." The sword of Major M'Donald, the Fergus MacIvor of Sir W. Scott, is in the possession of the Howard family at Corby Castle. Flora M'Donald, the attached sister of the Major, and who, after the fatal Culloden, was so instrumental in saving the life of Prince Charles Edward, stayed some time at Warwick Hall, and probably visited the Howards of Corby. Mrs Warwick, whose interest in the Stuart Prince was unhesitatingly manifested, was the daughter of Mr Thomas Howard of Corby, and Barbara, daughter of Viscount Lowther.

of some of the parties who took share in the '45 stuck over the ancient gates of the city—horrid mementos of a cruel and wrathful Government. The followers of the "Pretender" were not essentially Catholic, but as the Gaelic chiefs and clans prevailed over the Lowland contingent in the Stuart army, suspicion attributed a large amount of Catholic interest to the rebellious movement, headed by a French-educated Prince. Considering the early developed character and refined feeling of Master Howard, he could not fail to be painfully influenced by this degrading exhibition of Hanoverian hate to the partisans of a fallen dynasty; and possibly these bleached skulls gave a direction to his thoughts which in mature life found full utterance, and eventually led him to be one of the most prominent, as he was assuredly one of the most able, supporters of the civic claims of his co-religionists in Britain.

Henry Howard was placed by his father at the College of the English Benedictine monks at Douay in the spring of 1767. There were no Catholic schools in England adapted to the Catholic gentry. In passing through St Omer he saw the celebrated Alban Butler, author of "The Lives of the Saints." He spent six months at the University of Paris, and was transferred from thence to the Theresian Academy at Vienna—the date of his entry being December 17, 1774; the date of his leaving, September 5, 1777. The uniform of this noted academy was uncommonly gay; it consisted of a blue coat, red waistcoat and breeches, and gold lace at the pockets. It may be inferred that he had shown good parts, and obtained promotion in the academy, to claim such marked personal courtesy and kindness as he received from the famed Empress Maria Theresa* in her own palace. The academy was principally filled with Germans, Hungarians, Poles, and Belgians. Henry Howard was the only Englishman. There were several Irishmen. Howard's name, which stands so high in the philosophy class, is not prefixed by the word *Comes*, as he refused the title—enough of itself to mark his honourable character; but his Irish compatriots had no such scruples. The list is a curious study on account of the many distinguished persons enrolled, and the great parts they performed in Europe. Count Bethlem Gabor was one of his great friends at Vienna, and there he also met Marsigli, Rangoni, Montecucolli, and other distinguished men of various nations who afterwards became conspicuous actors in the events consequent on the great French Revolution. Placed among the *élite* of Vienna—*la crême de la crême* of European society at that period—he was flatteringly recognised, and on every side won friends of the highest order of blood and merit. He formed the acquaintance of Count Tablonowski, who, on parting, gave him the Polish

---

* The Empress Maria Theresa of Austria, speaking of the partition of Poland, in agitation when Mr Howard was at the Theresian Academy, said: " These gentlemen " (meaning her Ministers) " tell me it is the right course to take; but I see nothing in the measure but disaster and future evil." She was very strong in her feelings against the combination of the " Three Powers," of which Austria was one, from which her sense of justice revolted; but unfortunately she at last gave way to their importunity. It would have been well for the House of Hapsburg if she had stood firm by her private convictions; as it is, she should have the credit, so truly due to a brave woman, of acting only against Poland under the compulsion, more or less, of Russia and Prussia—both prone to extend their territories at the expense of their less fortunate neighbours.

cap of red cloth, with a gold tassel and band of very rare brown Astrakan lamb's wool, which his ancestor, who was second in command under John Sobieski, King of Poland, had worn at the siege of Vienna in 1683.

On leaving Vienna for a time, he went to Dijon, and from thence to Switzerland, along with his father and Monsieur de Montigny, who afterwards fell a victim to the guillotine. He visited Ferney six months after Voltaire's death, and was privileged to sleep in the "yellow stuff" bed of the French philosopher. There he learned much of Voltaire's private life from his chatty secretary, Monsieur de Florian, who used to shake his head on recounting the irritability of his master in his later years, as manifested by repeated bell-ringing during the night and other signs of impatience. It appears that Voltaire wrote *Tancrede* fifteen times over before he was satisfied; almost as careful a procedure as Henry Brougham's writing out his speech in defence of Queen Charlotte no less than seventeen times!

He studied in Strasburg for two or three years. There he met M. de Stackleberg, afterwards Russian Minister at Naples, and received much kindness from General Wurmser, by birth an Alsatian, and the Governor, M. de la Salle. During the protracted stay of his father and mother at Strasburg, he frequently visited the Cardinal de Rohan, who gave him a horse called "Henri." Subsequently, at Saverne, he enjoyed the princely hospitality of the Cardinal.

General Count Wurmser in 1781 tried to induce Mr Howard to join the Austrian army, and to get a commission in his famous regiment of hussars—a regiment that gained such laurels at Halbertstadt during the short war for the succession of Bavaria, in which the views of Austria were opposed to those of Frederick II. Wurmser, with his hussars, attacked two regiments of Prussians drawn up in line, with artillery both in their centre and at their flanks. He charged them at full speed (a kind of Balaclava charge, with different results), entered the battalions, and cut them to pieces, losing only forty of his own men!

In 1782 Mr Howard went with Prince Christian of Hesse-Darmstadt to the camp before Prague, consisting of 50,000 men under General Wurmser, who had Prince Poniatowsky (afterwards so celebrated under Napoleon I.), nephew of the King of Poland, as one of his *aides-de-camp*—thus having the opportunity of witnessing military evolutions on a large scale.

Having completed his education and sojourn on the Continent, he returned to Corby Castle, and with a strong *penchant* for military life. His ambition was to serve his country as a soldier; but England, as previously stated, would have no Catholic captain in her service, however worthy the claimant for honours might be. In the Appendix to his "Historical References in Support of the Catholic Religion," Mr Howard thus alludes to his early life and the bigoted prohibitions to which he was subject:—

"We (the Catholics) were all obliged before 1788 to seek for education abroad, and consequently seldom saw home or parents for six or eight years. The army being my choice, I did not see either for more than three days during ten years. I was sent to the Theresian Academy at Vienna; but neither my father, his relatives, nor the kind endeavours of that excellent gentleman, Sir Robert Murray Keith, our ambassador, under whose eye I had been for four years, could obtain leave for me to serve in our army. I even, in 1779, offered to serve as a volunteer in America, but did not receive any encouragement. .... In 1783, the late Duke of Norfolk tried to obtain for me admission into the German part of the military establishment of his Royal Highness the Duke of York. At last I had to give up my favourite object. Thus the best part of my life had passed away in unavailing attempts; and when later I endeavoured, through the kind offices of Sir George Howard, to procure a commission for a very fine young man, my brother, I found it still inadmissible. In the hope of more favourable times, he entered into the Sardinian service; but there, in a small village in Piedmont, was carried off by a fever, without having a single Englishman near him. .... A seat in Parliament in my neighbourhood was offered to me in a very flattering manner, with other advantages, which the law forced me reluctantly to decline. Like other Catholic gentlemen, when the laws respecting us began to be relaxed in their execution, I served in the militia, went to Ireland, and afterwards, by the friendship of many distinguished gentlemen of this county, who placed themselves under my command, I formed a volunteer corps (the Cumberland Rangers), and we served till peace broke us up. *Such, perforce, has been my inefficient life.*"

Such a narrative of personal experience as the above is calculated to embitter one's feelings. That a member of the highest family in England, acknowledged to be a man of superior education and honour, burning with patriotic zeal, nay, ready to sacrifice his life on behalf of his country, yet compelled to live an "inefficient life," and apparently for no other reason than that he was faithful to the religion of his forefathers! Truly, in those days, the altar of the Catholics, to men of worth and intelligence at least, was an altar that savoured of martyrdom. And as if to add to the mockery of the thing, the Catholics of England were living under an ancient monarchy, and a free constitution that boasted of a *Magna Charta*, and a broadly liberal national Church!

It was impossible for a person of Mr Howard's frame of mind and historical leanings to remain a passive observer of the great events then agitating not only England but the European family of nations. His politics led him to join the celebrated Society of the "Friends of the People," in conjunction with the Duke of Norfolk, Earl Grey, Charles James Fox, J. C. Curwen, and other uncompromising leaders of the Whig party. His name is said to have been among the first appended to the celebrated petition for Parliamentary Reform. With the Whig party he associated through life, and never swerved from being an active, zealous, and consistent advocate of civil and religious liberty. In Cumberland he took a prominent part at the elections, and at all public meetings for the redress of political grievances. The Liberal party might well rejoice in the hearty co-operation of a man of such noble character as Henry Howard—a host in himself.

Mr Howard took for his first wife Maria, third daughter and co-heiress of Andrew Lord Archer of Umberslade. The marriage was solemnised at Glaiston, Rutlandshire, on November 4, 1788. This lady was a truly beautiful and highly accomplished person. She died on November 9, 1789, in giving birth to an infant, and was interred in the Howard mausoleum in Wetheral Church. Mr Howard engaged Nollekens to erect a suitable monument to her memory; and in this work the sculptor surpassed himself. A lady, the portraiture of chastened feeling and beauty, her new-born babe, and an angelic form, constitute the monumental group. A tenderness and an exalted spirituality reigns through the composition of the work, so impressive and heart-touching.

Mr Howard married, secondly, Catherine Mary, the second daughter of Sir Richard Neave, Bart., of Dagnam Park, Essex, on March 18, 1793, and had issue—*Philip Henry*, the present owner of Corby, and for twenty-one years the earnest and faithful representative in Parliament of Carlisle; *Catherine*, married to the Hon. Philip Stourton; *Emma Agnes*, married to the Right Hon. Lord Petre; *Henry Francis*, now Sir Henry, Her Majesty's able Minister at Munich; *Adeliza Maria*, married to Henry Petre, Esq., of Dunkenhalgh, Lancashire.

Of Mr Howard's happiness with his highly beloved wife he offers due testimony in his "Memorials of the Howard Family," written upwards of forty years subsequently to his marriage :—" Before I close what relates to my own family, I must indulge in a grateful tribute to this beloved lady (his wife Catherine), my restorer to happiness, who might well be taken as a model of judicious, careful, and affectionate conduct as a wife and as a mother ; truly felt, returned, and, I trust, requited, by the love of us all."

Whilst hoping for the advent of better days to patriotic Catholics, he obtained, through his kinsman Charles Duke of Norfolk, whose biography precedes this, a captaincy in the West York Militia. In May 1795, accompanied by Mrs Howard, he joined his corps at Newcastle-on-Tyne. He continued in the militia till January 1800, during which time the 1st West York Regiment was stationed in several large towns in England and also in Dublin. After nearly five years absence, he and Mrs Howard reached Corby on the 24th February 1800, amid the hearty rejoicings of their friends and tenantry.

Though zealous in the service of His Majesty, he found time to refresh his mind with literary pursuits, and translated the *Wilde Jäger* of the German poet Bürger into verse,—" The Wild Huntsman's Chase." This translation appeared on the 26th October 1796 in one of the public prints ; and a few weeks afterwards Sir W. Scott's imitation of the same ballad appeared under the title of " THE CHASE." In 1798, Mr Howard issued his translation in a quarto form. The subject of this ballad, founded on a German legend, sets forth that the Wildgrave, or Earl Warden of the Chase, heedless of the mischief he occasioned to farmers and vassals, or of the profanation of the

Sabbath, pursued his sports at all seasons of the year, till at length the vengeance of Heaven reached him. Of the thirty-two stanzas, three are selected to show Mr Howard's versification. On comparing the two translations of the same ballad by Sir W. Scott and H. Howard, the Scottish bard appears more flowing and harmonious; on the other hand, Mr Howard has stuck more closely to the original, so as to convey a more German character, and thus to give to his work greater force and spirit.

"THE WILD HUNTSMAN'S CHASE."

"Halloo! on horse, on foot, away!
Shrill sounds the haughty Wildgrave's horn;
High rears his steed, brooks no delay,
And pawing snuffs the gales of morn.
They're off! the hounds loud op'ning cluster round;
With voices, whips, and horns the hills resound.

* * * * * *

"'Mercy, dread Lord! some pity show:
Reflect that in this pasture feed
The orphan's stock, the widow's cow.
Await! the deer I'll drive with speed:
Spare to the poor their all, their only trust;
In pity stay! be merciful and just.'

* * * * * *

"Appalled, the Wildgrave looks around;
His whip he swings, it makes no noise;
He tries his horn, it yields no sound;
He calls, but cannot hear his voice;
His steed he strikes and spurs, in vain he strove;
Fixed to the earth, no longer could they move."

RUNES AND ARCHÆOLOGY.

Archæological pursuits led Mr Howard to the study of Danish history, with a view to decipher the character of the Runes met with in Cumberland. The fact of his engaging in such a work proved his ardent zeal in the cause of historic literature. Notably superior to the order of country gentlemen living at home at ease, he threw aside commonplace reading and *belles-lettres* for the more recondite studies of Scandinavian lore. Much and lasting credit is due to him and others for having devoted their hours of leisure to the deciphering of the rude carvings and insignia of an unlettered people, whereby form and structure might be given to the hidden meanings of the historic past. In the exploration of these Runes, the modern observer is but studying the methods of inscription practised by our very ancient grandsires, seeking to convey to posterity their knowledge of the world and its doings, or what they wished to extol of the heroism and virtues of their race. Speculation has been rife on the origin of these runes; but whether invented by Odin or due to an artful priesthood, ever ready to profit by mystery and divination, the fact remains that they were devised by a Northern European people, to whom Englishmen owe some of their best blood, their hardiness, roving enterprise, and methods of colonization. The Anglo-Saxon blood is oft vaunted;—now there is something of the Saxon in these Danish runes, and the blending of the two nations offers another reason for our bestowing attention on their character. In Cumberland, at least, the mingling of tongues, British, Saxon, and Danish, is very marked; and the runes stand in more or less parental significance to our common dialect, if they have not a larger historical relationship. The utilitarian will ask, What behoves it that, on rising from their barbaric state, the Danes invented letters, shapely or shapeless, or inscribed on their Scandinavian shields illegible markings, for modern philologists to fight over, when we have our three R's in full vigour, and Bank of England imprimaturs? Is not the past all vanity and moonshine to the holders of railway scrip, the manufacturers of shoddy, and the big bellows-blowers of England? It may be so, but happily the world is not entirely made up of minds of the grosser sort, while the graspings of a mercenary age are daily softened by scholarly and ingenuous minds of the Henry Howard type, aiming at the promotion of letters and the higher culture of our race.

In order of date, it may be well to allude to Mr Howard's "Inquiries concerning the Tomb of King Alfred at Hyde Abbey, near Winchester," which were read to the London Society of Antiquaries (March 29, 1798), and published in the *Archæologia*, vol. xiii. pp. 309-312. After stating the fact of Henry I., A.D. 1112, having translated, with great pomp, the body of Alfred the Great to the magnificent abbey church which he built for the purpose, at a place called Hyde, near Winchester, he speaks with much regret and no small amount of indignation that, as late as the year 1788, the bones of the great Alfred had been scattered about by the rude hands of convicts, and were then probably covered by a building (new gaol or Bridewell), erected for the confinement and punishment of these outcasts. He gave a sketch of the ancient site of the abbey, and offered explanations of the different parts occupied by it. The coffins near the high altar had been broken up for the sake of their lead, which in its decayed state sold for two guineas; and the bones had been thrown about. These coffins, from the position they occupied, he conjectured contained the bones of the great Alfred, and also those of King Edward and Queen Alswitha. If so, the great bard is again verified :—

> "Imperial Cæsar, dead, and turned to clay,
> Might stop a hole to keep the wind away :
> Oh, that the earth, which kept the world in awe,
> Should patch a wall to expel the winter's flaw!"

On returning home from one of his visits to his hearty friend, John Christian Curwen, of Workington Hall, Mr Howard, on March 22, 1800, called at Bridekirk, near Cockermouth, to examine the antique font in the church. His observations on it, and the runic column at Bewcastle in Cumberland, were read to the Society of Antiquaries, London, and published in the *Archæologia*, vol. xiv. pp. 113-118. He had accurate drawings made of several sides of the font, and hoped Professor Thorkelind or some member of the Royal Society at Copenhagen, well versed in the runic language and characters, would be induced to interpret the inscription. These drawings of the font and the runic inscription on the Bewcastle obelisk are printed in the *Archæologia*; and probably are the most accurate facsimiles ever given to the public. The font he considered to be formed of the common red freestone of the country, and covered with a white cement or varnish. The scroll on which the inscription is engraved (*intaglio*), being sunk and safe from friction, is preserved entire, and as perfect as the day it came from the workman's hands. Bishop Nicholson deemed it a Saxon-runic inscription, and read it as follows :—*Er Ekard han men egrogta & to dis men red wer. Taner men brogten*; which he interprets, *Here Ekard* was converted, and to this man's example were Danish men brought.* Mr Howard looked upon the two last words before *brogten* as formed of compound letters, and meaning not *Taner men*, but *Nor men*, the general name given to the Scandinavian invaders. Mr Howard's views are given below in a foot-note.

* The difficulty seems to have been to find out who Ekard was; and Mr Howard, by joining the first two words of the inscription *Er Ekard*, which had no appearance of being separate, "thought it possible that the font might commemorate the fact that Erick, the son of Harald Harfagre, King of Norway (whose name is written in so many ways), having been expelled the throne of Norway, which he had assumed after Harald's death, by Haco his brother, sailed from that country, with all his friends, to seek his fortune and an establishment elsewhere; and in the piratical and predatory spirit of his countrymen, about the year 939, after having landed in the Orkneys, plundered the coasts of Scotland and northern parts of England. He was there met by ambassadors from Athelstan, who offered him the feudatory kingdom of Northumberland (then a fifth part of England). on the same conditions it had been held by Guthrum, whom Alfred had established over the Northumbrian Danes. Erick accepted the proposal, namely, that he should defend the country against the northern invaders, and previously, with his followers (a condition very usual in those days) embrace the Christian religion." Now, Mr Howard viewed the name in the inscription, the chief with the uplifted sword, and the messenger arriving in haste, as supporting the conjecture that the Bridekirk font was made for the ceremony. The female deploring figure may possibly represent the deeds of devastation, or the outrages he had already committed, and which Athelstan's ambassador was to engage Erick to put a stop to. That Erick reigned over the Northumbrian Danes, and was afterwards expelled, is acknowledged by the English as well as the Scandinavian historians; but they do not exactly agree in the mode or time of his establishment, nor of his expulsion.

F

He does not differ very much from his predecessors; but, if he be correct in his interpretation, the reader cannot but consider it as remarkable that Bridekirk, in the west of Cumberland, should have been selected as the church for the baptizing of Northumbrian Danes. How much their Christianity was worth when symbolized at Bridekirk font is another matter, and for State Church theologians to consider. The writer had proceeded thus far when he luckily fell in with Mr Hamper's views * on the said font, derived entirely from Mr Howard's exposition; and these he is disposed to look upon as more consonant with the facts than any previously expressed.

Mr Howard spent two days in exploring the inscription on the runic column or obelisk at Bewcastle. The obelisk is from the hands of a better artist than the font at Bridekirk; it is quadrangular, of one entire grey freestone, inserted into a larger blue stone which serves as its base. The greater base is 22 inches, diminishing to 21; the lesser 16 inches, and 12 only at the top; the shaft is 14 feet high. Little more than the vestiges of the inscription remain; the perpendicular parts of the letters are discernible, and

---

* In the 19th volume, pp. 379-82, of the *Archæologia*, Mr Hamper speaks in high praise of Mr Howard's description of the Bridekirk font; and, after doubting the opinions of Spelman, Wormius, Bishop Nicholson, and others, looks upon the font as bearing the sacred symbols of our faith, the baptism by St John, the expulsion of Adam and Eve, &c., whilst on the south side the sculptor of the work *in propria persona* is working with his mallet and chisel. That, instead of the inscription which has puzzled so many commemorating the conversion of Ekard and the Danes, it merely records the name of the ingenious sculptor who carved the font! Mr Hamper renders the runic into plain English—

"Richard he me wrought,
And to this form me diligently brought."

have probably been deepened by the rain; but the horizontal and other parts are nearly obliterated. Mr Howard did not venture upon any interpretation of the inscription.

Mr Howard's interest in archæological matters never abated. On 19th June 1839, he wrote a letter to the Antiquarian Society of London, giving an account, accompanied with careful drawings, of the hunting horns of Charlemagne; epitaph of the Empress Fastrada at Mentz; the sword of Charlemagne; the hunting horn of Roland; and a hunting horn at Greystoke Castle. This last-named horn differed but little from the figures on the golden horn at Copenhagen, given by Olaus Wormius.—(*Archæologia*, vol. xxix. pp. 368–70.)

THE CUMBERLAND RANGERS.

The historical reader need hardly be told that democratic Europe, at the close of the century, hailed the French Mirabeaus and Girondists as the pioneers of universal freedom; but the sacrifice of Madame Roland and Charlotte Corday, and the unutterable days of the guillotine, showed another side of the republican picture, which caused English reformers to ponder much, and eventually to doubt the virtues of the Robespierre-Goddess of Liberty. The Consulate, the passage of the Alps, and the seizure of Egypt, were but the initiative steps to the more startling usurpations laid down in the programme of the new Imperial Cæsar. The nations of the Continent might well hold their breath, nay, the world itself stood aghast at the daring efforts of the great military genius of the epoch. With a heaven-born minister of the Tory stamp, and an arbitrary king to guide affairs, England not only got into the European fray, but deeply engaged herself in the long and bloody fight. Then arose the usual doubts as to our military position, and what we should do to hold our own against the new Mephistopheles. The governing ministry, as well as the governed millions in these realms, got anxious and alarmed. At no time, perhaps, in our history, had the public mind of England been so agitated, and at no time was it more united and determined to meet the foe. To defend this sea-girt isle, as Cromwell with his Ironsides would have done, seemed to be the pervading thought of every citizen; and no *Marseillaise* could have infused a more martial spirit among his Majesty's lieges than the threatened invasion of Buonaparte. What with "the regulars," the militia, the yeomanry, and volunteers, scarcely a man in Britain, capable of bearing arms, escaped soldier's duty. None wished to escape, for all seemed to have imbibed the spirit of the poet who uttered these noble sentiments :—

> "Breathes there the man with soul so dead
> Who never to himself hath said,
> This is my own, my native land?"

Of the Cumbrians who came boldly to the front at this hour of danger, when the tocsin resounded from Penrith Fell to Christenbury Crags—from the heights of Black Coombe to the depths of Alston mines—was Henry Howard, of Corby, than whom no man could surpass in love of country and a patriotic desire to maintain this fair England of ours free and inviolate. Inclined to military training, he offered his services to the Government, and promised to raise a volunteer force in Cumberland. His offer being "graciously accepted," Mr Howard lost no time in developing his plans, and enlisting the feeling of the residents of his district. A corps was raised in 1802, bearing the title of "Edenside Rangers." It consisted of 220 effective men, to which were added a troop of cavalry. Shortly after the enrolment, the preliminaries of peace were signed at Amiens, so that the training of the corps was deemed superfluous. War again being declared, and Napoleon showing vast preparations for its continuance, Mr Howard, in May 1803, again tendered his services to the Government. "The principle of the proposed force was simply a revival of that which subsisted at the close of the last war under the title of the 'Edenside Rangers;'" but he wished "to extend the establishment to different parts of the county," so as to obtain a much larger body of volunteers. Lord Hobart, then Home Secretary, on 18th May 1803, replied:—"I am commanded to express the satisfaction his Majesty has derived from the zeal and public spirit manifested by this offer (of Mr Howard's), which his Majesty has been graciously pleased to approve and accept."

The towns of Cumberland had their special companies of volunteers, embracing professional men, tradesmen, and artisans, but there were numbers of persons scattered in the isolated rural districts whom it was desirable to enrol in the service of their country. Part of Mr Howard's plan in establishing the "Cumberland Rangers," was to secure the co-operation of the leading men of every hamlet and parish, through whom he might reach the subordinate class fit for arms, or zealous* to defend their homes and hearths.

The squirearchy, the yeomen, farmers, and their sons, hesitated not to enrol themselves in the ranks of the "Cumberland Rangers," that they might be placed under the command of so good a soldier as Lieutenant-Colonel Howard. They constituted a superior class of men, earnest at drill, and well imbued with the spirit of discipline. In point of general *physique*, in education, and respectability, they were worthy of the county that had contributed so many tall and stalwart fellows to the King's Life Guards. Seen standing side by side in soldierly attitude, or practising their respective manœuvres on inspection days, the bystanders of both sexes might be heard exclaiming, "What fine fellows, and how admirably trained! Who need fear 'Boney's coming' up the Solway, if the gallant Howard and his men are there to meet him and the French."

The Cumberland Rangers consisted of seven companies of infantry, about 600 strong, and two troops of cavalry. The head-quarters were at Corby Castle. The Colonel-Commandant saw the policy of assembling his corps in different localities—*e.g.*, Lanercost Abbey, Warwick Moor, Penrith, and the

---

* As illustrative of the spirit of the times, when the Carlisle Volunteers had to assemble at Penrith for a day's drill, men were known to start early in the morning for Penrith, pass several hours on the field of inspection, and return home the same night—thus, in addition to their day's drill, they walked thirty-six miles. Carlisle professional men —*e.g.*, the late Mr William Dobinson, solicitor, used to do ordinary sentinel duty in front of the Crown Hotel, Penrith, on market days. Such men, and they were to be found in thousands, were proud of their colours and the cause of their country.

Willow Holme at Carlisle, where numbers of people used to attend to witness the movements of "the crack regiment" of Rangers.

In compliance with the expressed wish of his corps of Cumberland Rangers, Colonel-Commandant Howard published a "System of Order and Training" for their private use, compiled from the Orders issued by Sir Charles Grey, and his Majesty's Regulations for Light Infantry, and the Regulations for Riflemen. In his address to the Cumberland Rangers he wrote thus patriotically:—"Should we be called out, by invasion, to the defence of our country, I trust an honourable post will be granted to us. We shall engage, on such an event, in a warfare under circumstances more favourable than have almost ever occurred, by which its attendant hardships would be greatly lessened. We should always have the best intelligence of the movements of the enemy; in every house we should find a friend; in every village numbers anxious to assist us, either as guides or pioneers; in every quarter we should find provisions brought to our hand; whilst our families at home would be cherished and protected by associations formed for that purpose.

"By regularity, attention to military discipline, ready and zealous obedience to orders, and by steadiness and coolness in action, I have no doubt but that this corps would merit the approbation of their country."

The many excellent men who served under Colonel-Commandant Howard should not pass unnoticed. Lieutenant-Colonel Lord Wallace, Major Sir W. Lawson, Bart., Adjutant Moss, and Dr Blamire, were on his staff. The troops of horse raised within the Corby, Carlisle, and Brampton districts were commanded by Captain Robert Warwick, of Warwick Hall, Captain H. Pottinger, and Lieutenant R. Lowry. Sir F. F. Vane, Bart., was captain of the first company raised in the Keswick district; Major John Losh of Woodside, Captains Robert Stordy and John Lowry, had charge of the three Carlisle companies; Thomas Benson of the Wreay company; Thomas Wybergh of the Brayton company; and John Thomlinson, with the Hon. W. H. Lyttleton as lieutenant, of the Corby and Warwick company.

As the Cumberland Rangers were in training for ten years, there would be changes in the corps during that time, the recognition of which would greatly extend the list just given.

Though Colonel Howard was well supported and as heartily respected by his officers, no one doubted that the perfect organization of the corps rested with himself. His equanimity and steady observation, his happy tact in the exercise of authority when firm decision was called for, told largely and happily. Moreover, his thorough knowledge of his work as a *bonâ fide* soldier claimed the admiration and esteem of all under his command. His administrative faculty was well developed, and its application tended greatly to the co-operation of interests, and the harmonious working of his subalterns and their companies. If his high character as a county gentleman sufficed to bring men from distant and isolated localities to his standard, thus making the Cumberland Rangers the largest force of volunteers, his mastery of both the principles and details in its organization contributed largely to its superiority and military excellence. Always at his post, and shrinking from no exertion or duty, he became closely linked with all the grades in his service. He encouraged his soldiers to do their best, and to act towards each other as brethren united in a patriotic cause—that of upholding the sovereignty of the nation and the interests of the commonweal.

In 1808, a handsome silver cup, with appropriate emblems, the gift of the officers, non-commissioned officers, and privates of the Cumberland Rangers, was presented to their Colonel-Commandant Henry Howard, in the castle yard, Carlisle. It bears the happy inscription :—" The Cumberland Rangers to Henry Howard, Esq., of Corby Castle, Lieutenant-Colonel Commandant, a testimony of affection and respect." The cup was presented in the name of the corps by Lord Wallace, who delivered an eloquent and spirit-stirring address on the occasion.

CORBY CASTLE.

Corby Castle is situated on the east bank of the river Eden, five miles E.S.E. of Carlisle; the pretty village of Wetheral occupies the opposite side of the same picturesque stream. In this part of its course, the Eden is bounded by red sandstone rocks upwards of one hundred feet in height; and upon a brink of this stratified facing stands the far-famed Corby Castle. With the exception of some massive walls, and a portion of the old tower or keep, the original nucleus of the ancient mansion, now lost in the general fabric, nothing is externally visible of the Castle that sheltered the Odards, De Harclas, and Salkelds : nor is there any very distinct trace of Lord William Howard's improvements, effected soon after he gained possession in 1624.

The Castle of to-day is almost entirely the work of Henry Howard, the subject of this memoir. It consists of a large square mansion, partaking of a Doric character, presenting two finished fronts, on the centre of the parapet of which is a pedestal, surmounted by a lion *statant-gardant*, the crest of the Howards. Over the Doric portico of the entrance to the castle is inscribed—

"SUIS. ET AMICIS.
H. HOWARD,
A.G. M.DCCC.XIII. D.D."

A motto truly appropriate to the hearty welcome offered all passers through the porch in Henry Howard's time, as it is to-day in that of his most estimable son, Philip H. Howard.

The view from the eastern front embraces a fine lawn and the park, that gradually rises to a great eminence, the Castle hill, and is studded with ancient oaks, the noblest of their kind;* the southern, and

---

* The trunks of many of the oaks on the Castle hill (measured in 1841) were found to vary from 12 to 18 feet in circumference. Some of them with stag-horns are supposed to have ornamented the Corby grounds for ten centuries. One of these showed a circumference of 30 feet—truly a giant of the forest, hardly to be matched in Cumberland.

Thomas Howard, about 1720, planted Scotch firs, which in 1841 had attained a growth ranging from 8 to 12 feet in circumference. Some of them were 100 feet high, and one of the largest showed a uniform thickness of stem for 30 feet above the ground! Silver firs and Scotch firs, planted in 1765, had, in eighty years, reached a size that formed stems nearly 11 feet in circumference; and in part of the grounds where Mr Henry Howard remembered a kitchen garden void of trees, he found, in 1826 (say after sixty years), a silver fir nearly 9 feet in circumference;

more favoured prospect, reveals a long reach of the river, admitted to be the finest in the whole course of the Eden, from its origin in the Pennine Chain to its fall in the Solway Frith. Standing solid on its verdurous precipice, while high around rise the noble woods, the Castle possesses a rare and, perhaps, unrivalled picturesqueness of position. It also commands a great breadth of holme and arable land, backed by the Fells of Cumberland and the southern range of Scottish mountains. The river Eden displays a thousand beauties: its broad silvery stream, gurgling and spraying over pebbles and boulders; its rapid sweep around prettily wooded islets, then seeking a meandering course, and gently merging into deep pools and silence; but for a time only, when the current starts afresh, falls impetuously across the bay, and dashes under the lofty arches of the elegant railway viaduct in its course towards Warwick.

An endless variety of scene and untold beauty meets you everywhere in Corby grounds. There strata of red sandstone stand like bastioned guardants to the river's swell; there they have become grey, lichened, and mossy, beneath the drip of overhanging foliage—the hard geological outlines in bold contrast with the green umbrageous living growth; there the sturdy oak, or graceful pine, are springing in grotesque fashion, with inosculated roots, from creviced rocks, and casting their boughs to the midstream, whilst lesser growths gracefully fringe the

a beech tree nearly 8 feet; and a larch nearly 7½ feet—and all thriving trees. The reader, who considers these measurements, will be the better prepared to comprehend the statements made in the text as to the beauty and magnificence of the arboreal growths at Corby.

water's edge. For a moment your eye is caught by fragments of hoary stone-work, then it rests upon the green slopes tufted with ivy and grasses, ferns and wild flowers; and whilst your path is along the carpeted greensward, shadowed with stately trees, you hear the brawling of the river, and through opening glades you mark the wooded banks and beauties reflected on its mirrored surface.

If you wish to mark individual forms, here is the gnarled oak, in towering magnificence, sheltering at its base the tiny plant, or "wee bit tippit flower;" the yew, with its partite stem, showing decadent streaks and hoary age, hiding the germs of cryptogamic growth, so pretty in their miniatured forms and variety; the towering ash, with stem entwined by ivy, stretching, climbing, and aye holding fast to its pabulum; the hawthorn, in its May blossoms, showing like clustered ornaments of white and pink hanging over the fringed green leaves, charming in their colour, and bright ushering in of spring; these again, yielding to the wild rose and honeysuckle, so that in her seasons Nature seems redolent of sweetness, and in rich display of growth and colour and harmonic gladness.

If Nature has been lavish in her gifts of mountain stream, rocky boundaries, and wild arborescence, Art, in the hands of Thomas Howard (Henry Howard's grandfather), a man of fine poetic and artistic taste, was made to play no insignificant part, in the construction of a broad terraced walk leading by the river's side to a Grecian temple, in the placing of statuary, and ornamental buildings, the formation of winding-paths and cells and grotto-like excavations in the rocks. Relph, the Sebergham poet, wrote of Corby walks:—

> "For Paradise's seat no more
> Let travellers search on Persia's shore;
> Its groves still flourishing appear
> *Upon the east of Eden* here."

The west side of the river is equally worth the visitor's attention, were it only for the advantage of seeing Corby Castle aright. Passing the remains of the ancient Priory of Wetheral, and on by the river's side to "the caves"—three cells excavated in a perpendicular rock, probably serving as hiding-places to monks and laymen alike—you reach a bend of the river, from which you have by far the best view of Corby Castle and its charming surroundings. Who can visit Corby and ramble amid the rich sylvan scenes revealed to him at every turn and walk, without having his æsthetic feeling gratified, his imagination exalted, and his mind enlightened! Thomas Howard laid out the Corby walks early in the last century; he spent large sums, even a third of his income, in decorating the grounds with statues of sphynxes, gods, and goddesses, &c. He also erected a grand amphitheatre, and sought to give a mythological meaning to his combinations of Art with Nature.* "Alas!" wrote Mrs Howard, wife of Henry

* The classical tastes of the Master of Corby seem to have infected the gardener with a love of the mythological along with his own vocation, as the following amusing story testifies :—"After the battle of Culloden, the Duke of Cumberland, on his return from Scotland, called at Corby Castle. The family being from home, the gardener showed his Royal Highness the curiosities of the place, and as they passed by the statues, observed, 'that having a poetical genius, he had written some lines on every one of them.' The Duke, curious to have a speci-

Howard, the subject of this memoir, "such are the destructive propensities indigenous to Englishmen, that when the pleasure-grounds were thrown open to the public, neither a seat nor the smooth bark of a tree were left unmutilated with names and low verses, and not even a statue or Roman altar escaped being broken to atoms." Hence Diana's grotto is now untenanted, and Polyphemus alone remains to lament his Galatea and the rest of the sylvan court.

Mr Howard might well call in request the Odes of Horace, and the poesy of Milton, for inscriptions on tablets to his grottoes and lawn seats; and if Milton had studied the Eden of Corby for the Eden of his "Paradise Lost," he could not have made a more faithful picture than this:—

> "There Eden's lofty banks,
> Now nearer crown with their inclosures green
> As with a rural mound, the champain head
> Of a steep wilderness, whose hoary sides
> With thickets overgrown, grotesque, and wild,
> Access deny; and overhead up grow
> Insuperable heights of lofty shade,
> Cedar and pine, and fir, and branching oak;
> Shade above shade, a woody theatre
> Of stateliest view."

Many of poetic fancy have contributed their meed of praise in sonnets and poems to the loveliness of Corby. One of these rhymsters deserves a place here, yet he only wrote a single line in its favour; but then

men of the gardener's poetry, asked him what he had written on the statues of Cephalus and Procris; upon which the gardener immediately turned to his common-place book, and read as follows:—

> 'He bent his bow, and he shot at random,
> And killed his wife for a memorandum.'"

—*European Magazine* for the year 1793.

that line truly confirmed the worth of the sentiment, that brevity is the soul of wit. David Hume, the historian, journeying from Paris to his home in Edinburgh, a hundred years ago, found it convenient to rest a day in Carlisle: he took up his quarters at the "Old Bush Hotel," situated in a narrow lane on the east side of Scotch Street. After being offered for breakfast coffee, and eggs that were half-hatched, he attended the Cathedral service, and afterwards inspected the city, its walls, and castle. None of these things at all pleased his senses; his smell and taste were both tried at his morning's meal; his hearing found no harmony in the notes of the choristers; whilst his sight of the Scottish gates thrilled him with horror. Seeking repose in the contemplations of nature, he repaired to Corby for the rest of the day. On his return to the "Old Bush," he inscribed on a pane of glass in the window of his room the following stanza, as a record of his personal experience of the Border city and its delightful environs at Corby Castle:—

> "Here chicks in eggs for breakfast sprawl;
> Here godless boys God's glories squall;*
> Here heads of Scotchmen guard the wall;
> But Corbie walks atone for all."

---

* Much of this second line is difficult to read, owing, it is said, to a jovial Parson who frequented the "Old Bush," and feeling indignant at Hume's reference to the godless boys, tried to scratch it out. The third line given in the text is the correct version. Sir W. Scott, on May 2, 1815, gave it to Mr Howard as, "Here Scotchmen's heads do guard the wall." How the inaccuracy arose cannot be explained. David Hume spelt Corby as any Scotchman would do—Corbie. The exact date of his record is not known, but at the top of the pane is "H. Evans. 2. Octr. 1769."

This pane of glass continued *in situ* till about the year 1848, when the writer's lamented friend, John Bell, solicitor at Brampton, on offering to put a clean pane in its place, got it from the landlord of the "Old Bush." Mr Bell being anxious for the preservation of this historical relic had the good taste to present it to Mr P. H. Howard. So this curious memorial of Hume's visit to Carlisle has now a place, among other costly and valuable treasures, in the possession of the Howards of Corby.

Hume was a hard-headed philosopher, never credited with much imaginative feeling, hence possibly his non-apprehension of the doctrines of the Trinity, and his entire disbelief in all theologies. His rising for once to the poetic strain, however doggrel his rhyme, would imply that there was a chord in his mental constitution which beauteous Corby had reached; the response was—

"Corbie walks atone for all."

With a kindness and generosity of feeling that is beyond all praise, the present owner of Corby, Mr Philip Henry Howard, opens his grounds to the general public every Wednesday during the summer season; indeed, access to them is not denied to travellers and persons of respectability on any day of the week. This free admission to one of Nature's rural gems is the greatest boon ever conferred on the inhabitants of Carlisle and the neighbouring towns; for holiday-seekers come from east and west, north and south, to enjoy a day in the far-famed walks of Corby. Who can measure the amount of positive enjoyment conferred on each visitor? and there are thousands annually. Robert Anderson, our ballad-maker, hit the popular sentiment when he wrote :—

"We've Corby, for rocks, caves, and walks, sae delightfu',
That Eden a paradise loudly proclaims;
O that sec like pleaces had aye sec like owners,
Then mud monie grit fwok be proud o' their neames!"

It may interest many readers to know that Corby Castle contains a fine historical library; highly valuable pictures by Da Vinci, Correggio, Sassoferrato, Nicolas Poussin, besides modern artists; family portraits of the Howards of the past, as well as of the Corby branch; many remarkable curiosities and articles of *vertu*—notably the massive gold rosary and cross worn by the unfortunate Queen Mary on her way to the scaffold; the grace-cup* of Thomas à Becket; the claymore of Major M'Donald, the Fergus MacIvor of "Waverley;" a cup of Edward the Third's time; and many more curious archæological relics.

* The grace-cup of St Thomas à Becket was bequeathed by the valiant Admiral Sir Edward Howard to Katherine of Aragon, the first Queen of Henry VIII. On her death it reverted to the Howard family. This curious relic of the twelfth century was given to Henry Howard of Corby Castle, by Barnard, Duke of Norfolk, on January 12, 1816, as a memorial of their friendship. It is of ivory and richly chased gold, of the chalice form, with a cover, and studded with knots of precious stones and pearls. Round the lid is engraved the restraining injunction, "*Sobrii estote*," with the initials T. B. interlaced with a mitre. The inscription round the rim of the cup is "*Vinum tuum bibe cum gaudio.*" An engraving of this cup has appeared in the *Archæologia*.
The authoress of the "Lives of the Queens of England" has portrayed (*Gentleman's Magazine*, March 1842) the grace-cup in eight flowing, if not rollicking stanzas.

G

RELIGIOUS VIEWS.

Mr Howard was a fervent believer in the doctrines and practice of Roman Catholicism. It can justly be said of him, that in every relation of life, political, social, or domestic, he showed the amiable and loving spirit of a true Christian. His faithful adherence to the Church of his fathers stood very much in the way of his worldly success, at least in early life. Occupying the position due to a Howard, and being pretty much alone in his advocacy of a proscribed creed, he became a marked personage, against whom the arrows of a bigoted Protestantism might be covertly and severely aimed. Had he shown but an equivocal regard for the countless religious institutions of the country, he might have held to his own persuasion without exciting much attention; nay, by a prudent reticence amid the prevailing shams and Pharisaisms of the day, got credit for a highly respectable Episcopal orthodoxy. Owing to the penal laws, nothing could be more unfortunate than the status of educated Catholics who sought the higher grades of English life—civic, parliamentary, or military; nevertheless, they bore their part as good citizens; and, whilst they were so often passed by, men of no professed religious belief, though outwardly ranking with Mother Church, could hold the highest offices in the State.[*] If ever there was temptation for men to be

[*] Lord Eldon, the Tory Chancellor for twenty-eight years, and stern defender of Church and State against all innovations of Catholic emancipation or political reform, used to pride himself on being one of the bulwarks of the Church. He was neither a church-goer nor a sacramental observer; so the clerical who listened to Eldon's boasting of being a pillar

lukewarm in belief, or positive hypocrites, it was surely at a time when the Catholics of England saw themselves denied all civic rights and political honours, for adopting a spiritual form of worship from which sprang the persecuting Church of Englandism, itself retaining nine-tenths of the old ceremonial. To the honour of Catholicism, its members remained steadfast to their principles. No overtures of state policy, much less of ambition gratified by military honours, could have allured the master of Corby from the faith and the shrine of his fathers. Guided by the family motto, *Sola virtus invicta*, he openly proclaimed his opinions, and, consistently with his own personal integrity and love of freedom, earnestly sought for the emancipation of his co-religionists.

Being persuaded that much misconception prevailed in this country regarding the tenets of the Catholic religion, whether owing to ignorance, or simple perversion of the history of her forms and discipline, he wrote an octavo pamphlet of sixteen pages, entitled, "Remarks on the Erroneous Opinions entertained respecting the Catholic Religion." These "Remarks" were printed for the "Defence Committee of the British Catholic Association," and issued by Bradbury and Dent. Having no pretensions to a study of divinity, Mr Howard submitted his opinions to several learned men of his own Church, who approved of the doctrines set forth, and sanctioned their publication. From a note in Mr Howard's handwriting, it may be

of the Establishment, quietly observed,—" Well, my Lord Eldon, if you are a buttress to our Church, it must be on the outside, as your bodily presence is not to be found among the congregations of either saints or sinners."

inferred that the first edition appeared in 1825; the fifth edition bears the date of 1829.

Whatever opinion may be entertained regarding the essentials or non-essentials of the Catholic Church, no one can rise from the perusal of Mr Howard's pages without admiring the fairness of his statements, and the generous spirit of his advocacy. There is no display of dominancy, no setting up of claims for infallibility, and no *odium theologicum* or rancorous polemic in Mr Howard's published opinions. In discussing the effect of the penal laws, he controverted the assertion that *the Constitution of England is essentially Protestant*, by showing that since the accession of Henry VIII. the religion of the State had varied six or seven times, and therefore the *essentiality* of the Constitution must as often have changed with it. On a page of his note-book, headed "Religious Liberty in England," he constructed a table showing the various changes in his religion, which were required by the statutes, of Henry Jenkins* of Ellerton-upon-

---

* Henry Jenkins was born in 1501, and died at the age of 169 in 1670; he consequently was required by law to adopt the following changes in his religious creed and practice :—From 1501 to 1534, under Henry VII. and VIII., thirty-three years a Catholic; from 1534 to 1547 (Henry VIII.), thirteen years a mixed religion; from 1547 to 1553 (Edward VI.), six years of Church of England; from 1553 to 1558 (Mary), five years Catholic; from 1558 to 1649 (Elizabeth, James I., and Charles I.), ninety-one years Church of England; from 1649 to 1653 (Interregnum), four years Independent; from 1653 to 1660 (Protectorate), seven years Presbyterian; from 1660 to 1670 (Charles II.), ten years Church of England! Surely the ancient Jenkins had more than a burthen of years to bear in the vicissitudes of a State religion; probably he consoled himself that with such a variety of credentials he might knock at the gates of heaven with perfect assurance of Peter's responsive keys.

Swale, in the county of York, in compliance with the principle that the English Constitution is essentially identified with the religion of the State, and "making it a bounden duty (of him and every subject) to conform to it if he wished to keep himself unsinged, uncut-up-alive, unhanged, unracked, unimprisoned, unexiled, unfined, unconfiscated, and unproscribed."

Without claiming the title of a student, much less the position of a teacher of theology, Mr Howard had evidently bestowed much attention on the questions affecting the Catholics of England; and personal as well as party considerations led him to a careful examination of the Scriptures and many religious works. After Catholic Emancipation had passed, and much had been accomplished in the direction of religious liberty, which he and his coadjutors laboured for previous to 1829, his pen did not remain idle for some years afterwards. Among some notes written in 1833, and which he probably thought of publishing, there is a postscript:—" To conclude, I am a Catholic on the same grounds that I am a Christian, from believing the divinity of our Saviour, and the certainty and permanence of His promises."

His largest effort in defence of the Catholic religion was entitled " Historical References in Support of the Remarks on the Erroneous Opinions entertained respecting the Catholic Religion, and to prove that its Principles are not adverse to Civil Liberty, and that Religious Liberty is a Civil Right."* This pamphlet consisted of ninety-four pages, and was printed by M. & J. Jollie, Carlisle, January 1827. It is full of

* To the words civil right, he meant in the second edition to have added the words, "and also the Best Policy."

historical references, and shows a large amount of real learning, and no small share of logical acumen. In his preface, addressed "To Friend and Foe," he assigns good reasons for publishing these "Historical References;" and, whilst assuring his friends of their position as religionists, he aims with a true conciliatory spirit to soothe and convince his foes. He agreed with the opinion expressed by Mr Wyse of Wexford in 1828, who said—"I know of no Constitution which is not for *all* the people. I can no more understand the meaning of a *Catholic* or *Protestant* Constitution than of a Mahomedan or Hindoo, or black or blue Constitution. I know of no just ascendancy which is not based on virtue, industry, and talent; any other may be a monopoly, but not a Constitution; it may, *vi et armis*, be the law, but not the right of the thing; and it is an open violation of *equality before the law*, which is the very essence of all free constitutions."

As a true Catholic, Mr Howard laments and condemns the conduct of those Popes who, in the dark ages, either guided by ambition and desire of power, or deluded by false notions, claimed a right to interfere in temporal concerns, and even to depose sovereigns and absolve their subjects from their allegiance. Intolerance he looked upon as proceeding "solely from state policy, the love of power and command, and the desire of exclusive possession." He writes: —"The Revolution of 1688 was a glorious event, the triumph of civil liberty over arbitrary sway; but, owing to the intolerance of the time, of which its leaders largely partook, not an advancement towards religious liberty." He instanced Germany and other countries to show that more toleration existed towards

Catholics than could be found in Britain, and the Catholic cantons of Switzerland as retaining their democracy, whilst the Protestant cantons favoured oligarchies.

He is full of admiration of Venice, her independence, her power of successfully repelling England, France, Germany, and the Pope, united in arms against her; and that without Venice one half of Europe would probably have been conquered by the Turks, and under a constitution essentially Mahomedan. "Venice, true to her faith, and exact in its exercise, always resisted the encroachments of the Popes, and all interference of the spiritual authority in whatever relates to temporals; *e.g.*, the resistance of the Republic in unison with its prelates and clergy to Paul V." Venice might well excite enthusiasm in the breast of such a reformer as Mr Howard, when Daru relates, in his history of the Republic, that Protestants, Greeks, Armenians, Mahomedans, Jews, and others were alike in the eyes of the law.

In Poland men of every sect or religious profession were eligible to "senatorial and royal dignity." Stephen Bathori used to say, when urged to intolerance, that "he was king of men, not of consciences." John Sobieski, the great Christian hero of his age, was equally tolerant of Greeks and Mahomedans.

Louis Philippe d'Orleans, who reigned over France from 1830 to 1848, was a correspondent of Mr Howard's, and in acknowledging Mr Howard's essay on the Catholic claims, wrote as follows:—

"PARIS, 15*th April* 1827.

"DEAR SIR,—Accept my best thanks for the books

which you have been so good as to send to me. I will read those publications with great pleasure and attention, particularly those that flowed from your pen. Nothing is worse for the success of a good cause than intemperate advocates, and unfortunately Catholic Emancipation has had many of that description. It was therefore an undertaking equally useful and worthy of you to present it in its true light, and to show, as you justly say, that *religious liberty is a civil right as well as the best policy.*—I remain, with great regard, your most affectionate

"LOUIS PHILIPPE D'ORLEANS."

This King of the French felt so amicably disposed to Mr Howard, that he presented him with his portrait and that of his Queen Amelie; and one representing the chief of the Orleanists as schoolmaster at Reicheneau during the imperial sway of Napoleon I.—a proof that he was not ashamed of pursuing an honest calling in the days of his adversity.

The Rev. Sydney Smith, whose writings in favour of Catholic Emancipation in the *Edinburgh Review* were considered the most telling of all that flowed from the pen of a Protestant clergyman and writer, was in frequent communication with Mr Howard, whom he highly esteemed.

Here is a characteristic letter from him, dated Aug. 13, 1829, Combe Florey, Taunton, and addressed to Mr P. H. Howard—"I am very sorry to lose so many good friends in Yorkshire. The only acquaintance I have made here is that of the clerk of the parish; a very sensible man, with great *Amen*-ity of disposition. If you come near here,

come and see me, and convert me to the Catholic religion, or be prepared to be converted yourself; and remember me with great kindness to your excellent father, the very model of what a high-minded gentleman should be.—Ever yours very truly,
"SYDNEY SMITH."

Henry Bathurst, Bishop of Norwich, wrote to Mr Howard in 1825 and 1826 on the same subject of the Catholic claims, and in a manner to prove his highest regard for his friend at Corby Castle. The strain of his correspondence is confidential, and his quoting from both Latin and Greek authors would imply that he was fully aware of his coadjutor's classical powers. The Protestant Bishop was a staunch supporter of the Catholics, and approved very highly of Mr Howard's labours and publications. In speaking of one of Mr Howard's valued essays, he writes to him:—"If Prejudice has either eye or ear, your 'Remarks' would satisfy her; at all events, they cannot but carry great weight with them to every candid mind."

Mr Howard's part in the great struggle for Catholic Emancipation was well known over the United Kingdom. He was earnest and faithful, yet no less conciliatory to the enemies of religious freedom—a cause which he upheld so long and arduously. The very circumstance of such a man as Mr Howard being linked with a political agitation gave it form and substantiality, and enlisted less energetic minds than his own to pursue the course that he had pointed out as beneficial to citizenship and true liberty.

When Parliament defeated, as it did repeatedly,

the efforts of the Catholics, he would cross the Channel and spend a few weeks in Paris or elsewhere. On one of these occasions he presented himself at the Court of Charles X. of France, in the year 1827, and was immediately recognised by the Bourbon King, who, after greeting him, inquired after the Duke of Norfolk, to which Mr Howard replied,—"*Très bien, Sire, mais un peu découragé du naufrage que nous venons de faire.*" (The Catholic Relief Bill had just been thrown out.) "*Et bien,*" rejoined the King, "*ramassons les debris, mettons les ensemble, et nous en ferons un radeau; cela nous menera au port.*" This was wonderfully smart on the part of Charles X., and is another instance of his power of repartee, for which he was oft credited.

When Catholic Emancipation had opened the doors of Parliament to members of the Catholic Church, Mr P. H. Howard, the son of Henry Howard, offered himself to the Carlisle electors in 1830, and became their choice. Carlisle honoured itself by sending to Parliament a man of such high principles—a good Catholic and honest Whig, and the representative of a noble house. Mr Philip H. Howard was the second English Catholic (the Earl of Surrey being the first) returned to Parliament. He served his constituency faithfully and well for twenty-one years; then arose a doubt, among the evangelical Whigs of Carlisle, owing to his natural advocacy of an English hierarchical direction of his Church, in opposition to Lord John Russell's Ecclesiastical Titles Bill; and that doubt induced him, in the most praiseworthy and honourable way, to give place to his able friend, Sir James Graham of Netherby. The writer cannot help expressing his regret, that a constituency which had done so nobly in electing a Catholic in 1830 should have so far stultified itself in 1852. Bigotry, however, is the essence of stupidity, against which neither gods nor men can contend.

A letter of the witty Rev. Sydney Smith, congratulating Mr Howard on his son Philip being elected M.P. for Carlisle, dated the 2d August 1830, is worth quoting.

"COMBE FLOREY, TAUNTON.

"MY DEAR SIR,—The intelligence we have received to-day, from the kind transmission of the Carlisle papers, gave us all here sincere pleasure. It is a pure pleasure to me to see honourable men of ancient family restored to their birthright. I rejoice in the temple which has been reared of toleration, and I am proud that I worked as a bricklayer's labourer at it, without pay, and with the enmity and abuse of those who were unfavourable to its construction. We are finishing here, and are in a very beautiful parsonage. Come and see me. You owe me some recompense for my zeal.—Ever yours,

"S. S.

"*P.S.*—You know Brougham had the offer of Algiers, and has refused it!"*

---

* This postscript was a capital hit at Henry Brougham, who was credited with being omnivorous for place, and not unmindful of pay and pension; it was also well known that he believed himself omniscient in science as well as in law and powers of government. Brougham oft suffered from Sydney Smith's jokes, and he would surely be wroth at the insinuation of his seeking to govern a community of swarthy Arabs and Barbary pirates when he fancied he saw "the Great Seal" looming in the distance.

FREE TRADE AND THE BALLOT.

On December 3, 1832, Mr Howard wrote a letter to the *Carlisle Journal,* assigning "reasons why agriculture should claim the support of all classes." Basing his arguments upon the statistical estimates of Mr Marshall, "that, out of 18,433,000 inhabitants of England, 6,000,000 are employed in agriculture, and 2,400,000 in the manufacturing interest," he held that the agriculturists more properly deserved the name of the PEOPLE than any other class. The impositions or burdens on the land in the shape of taxation next claimed his attention, and he argued that, as the manufacturers had a large share of protection, by taxes on importation on the articles they dealt in, the agriculturists should enjoy the same privilege. Like a truly liberal-minded landowner, however, he wished for a diligent, impartial, and unbiassed investigation of all matters pertaining to the Corn question. As proving that the depression of the comforts of the operative classes were owing to other causes than the relative prices of corn and provisions, he appealed to historical data in his possession.*

---

* "From the year 1770 to 1775, and after the American War, from 1791 to 1795, the prices of wheat for the Carlisle bushel (or three Winchesters) was from 18s. to 23s., and other produce bore the same proportion. At the present moment, in December 1832 (and with little variance for a few years back), the price for the same measure is from 19s. to 22s. ; while the price of labour, from 1770 to 1804 or 5, was, for labour in husbandry (without meat), from 10d. to 1s., and the carpenter had only from 1s. 4d. to 1s. 6d., the mason 1s. 8d.; in some instances the very same persons, then in their prime, now receive respectively 2s. for labour, and the carpenter and mason from 3s. to 3s. 6d. per day, with the advantage of now having apparel, furniture, and many other things at half the price they were."

On December 6, 1832, Mr Howard published his "Ruminations on the Ballot." Looking on the elective franchise as a trust, he wished for an open exercise of it, as consonant with the spirit of our Constitution, and advantageous to permanent freedom. The Ballot would destroy, in his opinion, the responsibility of the electors and the elected. In surveying the history of the question, he attributed the fall of the Roman Republic to the use of the Ballot, within a century of its adoption; and cited the fact that, in Greece, the best man, "the most disinterested patriot, Aristides, was exiled by ostracism, which was a ballot. In Venice, government was long in the hands of the people: they at length chose four hundred and seventy by ballot to govern the country, who perpetuated themselves in the same manner," and to the impairment of the interests of the republic. "On the contrary, in all the cantons of Switzerland that have from the fourteenth century preserved their liberties entire, all their elections are made by votes openly given." Mr Howard, like some of the best men of his day, at a time too when the rejoicings at the achievement of the "Reform Bill" had hardly subsided, wished for a fair trial of this large instalment of liberty without the risk of "newfangled theories" being attached to its working. In Cumberland, Sir James Graham, Mr Blamire, Rev. R. Matthews, and other leading Liberals, gave no countenance to the Ballot; and Mr Howard shared their opinions to the full. No one could give a more patriotic expression to his sentiments than the old Squire of Corby; and thus he concluded his short brochure:—" I speak as an Englishman who has at all times loved liberty, and I think understood it, and acted up to it. . . . .

I never, in public concerns nor in domestic life, knew any good to arise from concealment or secret machinations..... It is by the force of public opinion, openly and manfully given and acted up to, that we have on every crisis made our way out of all difficulties to success: that is our strength and advantage."

"MEMORIALS OF THE HOWARD FAMILY."

It was a happy thought that induced Mr Howard to gather the "Memorials of the Howard Family." No family in England has figured more largely in our national history; and among our highest nobility none have claimed more hearty respect and admiration. Mr Howard, with his natural diffidence, looked upon his inquiries as of little importance, beyond a "beguiling occupation to his mind;" and feared that his literary effort would prove "extremely deficient, and liable to many errors." To read and inwardly digest all that pertained to the lineage of his renowned ancestors was a large and laborious undertaking; it involved historical research from the time of Henry III., and the examination of countless papers and records. In this work of love he was naturally aided by his many noble kinsmen, with the further advantage of the family archives of all the Howards. Much was collected from the public records, the Heralds' College, and the labours of various historians and antiquaries, to all of whom he does ample justice in his "Explanation" or preface. He published the results of his many years' research in a handsome folio volume—"Memorials of the Howard

Family." This highly valuable and beautifully illustrated volume was designated " Indication of Memorials, Monuments, Paintings, and Engravings of Persons of the Howard Family, and of their Wives and Children, and of those who have married Ladies of the same name, and of the Representatives of those of its Branches now extinct, as far as they have been ascertained. By Henry Howard, Corby Castle. Dec. 10, 1834." The last passage in his prefatory explanation to the volume is well worth transcribing, as illustrative of the noble character of the author:—
"In making this collection relating to the Howard family, it is my sincere and anxious wish that what in them was religious, virtuous, honourable, patriotic, and trustworthy, may be imitated and followed by their posterity; and that whatever they may have done wrongfully, either in public or private life, may be carefully avoided. On these conditions, *Esto perpetua*."

Miss Strickland, with many other historians, have derived no inconsiderable advantage from the pages of Mr Howard's folio volume. Writing, in her " Lives of the Queens of England," of Mr Howard's high lineage, unwearied zeal, and indefatigable research, she adds, " His work ('Memorials of the Howard Family') is written in the pleasing and unpretending style of an English gentleman, with much candour, good taste, and excellent feeling." She speaks of her indebtedness to the Duke of Norfolk and Mr Howard, the descendants of Queen Adelicia, for some important particulars connected with the life of that princess which she obtained from the " Memorials." She adds: " To Mr Howard my thanks are peculiarly due, as well as to his accomplished son, Philip Henry Howard, Esq., M.P. for Carlisle."

The editor of the "Memorials of the Rebellion of 1569" records his thanks to Mr Howard for "obligations deep and lasting." There is reason to believe that the history of Leonard Dacre's part in the rebellion proceeded from the pen of Mr Howard of Corby.

PERSONALITY AND CHARACTER.

Mr Howard was a man of goodly form and stature; he was nearly six feet in height, and had a soldierly commanding presence. Seen among his own class, or in the midst of the old squirearchy and stalwart yeomen congregated on the hustings of a county election, Mr Howard was sure to attract special notice. His handsome noble face, his fair complexion, and his suave and highly intelligent expression, were such as are rarely met with in the best favoured English circles. The portrait accompanying this memoir satisfactorily displays the physiognomy of a man upon whom Nature had bestowed some of her choicest gifts. His features are animated, benignant, and thoughtful.

No gentleman in the county had more friends, and no one was better liked by all classes of the community. In every walk of life he showed good breeding, affability, and kindness; these were his natural habit, and could not fail to be manifested daily and hourly, publicly and privately. He was liberal and charitable in all things, and largely generous to the faults of both friend and foe. He was a pattern of a neighbour, and greatly appreciated beyond the precincts of

Corby. He was a warm friend; and lived through a long and eventful life without knowing that he had ever made an enemy. During his youth the writer of these pages never heard of Mr Howard except when his person and his virtues were cited as typical of "the true English gentleman," by birth, by education, and the conscientious discharge of every private and public duty.

Blessed with an affectionate wife, and amiable and loving children, his home was all that man could wish for. Hosts of attached friends gathered under his roof-tree. In his hands Corby Castle lost nothing of its ancient repute for a profusely liberal hospitality, elegant society, and all the pleasant amenities of life. As in the year 1634, so to-day (1872) there is a Howard-Philip Henry at Corby to do honour to his family name, and to enjoy the same high estimation that his father held in Cumberland; and happily, too, he has a son, Philip John Canning Howard, showing the promise of a studious and virtuous adolescence.

Mr Howard performed his share of magisterial duty, and lent willing aid to Sir James Graham in carrying out reforms, chiefly financial, in the management of county business.

Mr Howard filled the office of High Sheriff of Cumberland in 1832, and with the dignity characteristic of his nature. He was the first Roman Catholic in England to fill such an office since the repeal of the Test and Corporation Acts. He was a liberal contributor to the public charities of Carlisle and of the county at large, and in various ways ministered most kindly to the necessities of the poor. He subscribed handsomely towards the erection of the Catholic chapel at Warwick Bridge, designed by Pugin; and it was no small pleasure to him to witness the ceremonial of its being opened for divine service in November 1841.

Mr Howard could have boasted of as large a circle of friends as was ever enjoyed by an Englishman of rank and station. In Cumberland, he was universally esteemed by all classes of people; in London, Paris, Vienna, Rome, Naples, Bologna, &c., he had numerous friends, and throughout the capitals of Europe a large correspondence. He associated with the naval and military, the diplomatic and literary men of his epoch—one of the most remarkable and exciting in the world's annals. He knew many of those who played a prominent part in the French Revolution, and others who shone conspicuously in the eventful European history that sprang from the days of 1789. By Protestant and Catholic, by Tory and Radical, he was received as a man to be trusted and reverenced.

Though noted for his Whiggism and bold defence of the Catholic claims, Lord and Lady Lyndhurst rejoiced to visit him and Mrs Howard at Corby. It would be pleasant to note the many persons of distinction who have joined the Corby circle from time to time, were it only to show the great esteem in which Mr Howard was held, not only by his contemporaries and his own party, but by his political opponents performing the highest functions in the State.

Among as varied a correspondence as ever fell to the lot of any unofficial person, two short letters to Mr Howard may be quoted; the one is from Mr, afterwards Sir, Walter Scott, and the other from

Guiseppe Mezzofanti, the greatest linguist of Europe, and Professor of Greek in the University of Bologna. The Border Minstrel wrote from Edinburgh, 25th March 1806, to thank Mr Howard for a portrait sketch of "Belted Will Howard," in the following terms :—

"SIR,—I have to express my best and respectful thanks for the extreme politeness with which you have been pleased to gratify my hobby-horsical wish to be possessed of a sketch of your eminent ancestor, Lord William Howard. As minstrels are allowed to be invested with a portion of the second-sight, I am happy, but not surprised, at receiving from a descendant of Lord Howard an instance of the courtesy which I accounted one of his chief attributes."

Professor Mezzofanti's letter is dated Bologna, November 18, 1819, and is addressed to Mr Howard, then staying at Florence :—

"SIR,—The day I had the honour of making your acquaintance, and remaining some hours in your company, was very happy for me, and is always present to my memory. It is easy to conceive how great my satisfaction would be if I could have the good fortune of passing some days in your family, as you kindly propose to me in your letter, which I have lately received."

The monthly intelligence of the *Catholicon* for January, February, and March 1836 contains three very interesting letters of Mr Howard's, entitled "Anecdotes Collected in Rome and Italy in 1819-20." These letters afford much information relative to the incarceration of Pope Pius VI. and his cardinals by Napoleon I., also the cruel treatment to which they were subjected. Napoleon's rapacity, shown in his robbing both public and private galleries of pictures and valuables, and other acts of meanness, are shown up in their true colours. The crowning fact in the Corsican's disreputable history was his soliciting, with abject servility, the removal of the Papal excommunication in 1819, when he found himself caged in St Helena, and could no longer wage war against either Church or State.

During his long sojourn at Rome, he formed a pleasant intimacy with Sir Humphry Davy, the distinguished chemical philosopher, who, in his published volume, "Consolations in Travel; or, the Last Days of a Philosopher," alludes to Mr Howard as one of his companions at Rome, under the designation of "Ambrosio;" and as "a man of highly cultivated taste, great classical erudition, and minute historical knowledge; and in religion, a Catholic of the most liberal school." Ambrosio is credited with taking an active part in the Dialogues of Sir Humphry and his friends; occasionally, however, the sentiments assigned to him are not exactly in accordance with the political views known to be entertained by Mr Howard.

Among the compliments paid Mr Howard's literary and social character, mention may be made of Robert Anderson's dedicating his "Cumberland Ballads" to him; and also Mr F. Jollie's "small tribute of gratitude," evinced by his dedication of his "Cumberland Guide and Directory of 1811" to Mr Howard. All this was very different from his first experience of public life; for he relates that " on canvassing a Carlisle freeman for Mr Curwen in 1786, within my own manor at Corby, I was told by him, in circumstances nearly a pauper, that though he would give me his vote, it would not be creditable to him to be seen going into Carlisle with a Papist."

Mr Howard translated several odes and songs of Koerner, the German Tyrtæus, who fell in the service of his fatherland on the 26th August 1813, in the twenty-second year of his age. The last stanza in Koerner's " Volunteer Bond " may be quoted to show Mr Howard's translation:—

> " Now with speed to the fight,
> All that's earthy we close,
> Eyes and hearts to the light !
> Heaven opens above.
> A hand to each brother ;
> For this life fare-ye-well !
> True hearts meet each other,
> Steeled let every nerve tell !
> Hark ! the thunder we near !
> To the lightning rush in :
> In a better world's sphere
> Our next friendly meeting."

The threats of the French, at the beginning of Louis Philippe's reign, to take possession of the German Rhine, brought out the patriotic effusion translated below. Louis King of Bavaria was so pleased with the song, that he addressed the following autographic letter to its author, at the same time sending him a tankard as a present:—

" The words of your song of the Rhine will resound in all German hearts. This song will insure immortality to its author. I wish that you may frequently drain the silver cup which I send you, whilst you are singing, 'No, they shall not have the German Rhine.' I pray you to accept the assurance of my consideration.—LOUIS."

"CORBY CASTLE, 21*st March* 1841.
TO MISS ISABELLA HOWARD,
This attempt at a version of the Patriotic Song,
'THE GERMAN RHINE,'
Composed by N. BEETNER. Set to Music by R. SCHUMAN.

" No ! never shall they have our freeborn* German Rhine !
Let them like raven croak, or like him hoarsely whine ;
As long as peaceful flowing his green-clad bank he wears,
Nor whilst a helm resounding,† he on his bosom bears,
No ! never shall they have our freeborn German Rhine !
No ! never shall they have our freeborn German Rhine !

" No ! never shall they have our freeborn German Rhine !
So long as we enjoy thy spirit-stirring wine ;
As long as on thy shores thy rocks so firmly stand,
Whilst mirrored in thy streams high castles deck thy strand,
No ! never shall they have our freeborn German Rhine !
No ! never shall they have our freeborn German Rhine !

" No ! never shall they have our freeborn German Rhine !
Whilst lads and lasses shall in merry pleasures join ;
As long as in thy stream a single fish shall play,
Or while one German bard pours forth his civic lay ;
No ! never shall they have our freeborn German Rhine !
Until thy flood shall hold the last man of our line,
   The last man of our line,
   The last man of our line."

This song was translated by Mr Howard in the last (the 84th) year of his life. The handwriting in which

---

* The Rhine rises in Switzerland.

† The helm of the old vessels on the Rhine is a long oar, which the steersman works with some noise and splash.

he couched it to Miss Howard not only gives no indication of advanced age, but is so marvellously round and beautiful, that those unacquainted with the caligraphy would attribute it to a youthful or middle-aged person.

Mr Howard was a man of high literary attainments and fine æsthetic taste. His historic researches were of value to Dr Lingard in his last edition of the "History of England;" to Mr P. Fraser Tytler in his "Edward VI. and Queen Mary," and "History of Scotland," vol. vii.; to Sir Cuthbert Sharp in his "Memorials of the Rebellion of 1569;" to Mr Tierney in his edition of "Dodd's Church History;" and Miss Strickland, author of the "Lives of the Queens of England." It is probable that his literary fame will principally rest on the elaborate and truly historical work, "Memorials of the Howard Family." His command of languages and skill in reading old manuscripts were well known; and his researches in various departments of learning fully entitled him to the creditable distinction of being a scholar ardently devoted to history.

Mr Howard enjoyed an unusual amount of good health. It was not till the spring of 1842 that eighty-four years of active life began to tell on even his vigorous constitution. "His last days were those of peace and Christian resignation. He watched the approach of death with calmness and without apprehension. His faculties remained entire to the last; and he may be said to have passed into eternity without pain or suffering, for so tranquilly did he pass away that his attendants were for some time unconscious that the vital spark had fled." He died on

1st March 1842. His remains were interred in the family vault in Wetheral Church, on Tuesday, the 8th March. Though the invitations to the funeral did not extend beyond the tenantry of the estate, great numbers of people from Carlisle and the neighbourhood found their way to Corby. The Corporation of Carlisle had a special meeting at the Town Hall, and resolved to attend the funeral as a mark of the respect and veneration in which Mr Howard's memory was held. Everything was conducted in a manner worthy of the deceased. In addition to thirteen carriages for mourners, and pall-bearers, the tenantry, wearing black hat-bands and gloves, and several hundred persons of respectability, joined the funeral cortége. It was truly said that "the tomb closed upon one full of years, and who had earned for himself the love and veneration of all with whom he had ever come in contact—whose life had been as blameless as his end had been happy, dying in peace with all men."

Mr Patrick Fraser Tytler, the well-known historian, had the highest esteem for Mr Howard, from whom he occasionally obtained valuable information respecting both genealogy and history. These two ardent friends often worked in the same literary groove, and were at all times ready to render each other mutual help. How deeply Mr Tytler felt the loss of his friend and coadjutor is evinced in a letter addressed to the present Mr Howard of Corby, from 34 Devonshire Place, London, 17th November 1842, which contains *inter alia* the following :—

"I have resumed my labour at the State Paper Office, where I am now alone, and often in my studies the image of your excellent father rises to my mind's eye. We used to sit in the same room, and found mutual pleasure in communicating our thoughts, or (as sometimes we ventured to call them) our discoveries to each other. These were very happy hours, and I cannot even now think of them, or of him whose friendship I felt an honour, without a shade of tender regret passing over the memory.—Believe me, dear Mr Howard, ever most sincerely yours,

"PATRICK FRASER TYTLER."

"The cause of historical literature," writes Miss Strickland of her deceased friend, "has lost one of its noblest votaries and friends by the much-lamented death of this venerable gentleman, Henry Howard, Esq., of Corby, who died March 1st, full of days and honours, carrying with him to the tomb the admiration and esteem of all parties, and the lasting regrets of those who were distinguished by his friendship.

> 'It is not the tear at this moment shed,
> When the fresh sod has just been laid o'er him,
> That can say how beloved was the spirit that's fled,
> Or how deep in our hearts we deplore him.'

"The late Mr Howard of Corby derived his descent in a direct line from nine of the queens of England, whose memoirs have appeared in the first and second volumes of this work. His 'Memorials of the Howard Family' (a splendid folio volume, printed for private circulation), has proved a most valuable addition to the historical references connected with the 'Lives of the Queens of England.'"

Mr Howard was a Director of the Newcastle and

Carlisle Railway, and took a deep interest in the work throughout. His colleagues, in recognition of his services, and their high esteem for his character, placed the following inscription on the parapet of the Wetheral Bridge spanning the Eden:—" In testimony of respect to their late colleague, Henry Howard, Esquire, of Corby Castle, who, on the 25th March 1830, laid the foundation-stone of this bridge, the Directors of this railway place this tablet."

MRS HOWARD.

Though no man was more lamented by his family and friends than Mr Howard, the greatest share of sorrow fell to her who had been his affectionate wife, his daily companion, and home-solace for nearly fifty years. Mrs Howard's good breeding and accomplishments enabled her to reap all the advantages of her husband's intellectual status, and the many enjoyments that his society of choice friends conferred. Her motherly feelings and affections sought expression in a daily record of passing events, for the perusal of her children in after life. These private journals, the effusions of a maternal heart, so gratified those whom they concerned, that she published them under the title of "Reminiscences for my Children." They occupy two octavo volumes, and were meant for private circulation only. The mode in which she fed and brought up her children (in this she greatly excelled, by adopting natural food), their amusements and associates, her own interpretation of society in which she so freely mingled, and the more striking events which engaged her husband in the earlier years of their married life, are all set forth in simple narrative, not without the somewhat gossipy character incidental to any record of social meetings in which ladies form the chief feature. Her volumes are interesting in various ways: they show a lady's good-natured view of the society in which she moved, affording anecdotes and other characteristic traits of the more distinguished men and women of the day. Accompanying her husband in his militia experience for five years to different quarters of the United Kingdom, gave her an insight into military life when all was tip-toe expectation as to Napoleon's movements. Then their travels abroad, their intercourse with the notabilities of the French and other European courts; their London life, and associations with the English aristocracy, afforded countless subjects for pleasant comment, and reflective of the age, its men and manners. On her introduction to court by the Countess of Carlisle, for the first time after her marriage, Mrs Howard was agreeably surprised by the Queen of George III. asking her if she had as yet been to Corby, adding she had heard " it was a very pretty place." Mrs Howard had previously, when young, along with her father and mother, Sir Richard and Lady Neave, been presented to the unfortunate Marie Antoinette at the Tuilleries.

She entered with zest into all her good husband's plans and thoughtful considerations, his public efforts, and his private generosities. Her children were all that could be wished, and she naturally doted on them, and might well be excused saying, " Surely these favoured beings are descended from a truly virtuous race." Nor was she unmindful of their ancestors. Thus she writes :—"I must here pay a tribute of respect and affectionate gratitude to the memory of their revered grandfather, Philip Howard, whose suavity of mind and manners, piety and learning, will, I hope, descend to them and their children, with the virtues of their excellent father, Henry Howard, who has so anxiously exerted himself for their future welfare, and the restoration of, and acquisitions to, their family property."

This excellent lady survived her husband nearly seven years. Retaining her faculties till near the close of her eightieth year, she had only been seriously ill for two or three days, when death overtook her, on January 16, 1849, at her house in Lower Brook Street, London. Her remains were interred in the Howard mausoleum in Wetheral Church on February 1st, 1849.

Very faithfully Yr.
Carlisle

GEORGE WILLIAM FREDERICK HOWARD,

Seventh Earl of Carlisle, K.G. and K.T., &c.

> " Thy blood and virtue
> Contend for empire in thee, and thy goodness
> Share with thy birthright."
> —SHAKESPEARE.

THE Carlisle branch of the Howards is derived from Sir Philip Howard, the oldest son of Lord William Howard of Naworth Castle, "the Civilizer of the English Borders." Sir Philip's grandson, Charles Howard, born about 1622, was a colonel in the service of Cromwell; but, after the death of the Protector and his son, became very instrumental in the restoration of Charles II., who, on April 30, 1661, created him Baron Dacre of Gillesland, Cumberland, Viscount Morpeth of Northumberland, and Earl of Carlisle. This Charles, the first Earl of Carlisle, acted as ambassador to Russia, Sweden, and Denmark, and also as Governor of Jamaica. He died in 1685 or 1686.

Edward, the second Earl of Carlisle, was First Lord

of the Treasury in 1701, Lord-Lieutenant of Cumberland and Westmoreland, and Governor of Carlisle. He died in 1692.

Charles, the third Earl, was First Lord of the Treasury, Constable of the Tower, and Governor of Windsor Castle. He is mentioned among Horace Walpole's noble authors. The best memorial of him is the building at Castle Howard, the laying out and planting of the park, and other ornamental decorations to the property there. He died on May 1, 1738.

Henry, the fourth Earl of Carlisle, married, as his second wife, the daughter of the fourth Lord Byron, and through this marriage the illustrious poet Lord Byron became connected with the Howards, being moreover a ward of the Earl of Carlisle, a nobleman whom he ungratefully treated.

Frederick, fifth Earl of Carlisle, was made Knight of the Thistle in 1768, Knight of the Garter in 1793, and subsequently Lord-Lieutenant of Yorkshire. He was a connoisseur in painting, and a great patron of artists both of his own and other countries, and became the owner of the famous picture by Caracci, "The Three Maries." His literary powers were shown in two tragedies,—"The Father's Revenge," and "The Stepmother;" and two small volumes of miscellaneous poems, some of which show a considerable amount of merit.

George, the sixth Earl of Carlisle, born in September 1773, married, on March 21, 1801, Lady Georgiana Dorothy Cavendish, the eldest daughter of William, fifth Duke of Devonshire. This noble pair had six sons and six daughters born to them, of whom they might well be proud, as no finer family could be met with amongst the English aristocracy. Their first child, George William Frederick Howard, born April 18, 1802, in Hill Street, Berkeley Square, London, is the subject of the following pages.

In sketching, however briefly, the leading facts in the history of the seventh Earl of Carlisle, it is hardly possible to overlook his affectionate consideration for all his family, and, most of all, his sisters. In contemplating his own lovable character, your mind seems instinctively to rest on the charming gifts and no less charming graces of his sister, Lady Harriet Elizabeth Georgiana Howard, the lady who married (May 27, 1823) George Granville, Duke of Sutherland, and who, as Duchess of Sutherland, and Mistress of the Robes, held through life the honourable position of a confidential friend of her gracious Majesty Queen Victoria.

England has been credited with producing, under favourable conditions of ease and culture, the finest women in the world. The family of Howard might well be cited by foreigners as embodying types of the prevailing sentiment. Among modern examples, the late Duchess of Sutherland claimed an unfeigned admiration; and not more for her captivating form and beauty than her charming disposition and goodness. The Duchess presided with unrivalled elegance over the acknowledged optimacy of Stafford House, in whose stately saloons oft assembled *le beau monde*, —men of the first distinction and women of the noblest quality, there presenting a *tout ensemble* that rivalled the magnificence of the gayest and grandest courts of Europe. An introduction to the Duchess of Sutherland was the most coveted of all favours to Americans and foreigners visiting London. The eminent in science and in art, in literature and philosophy, diplomatists, military chiefs, and the renowned of every country, rank, and sex, held Stafford House as the greatest *desideratum* in English aristocratic society. The good Duchess gave a true significance, nay, more, a virtuous halo, to every cause she espoused. She headed the philanthropic efforts of the metropolis, and willingly joined all schemes for the amelioration of her countrywomen and the best interests of humanity. She understood English feeling, and oft directed its foreign tendencies and sympathies, notably aiding the enterprise of Garibaldi and the struggles of the Italians for their unity and independence.

Other sisters, besides the Duchess, could hardly fail to exercise a happy influence on both the future Earl and his brothers. Of these highly favoured ladies, who are now filling positions in English society due to their noble birth and virtues, the writer is afraid to speak, lest he disturb the equanimity of the Howard mind, ever disinclined to accept the faintest praise. In holding this disposition of rare and estimable diffidence, the Howards stand in marked contrast to another political House with which Cumberland is far too well acquainted.

The Honourable Mr George Howard was educated at Eton, the nursery of so many of our famous statesmen and scholars. He spent six years there, and became one of its distinguished *alumni*. He was no less conspicuous for his moral rectitude and genial nature. Practising a studious diligence at Eton obtained for him a sound scholarship, which proved of infinite service to him in his career of statesmanship.

He seems to have been more than a schoolboy in thought, and in his earliest years to have shown great zest for classical studies. The noble achievements of the Greeks in art, history, and philosophy; the martial and colonizing spirit of the Romans, might well absorb a youth so well skilled as he was in transforming the sentiments couched in an ancient language to the embellishments of a living tongue, and that the wide-embracing Anglo-Saxon. His penchant for English prose and poesy was no less marked than his ardent love for classical literature; and whether owing to Etonian indoctrination, or his own culture, he acquired a mastery over the English language that few men of his own time possessed. He early sought to establish the groundwork of correct composition; and as he grew in years he matured a style of prose elegance and poetic purity that often elicited remark, and not unfrequently the high approval of able critics. His powers of versification were remarkably good and innate—*poeta nascitur, non fit*—as is well evidenced in his "Farewell to Eton," written at the dawn of his seventeenth year, a few lines of which are here subjoined:—

> "Thus must I leave my lyre, so often strung
> To the soft numbers of the Latian tongue;
> Yet will I breathe its last, its parting tone,
> The heart must speak—the language be my own.
> . . . . . .
> Yes! I must grieve; and who that e'er has strayed
> In sportive joy, and through thy classic shade,
> Breathed the light gales that float thy banks along,
> Hallow'd to science and beloved by song,
> Wove the light verse, or roamed the shady grove
> In mutual friendship and confiding love.
> Could e'er those happy hours and scenes forget,
> View without fondness—leave without regret!

Mingling with his regrets at leaving Eton, he seemed hopeful for the future of some of his loved companions. This is elegantly expressed in the following:—

"Here youthful warriors, youthful statesmen dwelt,
Here bards the tide of inspiration felt;
Here first the eagle-pinioned lyre of Gray
Poured to his own loved 'Father Thames' the 'lay;'
Here Fox's eloquence first learned to flow,
And Wellesley's spirit caught its martial glow.
My loved companions! still may Eton view
All that she prized in them revive in you;
Still may she see you, ever as in youth,
Bold in the cause of freedom and of truth;
With lettered science, or with patriot zeal,
Upholding Britain's fame, and Britain's weal,
First in her Church, her Senate, or her Bar,
In peace her wisdom, and her strength in war."

In 1819 he entered Christ Church, Oxford. In 1821 he obtained the Chancellor's prize for Latin verse, and also the Newdegate prize for English verse. His "Eleusis" and "Pæstum," the subjects of these prize poems, served to establish his reputation at Oxford as one of the coming men of the time—another Howard born to enjoy the inspiration of the muse, and to realise for himself a share of the ancestral honours of his noble house. Here are a few passages from his prize poem "Pæstum" to show its character:—

PÆSTUM.

"'Mid the deep silence of the pathless wild,
Where kindlier Nature once profusely smiled,
Th' eternal temples stand—untold their age,
Untraced their annals in historic page;
All that around them stood now far away—
Single in ruin, mighty in decay;
Between the mountains and the azure main,
They claim the empire of the lonely plain.

> In solemn beauty, through the clear blue light,
> The Doric pillars rear their massive height,
> Emblems of strength untamed; yet conqu'ring Time
> Has mellowed half the sternness of their prime,
> And bade the lichen 'mid their ruins grown
> Imbrown with darker tints the vivid stone.
>
> . . . . . .
>
> Not always thus—when beamed beneath the day,
> No fairer scene than Pæstum's lovely bay,
> When her light soil bore plants of every hue,
> And twice each year her storied roses blew;
> While bards her blooming honours loved to sing,
> And Tuscan zephyrs fanned th' eternal spring.
>
> . . . . . .
>
> 'Tis past—the echoes of the plain are mute,
> E'en to the herdsman's voice or shepherd's flute:
> The toils of art, the charms of nature fail,
> And Death triumphant rides the tainted gale;
> From the lone spot the trembling peasants haste,
> A wild the garden, and the town a waste."

Having obtained first-class honours, he graduated at Oxford in 1822 with the highest distinction. He proceeded to his M.A. degree in 1827.

Though freed from the restraints of his *Alma Mater*, and naturally brought in contact with the aristocratic gaieties of London life—that terrible vortex for the youthful nobility wanting intellectual culture and moral powers of guidance—he remained faithful to his scholastic training and Oxonian indoctrination. If, as a member of the nobility, he responsively joined in the round of graces constituting the higher English life, and helped to make that life more charming and virtuous; he still held by his early love of the muse, his affection for the literature that would enliven his thoughts, and the classical history that would enlarge his understanding and ennoble his patriotism. He would have been the last of his order to indulge in the *dolce far niente* of patrician life. As if prefiguring the part he was to play in the service of the crown, he gave large attention to passing events, and these were of no ordinary magnitude after he had attained his majority. He had excellent opportunities of studying the chief actors in the arena of his political dawn, the machinations of state parties, and all that bore upon the present policy and future guidance of England.

Wishing to enjoy in his early adolescence the full advantages of travel, he left home in 1823 for the southern parts of Europe, and lingered long by the shores of the Mediterranean, around which, as every one knows, the great events of history have for so many centuries been clustered. He spent much time in Italy exploring its noted cities, and above all, its great capital—Rome.

And if ever any one was susceptible of the happier influences arising from the contemplation of historic phenomena illustrated by galleries of art, Pagan temples, Christian basilicas, amphitheatres, and other architectural achievements; or recalled by scenes hallowed by heroic deeds or the display of classic and forensic eloquence—it was surely he who, in his early teens, had set forth in admirable verse the characters of Eleusis and Pæstum, and gained the highest honours at Oxford. One might be disposed to envy the Hon. Mr Howard, the man of classic thought, æsthetic culture, and rich fancy, visiting lands of world-wide repute, and under skies of almost permanent sunshine, where Nature seemed to reflect in her clear brightness the spirit of those humanities who in days of yore gave a large personal significance to mundane events. In his journeyings he made free inquiry into the merits of national institutions and liberties; and if modern Italy revealed but fragmentary illustrations of her ancient glory, he might, like the palæontologist examining the relics of a former geological epoch, gather from the debris of to-day the life of an historic past. Sagacious as a traveller, every line and streak of colour in the lights and shadows of society would fall upon his impressionable nature like a receptive canvas, or serve as a mnemonic syllabus, in hours of leisure, to an interpretation of the varied national life.

In 1825 family changes supervened to affect Mr Howard's position. By the death of his grandfather (fifth Earl of Carlisle) on September 4 of that year, his father became the sixth Earl of Carlisle, and moved to the Lords, whilst he himself succeeded to the dignity of Lord Morpeth, by which title he will now be spoken of. He was long and most estimably known to the British public as Lord Morpeth—a name associated with noted electioneering contests, and, with one exceptional instance, always allied with victory—nay, crowning success. Prominent as a Minister, abiding by the standard of civil and religious freedom, Lord Morpeth was universally known for his immaculate conduct and praiseworthy public services. Under the same propitious title he achieved for Ireland a vast amount of amelioration and positive good, and so won his way to the affections of the Irish people as to gain crowns of laurels where too many Government officials had reaped but thistles and rue.

The Parliamentary Session of 1825–26 showed more

or less deterioration in the ranks of the Tories, and a bolder attitude on the part of the public out of doors crying loudly for the redress of grievances. This was a fitting opportunity for the promising Young England of politics to come forth and take their position on the platform of state government. The clubs and the associations of parties, especially of that party named the Progressive, from being in accord with the spirit of the times, sought for representative men to advocate their principles and the popular cause; and among those deserving of distinction and indicating a noble promise from a noble stock, was the young Lord Morpeth.

Lord Morpeth attended the coronation of Charles X. of France at Rheims, little auguring that the splendid paraphernalia of the ceremony were but the dying embers of the ancient Bourbonic fire, and that five years more would sweep away the tinsel, the theatrical shiftings, and Jesuitism of this infatuated race, into the unutterable future.

He accompanied his uncle, the Duke of Devonshire, to St Petersburg, to pay English official respect to the Emperor Nicholas on his being crowned in 1826. There he saw the forces of the Eastern potentate in transcendant array, the new Romanoff bidding for full honours to his house and larger amplification to his domains; and in his emulating the ambition of a Western Pope, realising *per se* the autocracy, if not semi-divinity, of the Primitive or Greek Church.

Born to the service of the state, Lord Morpeth's training had been directed to make that service worthy of the high repute of the Howards, and of the important parts they had played in English history. The baubles and blazonry of the French and Russians had given him an insight into the characteristic emblems and proclivities of the greatest of European courts, and enabled him to compare the Eastern patriarch, to whom millions bent the knee, with the last representative of the famed Bourbon who declared —"*L'etat c'est moi.*" In other continental states he saw much that was calculated to arouse his sympathetic adolescence, and to give him food for thought. At home, events were marching apace. Eldonism had lost something of its terrors, and Toryism a good deal of its ancient vigour. The Cavendishes, the Howards, and the Greys were making themselves heard in the House of Peers; the Russells, Cannings, and Broughams were trying to revive the old spirit of Charles James Fox in the Commons; whilst outside the walls of Parliament, William Cobbett, Henry Hunt, and the Radicals were fighting hard against oligarchical rule, trade monopolies, and restricted liberties. The framework of the constitution and the feeling of the time were getting out of gear— new operatives were being inquired for, and fresh machinery had become essential to the renovation and validity of the state-coach.

Whilst Lord Morpeth was returning from the Russian mission, the general election of 1826 took place, and in his absence he was nominated and elected M.P. for the borough of Morpeth. His address thanking the electors was held to be worthy of him in every way; and his popularity in the Morpeth barony not only was unbounded, but truly warm and affectionate. He sat for Morpeth till 1830, and during this his first experience of Parliamentary life, aided the Whigs in carrying the Catholic Relief Bill, the repeal of the Test and Corporation Acts, and other measures of needful reform.

Though his speeches in the Commons were neither numerous nor lengthy, he fully sustained the high character he had earned at Oxford, and was looked upon as affording healthful promise for the future. He avoided the diffusive and parenthetic style of rhetoric, as well as the sentimental—blemishes to be met with in older hands, and notably in Mr Disraeli of to-day. He aimed at a clear definition, and never lost sight of his argument; his sentences were well measured, and naturally told for whatever they were worth; and inasmuch as he never dealt in ambiguous phrases and useless circumlocution, they told happily and well. From the first it was apparent that the aids to his rhetoric displayed more of the literary than the forensic element in their character. His quotations from his favourite poets or classical authors were among the most successful of their kind, and could not fail to awaken interest in an assembly that, in those days at least, boasted of scholars and men of classical fervour and enlightenment.

He was at no time an idle man, and university studies were still dear to him. Occasionally embracing the pleasures of the muse, he contributed to the illustrated Annuals and other channels of more *recherché* literature. His imaginative faculty found a theme in the second vision of Daniel, which he paraphrased in verse, adding numerous notes and explanations of the text. In 1828 he wrote a tragedy—" The Last of the Greeks; or, the Fall of

Constantinople." There are many admirable passages in his tragedy, had space permitted of quotation. The "Last of the Greeks" was hardly suited, and was not intended by its author, for dramatic representation.

His studies were not confined to polite literature, but assumed a large range of history and political economy. His eyes were specially drawn to the great political problems then agitating the public mind, and calling for speedy settlement. Thus, he laboured in the initiative to a position in public life to which he was no less destined by birth than by the possession of natural talents of a high order. The breathings of his youthful Etonian verse, portending lofty paths for his school companions—

> " With lettered science, or with patriotic zeal,
> Upholding Britain's fame or Britain's weal!"

would lose nothing of their force in his adolescence and personal applicability, but derive increased strength from his associations with the aspiring men of the epoch.

Owing to the family interests of the Howards prevailing at Morpeth, his Lordship's seat for this Northumbrian borough might be held both safe and prizeable. However, with the swelling tide of Reform sweeping across the kingdom, and affecting both county freeholders and city freemen alike, the Whigs anticipated that small boroughs like Morpeth would take care of themselves in the struggle for an enlarged franchise, whilst county interests would require special considerations. Any assault upon the old Tory constituencies was so far precarious that the reformers of 1830 could only hope to succeed in contesting them by offering their ablest advocates for the county suffrages. It was deemed a bold policy to try and upset the Lowther influence in Cumberland; but many thought the proposal of the Whigs to carry the great county of Yorkshire vastly more rash. In the character of their candidates lay their only hopes of success. The one was a veteran well known for his services in the cause of education and freedom, and at that time the most popular champion of the people's rights in England—Henry Brougham; the other was a young politician, only twenty-eight years of age, heir to a Yorkshire property and a good name, and whose personal character held out a great senatorial promise—Lord Morpeth. It was a singularly high compliment to his Lordship to link him with Brougham in contending Yorkshire. The Whigs by their choice apparently wished to test the feeling of the people on the subject of Reform, by the crucial example of the election for the largest and most influential constituency in the kingdom. They were right in their diagnosis of the popular sentiment, and the return of Lord Morpeth and Henry Brougham to Parliament was the most crowning triumph of the day that witnessed the downfall of the last prop of political feudalism in England.

On addressing the electors of Yorkshire on August 5, 1830, he said *inter alia*—

"We are sometimes accused of taking a foolish pride in our county—a pride in our county I hope we shall always feel; but it would be a foolish pride if we placed it exclusively, or even principally, on the richness of our soil, the extent of our borders, the beauties of our scenery, or even the products of our industry; but it ceases to be a foolish pride if we make it consist in setting an example to England of maintaining the purity of the elective franchise, of befriending the claims of humanity, and of vindicating the cause of freedom."

Speaking on the corn laws he said,—

"I know that I am addressing a mixed assembly, both of consumers and producers of corn; but you are, gentlemen, one and all of you, eaters of bread; and it never can make a country rich, it never will enable our industry to thrive or commerce to extend, if we unnecessarily raise the price and stint the quantity of the daily bread we eat. But believe me, gentlemen, whether you belong, like myself, to the landed interest, whether, as workmen, you handle the spade or the shuttle, or whether, in higher ranks of society, you live upon the labours of an industrious tenantry, or the honourable enterprise of commerce, our interests are not separate and single, but reciprocal and united. ... It is this sympathy which, above all things besides, I wish to see exist and grow among all classes and all ranks, when the wealthy portion of the community shall feel that their most real security is in the comfort of the industrious, and when the higher classes shall know that their most true support is in the contentment of the lower. It is this same feeling which leads me to entertain a decided hostility to the present system of the game laws. ... Gentlemen, while, as a patriot and a philanthropist, I cannot help expressing my general wishes for the triumphant and bloodless march of freedom in every corner of the globe—whether it sweeps away a Bourbon, a Don Miguel, or a Grand Turk—whether it inspires France, or revives Portugal, or regenerates Greece—we must not forget that it is a still more especial duty of our own to take care that the blessings of freedom should be extended and felt in our own dominions, and among our fellow-subjects."

On the declaration of the poll, Lord Morpeth (at the head of the poll) had 1464 votes; Henry (afterwards Lord) Brougham, 1295. Their opponents,—Mr Duncombe, 1123 votes; and Mr Bethell, 1064 votes.

On his second appearance before the Yorkshire electors, May 6, 1831, he argued for the principles of the Reform Bill with great earnestness, and in great hopes of its becoming the law of the land. In reference to the tactics of the Tories, who had been crying revolution, he concluded his speech in the following words:—

"We are branded as disaffected and disloyal men, enemies to the Constitution, and traitors to the Throne. Gentlemen, I will not insult you by endeavouring to refute that charge in your behalf. Allow me to say one word in my own. It so happens, by the chance of my birth, that I share in the accident of a high and historic name. I feel put upon my defence, and you will excuse this personal reference; but often as the name of Howard may be found on the page of British story—though it has been the rallying shout of many a well-fought field—though it rose above the wrecks of the Armada—it never appeared in a more ennobling crisis, and never performed a more acceptable service, than when he who is now its head, the present Duke of Norfolk, stepped forward, and in the place in Parliament, to which he had lately been restored, sacrificed the oligarchical privilege which he had inherited from his ancestors for the benefit of that community of which he thinks it honour enough to be the foremost citizen; while I, who bear his name, but cannot emulate his sacrifice, feel that I shall most nearly tread in his steps by joining heart and hand with you, my countrymen, in accomplishing the work before us, which, as it strengthens the Crown by basing it upon the love, so it will support the aristocracy by inciting them to win the respect, of the people. And I will only add a prayer to Almighty Goodness, that He may deign to sanction this attempt to achieve a great act of national conciliation, by infusing amongst us, in every walk and every work of life, such a spirit of order, such a spirit of union, such a spirit of piety, as can alone make us capable and worthy of enjoying all those blessings of peace, and prosperity, and plenty, which He alone can give."

Nothing could more clearly establish the high confidence of the Whig party in the administrative powers of Lord Morpeth (then only in his thirty-third year), than his appointment to the Chief Secretaryship for Ireland. This post, at all times important and onerous in responsibility, was specially so in 1835, when Mr O'Connell was in all his glory as chief counsellor for the Irish people, with demagogism rampant over the land, and the Roman Catholic hierarchy incensed by what was looked upon as tergiversation on the part of Lord Stanley and Sir James Graham. It is no exaggeration to say that Lord Morpeth undertook the most difficult post in the Melbourne Ministry; for as Secretary for Ireland he was the principal representative of the Irish Government in the House of Commons, and daily liable to be interrogated by the Irish agitator and his allies,—described in those days as O'Connell and his *tail*. Lord Morpeth fulfilled the highest expectations of both his political party and his personal admirers. He earned, as he certainly merited, success in all his efforts to render justice to Ireland. His popularity gained daily in strength, and in the accession of friendly supporters. His policy had a clear, intelligible meaning; it was firm, yet conciliatory; it recognised the Irish people not as sectional, denominational, or tripartite, but as a whole and indivisible portion of the United Kingdom. His kind, genial nature and the hopefulness of his sympathies found a responsive chord in the Irish heart; and that heart being gained, his course became facile and comparatively cheerful.

His administration of Irish affairs continued over the unusually long period of six years (1835-1841), and not only satisfied the Liberal and more decided "Irish party," but obtained for him no small amount of commendation from his political opponents.

On June 26, 1835, Lord Morpeth brought forward

a motion which had for its professed object the settlement of the question of Irish tithes, and the future regulation of the Irish Church Establishment. His speech occupied four columns of the daily press, and was characterised by "a simplicity of expression, a collected force of enunciation, an unaffected dignity and calmness and determination of manner, which captivated the attention of the House." The *Morning Chronicle* went further :—"We heard several of the senior members of the House acknowledge that they had seldom heard a Cabinet measure explained with so much clearness, or with more of that passionless earnestness which bespeaks the formed statesman, than they did on this occasion." After congratulating Ireland on having obtained in Lord Morpeth a sincere friend, a discreet adviser, a devoted and most efficient advocate, the writer of this leading article (June 27), adds :—"The subject afforded little field for eloquence; but the language that best suits wisdom, the unsought but pregnant phrase, the deep feeling of important responsibility, the inflexible resolution to do that which was right, no matter whom it alienated or attracted, combined to bestow a character on Lord Morpeth's official *début* of which his family and his country may be proud." The Commons showed their appreciation of Lord Morpeth's maiden effort in official life by cheering him for several minutes after he concluded his excellent and well-argued speech.

Lord Morpeth was not wanting on occasions as important as the delivery of a set speech; he was not slow to accept the challenge of the most fearless of the Opposition, and showed himself fully able to hold his own against all comers. In all the debates on Irish affairs Lord Morpeth took a prominent share, and fairly earned the character of being a reliable Minister.

In addition to the ordinary tear and wear of official routine, he carried through the House of Commons the Irish Tithe Bill, the Irish Municipal Reform Bill, and the Irish Poor-Law Bill, any one of which would have been a fair test of his application and good management. On looking back to these troublous times, such an amount of work was a truly great achievement, which the future historian cannot fail to recognise as highly worthy of record, and with the more satisfaction that previous Governments could only show years of misspent legislation and a discontented people.

Though anticipating four years, noticeable for the Yorkshire contests, the reader will probably concur in the judiciousness of saying all that requires to be said on Lord Morpeth's Irish Secretaryship at this stage of the record.

The best proof that could be adduced of the success of his Irish administration—a success altogether unprecedented since the establishment of the Union—is to be found in the fact that the Irish people, headed by the best men of the day, and the best representatives of Irish feeling, presented Lord Morpeth with a farewell address previous to his departure from Dublin, September 12, 1841, occasioned by the accession of the Ministry of Sir Robert Peel.

The Duke of Leinster, on presenting the address to Lord Morpeth, said that " it gave him the greatest pleasure to have had the honour of being chairman of the meeting at which the address was adopted. To the address were appended no less than 257,000 names—57 peers, 29 honourables, 25 baronets, 97 deputy-lieutenants, 102 magistrates, 12 Roman Catholic bishops, together with a considerable number of Protestant and Dissenting ministers of various denominations."

Lord Morpeth might well be overpowered by such an exhibition of kind feeling towards him. A memorial consisting of 400 feet of parchment, and signed by upwards of a quarter of a million of Irishmen,—by persons of the highest rank and station, and of every religious persuasion,—being presented to a Government official not soaring towards the zenith of his career, but retiring from his position, nay, despoiled of power, is the most remarkable thing of its kind in the annals of Britain. In his reply to the address, he claimed the desire to give both permanency and efficacy to every development of the paramount principles of civil and religious freedom, and the practical exercise of political and social equality between man and man, between class and class, between creed and creed, and between country and country. In conclusion he said—"I have found among you everything that could most excite and rivet attachment. And now, all that remains for me is to renew my assurance that through the whole course of my life I shall seize with alacrity any opportunity that passing events may supply for evincing it; and I shall retain this honoured document as its best memorial and incentive, and as the the richest heirloom I could bequeath to the name I bear.

A great banquet was given to Lord Morpeth on the same evening, at which the Marquis of Clanricarde presided. To the toast, "Our distinguished guest, Lord Morpeth," the noble lord replied, *inter alia* :—

"But I am here to-night, gentlemen, having filled for a longer period than any of my predecessors the office of Chief Secretary for Ireland; and knowing, by my personal experience, the responsible and difficult nature of the delicate duties which it involves, and remembering the feelings of anxiety, and even of misgiving, with which I first entered on their discharge, and conscious, above all, of the many errors and imperfections which a retrospect of the whole intervening period affords, and which I cannot fail to conjure up before my memory, I own I cannot wholly suppress the thrill of pleasure and exultation with which I look at this brilliant scene before me as the rich reward of all my exertions."

He traced the history of his official career till he came towards its close; and speaking of the transfer of the power the Whigs had held into other hands, he gave the following advice to his successors :—

"Improve upon the errors of which we may have been guilty in our management; correct the abuses which we may have left unremoved, and carry the fortunes of the Irish people further and higher than we have been able to do ; but, above all, do not suffer the sacred deposit which has been intrusted to you to be tarnished in your hands. But I say to you, above all, keep clear—knowing, as I do, some of the companionship with which you are connected—I say, keep clear of the blighting breath of bigotry—foster the seeds of religious peace and good feeling which have been generally disseminated throughout the land, and which, with prudent and careful culture, may fill the furrows of the country with plenty, and its heights with verdure, and make this great people happy and united. . . . When I look back on the past history of this country, and her present capabilities—on all she has suffered, on all she may be destined to become—when I perceive how much she has contributed in some ways to the weakness, in other ways to the strength of

England—how she has shed on every page of their blended history the traces of her power and her intellect—the light that still flashes from the sword of Wellington, and plays around the lyre of Moore—when, I say, I recollect these things, I can form no wish but that two nations so circumstanced should enter into mutual participation of every civil right and every national privilege. . . . As for myself, individually, it is a painful, yet a grateful office to bid farewell to those associates whose prompt and active zeal has lightened the load of business and soothed the responsibilities of office—to friends whose steady and assiduous kindness has gladdened my hours of recreation, and furnished me with stores of pleasurable recollections—and to the Irish people, who must ever command my respect, affection, sympathy, and gratitude, whenever I have the means of serving them, and as long as I have the power of remembering them."

At a great Reform banquet given to the Members of the West Riding of Yorkshire at Leeds, January 18, 1837, a meeting attended by upwards of two thousand gentlemen, Lord Morpeth was called upon to respond to the toast, "Lord Melbourne and His Majesty's Ministers," and thus adverted to the Tories and their professed patriotism :—

"Is the vessel of the State so utterly valueless in your (Tory) eyes that you can see her without emotion—nay, with seeming complacency—dashing dreadfully on the breakers, or madly rushing aground on the quicksands, without attempting even to do what you fully proved to your own satisfaction you could do—either re-manning her crew, or altering her dangerous and destructive course? Contrasting one series of your representations with the other, are you not, on your own showing, the most abashed of foul libellers, or the most pusillanimous of recreants? Was there ever before so much swaggering and so much shrinking in any body of public men? So much pealing of trumpets to the fray, and so much backwardness to the onslaught? Haste on, magnanimous men, to the battle if you will—we still keep the field, and still hold the helm."

Speaking of the condition of Ireland and the introduction of a system of poor-laws into that country, he said :—

"It is by legislating thus—in a spirit of enlightened consideration for that country—in a spirit of sympathy with its rights, and of confidence in its gratitude—that we may hope for what we shall then deserve, that she will be in the future, instead of a sore and a blot in our side, a blessing and a pride—our partner in all the arts which grace the empire, and our competitor in all which contributes to our national greatness and glory."

His peroration was as follows :—

"As for myself, I am prepared to persevere in that course of conduct which has been hitherto tried by you. I value, and will to the utmost of my power maintain, the integrity of the Constitution ; but under its broad and expansive shade I would remove every obstacle—would clear every path to each rank, creed, and class which owns its sway and courts its shelter. I would persist in reducing and removing all the remainder of the system of exclusive privileges and monopolies by which one small portion of the community are benefited to the detriment of all the rest. I would give to religious as well as to civil liberty the widest and most unobstructed range. I am, above all, most desirous to brush from our temples and our altars those sordid disputes and clerical bickerings which desecrate and disgrace them ; and while I thus advanced with the spirit of the age, I would adapt the framework of my polity to surrounding circumstances—I would cling to no abuse because it was ancient, and shrink from no improvement because it was change ; but I should, at the same time, feel little disposed to desert that party whom it has pleased some to predicate are verging on extinction, never more to rise to power or popularity in England. Be it so. The destinies of parties as well as of empires are beyond the scan of human calculation ; but to whatever depth of obscurity my friends and myself may chance to be consigned, it will be sufficient for me, as an individual, to remember that in four successive elections I bore your colours on to victory. It will be sufficient for me, as a member of a party, to know that in four short years we have reformed the representation of the people in Parliament—that we have reformed and opened the municipal corporations of England and Scotland—that we have swept from our blushing records the demon code of negro slavery—that we have opened trackless seas and boundless shores in the most distant parts of the globe to British trade, British industry, and British enterprise—that we have, in a word, done all these things upon the imperfect and hesitating assent to which Sir Robert Peel, their sole champion, alone rests his defence of the House of Lords, and that the legislation of four years, the far and dim-seen results of which will enrich and bless the future as well as the present time—generations yet unborn and ages yet uncounted—has all been achieved without a single form even of the Constitution having been violated, a single breach of the law having been countenanced, or a single drop of human blood spilt. Constituencies of England, send us on in the same path! It is a career too lofty and too glorious for us to desert while there is a remaining triumph of good government, national freedom, and human amelioration to be accomplished. I may be thought too much of a party interested to urge on you a vigilant attendance on the courts of registration, or to impress on your minds the necessity of unity and co-operation among yourselves. These parts devolve on you as electors—they are the parts allotted to a free people. It is for the Ministers of this great empire to perform their parts with honesty, fearlessness, and zeal—jealous of your interests, guardful of your rights, anxious always to promote your advancement,—to consult your permanent rather than your temporary advantages, however momentarily tempting the latter may be—to watch over the ægis of British freedom, and keep it from taint or tarnish—to array it with all the mild and manly acts and virtues which at once adorn and ennoble our nature,—to be as devoted to you in the senate as your soldiers are in the field or your seamen on the billow—or, to sum up all in one short word,—to be worthy of such a country."—The noble Lord then sat down, much cheered.

On the motion of want of confidence in the Whig or Melbourne Ministry, introduced by Sir J. Yarde Buller, January 28, 1840, and strongly supported by Sir Robert Peel and the Tories, Lord Morpeth took his part in the defence of the Irish policy of his party, and said, *inter alia—*

"If Ireland be in a state of tranquillity unprecedented, and if the keystone of ministerial policy be the impartial administration and vigorous enforcement of justice between all creeds and parties, and an anxious endeavour to raise Irishmen, in point of rights and privileges, to an equality with their British fellow-countrymen—if such was the condition of Ireland, and such the guiding principles of those who governed her, then he felt proof against all the sneers and clamours of the Opposition, and would leave everything else to the evidence of facts and the appreciation of a liberal and intelligent people."

He then reverted to the difference of opinion amongst the Conservative party, and continued—

"And did we not hear, a few nights afterwards, the Right Hon. Baronet (Sir Robert Peel) declare that if he undertook the government of the country, Ireland would be the chief source of his difficulties? And do you think that, in the intervening period, Ireland has been so soothed by the dulcet strains of sympathy and consolation which have been poured forth through all your organs and from all your gatherings? Do you think that the mind of Ireland has been so enlightened, so irradiated by the glimpses you have let fall upon her of the sentiments you entertain towards her, and of the purposes you cherish in her behalf, that the difficulties to which the Right Hon. Baronet alluded in so emphatic a manner are removed—that the dark cloud will pass away which before closed round his accession to office, and open a horizon of serenity and confidence where all was mistrust and alienation? Have there been no indications of late from England and Scotland as well as from Ireland? . . . We hail (continued the noble Lord) with right good-will from the different constituencies which have been consulted their commentary on the motion of to-night. And if it pleases you so to continue it—if, heedless of 'the better part' which is still open to you, you decline to co-operate in the work of assisting to smooth the difficulties and to lessen the obstacles which, we do not dream of denying, beset and impede many of the complicated relations of our internal, our foreign, and our colonial policy—to soothe the irritations which prevail in the public mind—to disarm jealousies—to allay dissensions—in one word, to consult together for the public good, why we, as a party, and in a selfish point of view, have only to bid you go on—to stir up, or rather, perhaps, to suffer to be stirred up, the fierce embers of past intolerance—to re-illume the fires of expiring bigotry, and scatter the elements of mistrust amid the inhabitants of the same soil—the children of the same Creator. And while you adopt this course, we, on the contrary, shall put our trust in the increasing spread of intelligence, in the confirmed sway of toleration, and in the returning sense of a disabused people."

At the election for the West Riding of Yorkshire, held at Wakefield, June 28, 1841, Lord Morpeth spoke in favour of removing the restrictions on sugar, corn, timber, &c., and in general defence of the ministerial measures; but failed to convince the constituency, and for the first and only time in his electioneering contests, suffered defeat.

In addressing the electors at the declaration of the poll, he did not attempt to conceal the magnitude of the triumph gained by his opponents, but, on the contrary, looked upon it as the most signal and decisive one attached to the car of Conservative reaction. Not less in his hour of defeat than when he anticipated victory, he felt persuaded that the opinions and measures which he had advocated were hastening on to their accomplishment; and though the verdict of the West Riding might postpone the time for gathering the first-fruits, and aggravate the burthen and inflame the heat of the day, he believed that the cause of truth and justice was sure in the long run to prevail; for if there was one subject more than another on which a nation was most likely to see itself righted, it would be on that which concerns its food.

After speaking of the period of his connection with the constituency—lasting through eleven years and five Parliaments—he turned to personal matters, thus :—

"I am willing to flatter myself that even with my political opponents I leave behind nothing but political difference, and that we separate without any ground for angry retrospect, or for personal offence. But as to those with whom I have had the greater happiness of agreeing, now that so many recollections of considerate kindness, of disinterested zeal, of generous forbearance, of past struggles and of past victories, are rushing at once upon my mind, I feel what language cannot embody and thanks cannot convey. I have learned, gentlemen, to love even the inanimate features of your lovely landscapes, with which I have grown familiar during my repeated canvasses among your heath-clad hills and your wide-spreading valleys; but how much more has my spirit bounded in answer to the cheers which roused the mountain echoes, or to the welcome which ushered me into the busiest haunts of your living industry! I trust I need not debar myself from the hope that, in the various courses of life, opportunities may present themselves to me of showing an abiding sense of gratitude for your past favours; and I cannot help declaring, though it may seem to bespeak a more poignant sense of the loss I have sustained, that I do not think I could reconcile myself, for the present, to occupy any other seat, or to represent any other men. And now, gentlemen, that I have to take my leave of you, bear with me if I adopt for one moment a more solemn tone than I might otherwise have thought it fit to use on such an occasion; but I cannot refrain from putting up one fervent petition that the Disposer of all events and the Giver of all good may visit each and all of you with His choicest and most abundant blessings! May He store your garners with increase, and reward your industry with plenty! May He scatter the seeds of order, of temperance, and of domestic and public virtues far and wide amidst all your dwellings! May He crown each hearth and home with peace, with comfort, with content, and with thanksgiving, and ever supply you with those who can, I will not say more faithfully, but more efficiently, serve you! These, gentlemen, are my latest words. Thanks again—fare you well, and all good be with you!"

In reference to this election, and Lord Morpeth's address, the *Daily News* thus wrote—

"There are many Yorkshiremen who say that Lord Morpeth's speech after his defeat has never been equalled in the history of elections. Some of us, who did not hear the address, but only read the report of it, are almost disposed, even while remembering Burke, to agree to anything that the actual hearers can say. It was a natural occasion for the magnanimity of the man to appear; and its effect on the election crowd was just what it was every day on those who lived in his presence. The feeling of many hearers was that it was a happier thing to endure a defeat, even of a ministerial policy, in such a spirit of enlightenment and philosophy, than to enjoy the most unexpected triumph, merely as a triumph."

The freeholders felt much chagrined at the result of the election, and decided upon showing their affectionate regard for Lord Morpeth by presenting him with a splendid casket, or wine-cooler, of bog-oak, found in one of Lord Carlisle's estates in Yorkshire, and mounted in massive silver. On each side of the casket are his Lordship's arms in relief, and around are the arms of the twenty-five polling-places into which the West Riding is divided, and the number of voters polled upon the occasion.

"This casket, with the address which it contains, is presented

To THE RIGHT HON. GEO. WILLIAM FREDERICK,
VISCOUNT MORPETH,

By his friends and supporters in the West Riding of the county of York, in respectful testimony of their sincere attachment to his person and esteem for his character, and of their deep regret for the loss of his valuable services as their representative in Parliament, and the advocate of a liberal and enlightened policy in Her Majesty's councils.

A.D. 1841."

In the autumn of 1841, Lord Morpeth sailed to North America, and spent one whole year in visiting the United States, the Queen's dominions in Canada, and the Island of Cuba. He kept a journal of his travels, but did not think it of sufficient interest to be published. His principal observations were conveyed to the English public by a lecture on America, which he delivered to the Leeds Mechanics' Institution and Literary Society on December 6, 1850—a lecture admirably suited to his audience.

He saw nearly every one of literary, scientific, and political repute in the States, and was received with uniform civility and attention—nay, with real warmth and openness of heart. At Rochester he stumbled on a home association, by seeing the word theatre written on a wall, and, being tempted to enter, felt great surprise on seeing (in a rude playhouse of strollers, at a town nearly five hundred miles in the interior of America, which, thirty years before, had no existence) upon the drop-scene a most accurate representation of Naworth Castle!

Lord Morpeth was too staunch an advocate of freedom to make any compromise regarding his opinions on slavery; he paid special respect to the leading abolitionists. On the other hand, he looked upon the planters of the Southern States as having much more of the manners and courtesy of the English country gentleman than any other class in the Federal Union. He was not afraid to speak of the characters of the great public men of America, but always in a tone commensurate with dignity. His description of the grand natural scenery of America is worthy of his literary pen, poetic feeling, and characteristic appreciation. Though ready to praise the devotion of the Americans to habits of industry and practical business, he could not help seeing that the empire of dollars and cents held a very preponderating sway, to the exclusion of art and the more graceful accomplishments and amenities of life.

The last topic in his lecture was the mortal plague-spot—slavery; the evils of which he foresaw were calculated to distract the national councils, and to threaten the permanence of the Union, and to leave a brand, a by-word, and a jest upon the name of freedom.

He concluded his lecture by saying—

"*Causes are occasionally at work which almost appear to portend a disruption of the Federal Union;* at the same time, a strong sentiment of pride about it, arising partly from an honest patriotism, partly from a feeling of complacency in its very size and extent, may tend indefinitely to postpone any such pregnant result. But whatever may be the solution of that question, whatever the issue of the future destinies assigned to the great American Republic, it is impossible to have contemplated her extent, her resources, the race that has mainly peopled her, the institutions she has derived or originated, the liberty which has been their life-blood, the industry which has been their offspring, and the free gospel which has been published on her wide plains and wafted by her thousand streams, without nourishing the belief and the hope that it is reserved for her to do much in the coming generations for the good of man and the glory of God."

On May 1843, an address of the electors and inhabitants of the West Riding, agreed to at a public meeting in Wakefield, at which Earl Fitzwilliam presided, was presented to Lord Morpeth, expressive of appreciation of his Lordship's private virtue and public conduct during the time he represented the West Riding.

The destructive fire at Naworth on May 18, 1844, brought Lord Morpeth to Brampton, where, on the 29th, he received an address, conveying to his father and himself the sympathies of the people of the barony of Gillesland, and of the citizens of Brampton and the neighbouring gentry, on the great loss sustained by the House of Carlisle. Brampton had no room sufficiently large to accommodate the numbers of sympathising friends who met on the occasion to prove their high regard for his Lordship and the Howard family. Lord Morpeth could not fail to be deeply moved by so touching an address, and so unfeigned an exhibition of the kindness of his neighbours. His reply was appropriate and hopeful. As the "towers of Belted Will" were untouched, and the whole circuit of the outer walls remained in their full impressiveness and grey simplicity, he looked forward to a renovation of their ancient dwelling-house on the Borders.

The traditions of Naworth Castle might well endear it to the Carlisle family of Howard; for though their principal residence was in Yorkshire, where they have large possessions, the head of their house derives his Earldom from the chief city of Cumberland. Whilst all the family showed their intense regard for the old Border keep, around which are clustered so many tales of romance and chivalry, Lord Morpeth was ever credited with having a truly warm affection for the venerable fabric that his progenitor, "Belted Will," had surrounded with an historic halo. When free from official cares, he came to Naworth in the autumn, and made the room of his famed ancestor his sleeping apartment. Everything around the old castle harmonised with his tastes. He liked its quiet seclusion; he liked his neighbours and tenantry, among whom he moved with the native ease and unaffected friendliness of true nobility.

To render Naworth Castle again worthy of its ancient repute, and to strengthen those many ties of good feeling subsisting between the Howards and the people of Cumberland, Mr Salvin, the eminent architect, was engaged to effect the restoration of the fabric, and, as far as possible, in accordance with the lost antique. This was done in 1849, and the Earl of Carlisle entertained his friends in celebration of the completion of the work. Over the spacious fire-place in the grand hall, the following appropriate words are inscribed on a roll bearing the date 1844:—

"Our beautiful house, where our fathers praised Thee, is burned up with fire."

On a scroll bearing the date 1849—

"Thou shalt be called the repairer of the breach; the restorer of paths to dwell in."

In connection with this restoration, Lord Morpeth's beautiful verses on the jessamine tree, which spreads its modest flowerets over the doorway of the great hall, may be quoted here. They have not only become a part of our literature, but figure in all the American books of poetry, and are read with delight at the Anglo-Saxon antipodes.

"TO A JESSAMINE TREE.

"My slight and slender jessamine tree,
That bloomest on my Border tower,
Thou art more dearly loved by me
Than all the wreaths of fairy bower.
I ask not, while I near thee dwell,
Arabia's spice or Syria's rose;
Thy light festoons more freshly smell,
Thy virgin white more purely glows.

"My wild and winsome jessamine tree,
That climbest up the dark grey wall,
Thy tiny flowerets seem in glee,
Like silver spray-drops, down to fall.
Say, did they from their leaves thus peep
When mailed mosstroopers rode the hill,
When helmèd warders paced the keep.
And bugles blew for 'Belted Will?'

"My free and feathery jessamine tree,
Within the fragrance of thy breath
Yon dungeon grated to its key,
And the chained captive sighed for death.
On Border fray or feudal crime
I dream not while I gaze on thee:
The chieftains of that stern old time
Could ne'er have loved a jessamine tree."

In 1846, a vacancy occurring in the representation of the West Riding of Yorkshire, the constituency received Lord Morpeth with open arms and hearty welcome. He had no opponent. The *Leeds Mercury*, February 4, 1846, thus referred to the great triumph obtained by Lord Morpeth:—

"The great injustice of 1841 is repaired; the stain on the Opposition banner is wiped out; and on the very principles on which the noble Lord was defeated four years back, on those same principles, only carried out to a fuller consummation, is he restored to his seat, amid the enthusiastic acclamations of the

Riding. How rapid has been the progress of truth! how beautiful are its victories!—involving, in the present case, a full and honourable reparation to a public servant for the ingratitude he had experienced, the restoration of this great community to its proper place among the supporters of commercial freedom, and the retrieving of a noble cause from defeat, to crown it with sudden and splendid triumph.

"The noble Lord is regarded by the people of Yorkshire with a warm personal affection—an affection which has its source in the goodness, kindliness, and magnanimity of his nature, and which has been exceedingly heightened by the events that for a time separated the member from his constituents. They remembered his exemplary discharge of the duties he owed to them and to his country, and the unequalled success with which he conducted for six years the difficult affairs of Ireland.

"For the sake of the man, therefore, as well as for the sake of principles which they hold most dear, the electors of the West Riding have delighted to do honour to Lord Morpeth; and if the brightest triumph is that which leads the hearts of men in willing homage, that brightest triumph was enjoyed by the noble Lord this day."

In July 1846 Lord Morpeth was appointed Commissioner of Woods and Forests, an office which he held till March 1850. He turned his position to good account in draining and beautifying the parks of London, in which work he had the hearty co-operation of his friend Mr Blamire, the Tithe Commissioner.

Among many important services rendered to his country by Lord Morpeth, not the least were his indefatigable exertions in the cause of sanitary reform. If anything special was needed to prove the philanthropic character of his Lordship, it was his entering upon a field of inquiry so devoid of every feature of agreeableness, and casting his lines of legislation in muddy waters, surrounded on every side by vested interests and popular ignorance. Cleanliness and health were assuredly worthy of the notice of any English statesman, seeing that these had an important bearing on the physical aptitude of our people for the labours of life, and were not less relevant to the moral attitude and religious feeling of the country at large.

Lord Morpeth had duly considered the question, and was prepared to do his best to promote a cause that stood so largely in need of legislative help. He was Commissioner of Woods and Forests, and officially connected with the supervision of the public parks of London; and along with their orderly development and the full realisation of their oxygenating influences, arose the larger question of securing the greatest amount of health to the metropolis itself. Then again it was obvious that whatever was beneficial to London would be equally valuable to the provincial towns and the kingdom at large. Medical men of philanthropic motive throughout the country, and notably those conversant with the degraded condition of such cities as Liverpool, Edinburgh, and Glasgow, had, from time to time, tried to rouse public opinion to the dangers accruing from lethargy and indifference, so generally prevailing on such subjects. Not a few of these professional enthusiasts laboured day after day, and under circumstances as loathsome as they were dangerous, to obtain data upon which they might claim a hearing from the authorities, be they civic or parliamentary, and their sanction to schemes for the improvement of the dwellings of the poor, the formation of hospitals, or the adoption of other means to preserve the life of our artisans, and stave off the risks of widowhood and orphanage.

The general registration of births, marriages, and deaths, dating from 1838, had brought to light the astounding fact that thousands of our countrymen died from causes that were preventible or remediable; and the cellars of Liverpool and the filth of Glasgow offered special corroborations of the danger of neglecting the simplest of hygienic principles. These incontrovertible facts should have sufficed to awaken the public mind to the danger of our situation. It was not so, however, and John Bull continued to sleep over pools of poison, and in the midst of noxious atmospheres, and a physical degradation altogether irreconcilable with his loud profession of being a Christian and a tolerably educated personage.

Lord Morpeth was, of all men in Parliament, the best qualified to take up this national question. He was painstaking, conciliatory, and, if earnest, not less good-natured and regardful of conflicting interests. As usual with him, before venturing to attempt legislative measures, he collated all the information, private and public, that bore upon disease and mortality; and thus adequately prepared for the task, he introduced his Health of Towns Bill to Parliament. He addressed the House of Commons for hours together, strengthening his historical reasoning by statements capable of verification, and by data no less irrefragible. He had a difficult subject to handle, and he handled it with his usual ability and success. Through his unwearied zeal for the moral and physical welfare of the labouring classes, the bill became law; and upwards of twenty years' application of the principles he laid down have not only created no valid opposition, but received the full sanction of a discerning public. It is doubtful if any other English Minister could have attained half the support so freely accorded Lord Morpeth, whose perseverance, forbearance, and unruffled temper brought a question of national interest, and surrounded with countless difficulties, to a successful issue.

In 1847, he received the appointment of Lord-Lieutenant of the East Riding of Yorkshire.

Another election for the West Riding of Yorkshire came off on August 7, 1847. 'Standing side by side on the hustings on that occasion were Lord Morpeth and Richard Cobden, in honourable alliance for the cause of free-trade and the best interests of England. On his first appearance as a candidate for Yorkshire honours in 1830, he had a colleague in Henry Brougham; on his last opportunity, he was linked with Cobden, and on both occasions bore Whig colours on to victory. No public man in the century could have boasted of a prouder position than Lord Morpeth enjoyed as the representative of Yorkshire. It was highly characteristic of him to use his signature "Morpeth" for the last time of his life in his farewell address to the electors of the West Riding, —so grateful an acknowledgment could not fail to be heartily appreciated.

In reviewing the session of 1848, Mr Disraeli made some pretty strong comments on the Whigs, but was more considerate to Lord Morpeth, who merited the compliment of having introduced thirteen bills and passed them all!

By the decease of his father, in October 1848, he succeeded to the Earldom of Carlisle, and of course took his seat in the House of Peers.

L

EARLDOM OF CARLISLE.

The Earl of Carlisle's portrait graces the frontispiece of this volume. It is an admirable likeness of a thoroughly intellectual and noble head. The general expression is no less spirited than attractive; an exalted feeling and refinement reign in every feature of the physiognomy. The forehead is specially fine in development, and in thorough harmony with the facial contour and bust. The portrait reflects the *beau-ideal* of the high-bred, thorough English Saxon of true patrician blood and type. The artist of the original portrait,[*] from which this is taken, has done every justice to Lord Carlisle, so that posterity, aided by it, and the admirable busts and statues carved by Mr J. H. Foley, may for ever call to mind the representative Howard of the Carlisle family during Victoria's reign.

The Earl of Carlisle was Vice-President of the British and Foreign Bible Society, and an active coadjutor of various societies of a similar nature. He took great interest in medical education, in the establishment of museums, and the promotion of experimental and natural science. To all institutions having for their object the diffusion of sound information and learning, he lent willing aid, as he believed such to be the best groundworks of our national prosperity.

His patronage of the fine arts was often evinced

[*] The portrait alluded to was published by P. & D. Colnaghi & Co., Pall Mall, E., from a drawing by G. Richmond, engraved by F. Holl. It is an excellent work of art, and one of the most spirited of portraits. The publishers have done wisely to issue it at the reasonable price of a guinea.

by his subscriptions to the formation of exhibitions, and by the purchase of pictures; nor was that patronage less happily bestowed when he presided at the annual meetings of the Academies of Painting, and infused an æsthetic spirit into the minds of the assembly present. He was the first to suggest that memorials of a substantial kind should be erected to Irishmen of genius; and the prominent part he took in the inauguration of statues to Goldsmith and Moore gave great pleasure to the citizens of Dublin and the Irish generally.

He was earnest in all matters pertaining to a true social science, *e.g.*, the maintenance of health and the physical and moral elevation of the industrial classes; the formation of schools, reformatories, blind, and deaf and dumb asylums; and other institutions claiming the attention of private charity or public support, on the recognised assurance of ameliorating the sufferings of humanity in every walk of life.

> " He had a tear for pity, and a hand
> Open as day for melting charity."

He gave a site on his own estate of Castle Howard for a reformatory school, and looked upon the work he had promoted with the greatest possible pleasure. The largest audience he ever addressed was the Sunday-School Union meeting at Halifax, in May 1846, where the numbers present were estimated at 25,000, including scholars, teachers, and their friends; and one of his best speeches, delivered October 30, 1861, was in favour of a Yorkshire school for the blind, founded in memory of Mr Wilberforce.

A mere list of the occasions on which he acted as

president of different British societies, or took part at public meetings, would fill several pages; and it would be difficult to name any institution, either in England or Ireland, whose object was the furtherance of humanitarian interests, social, civic, educational, and progressive, to which Lord Carlisle did not lend a helping hand. He was truly philanthropic, in the broadest sense of the term, caring not for sects or denominations or parties, but guided in his wish to do good by as loving and admirable a spirit as ever marked the life of a zealous and faithful Christian.

> " His life was gentle, and the elements
> So mixed in him, that Nature might stand up,
> And say to all the world, *This was a man!*"

Among many gratifying circumstances in the history of the Earl of Carlisle, not the least was the Queen's visit to him at Castle Howard, on August 26, 1850. Her Majesty, accompanied by Prince Albert and some of her children, spent three days very happily in Yorkshire under the hospitable roof of the worthy Earl, whose guidance to the scenery around lent a pleasing charm to one of England's fairest lands and landscapes.

As a politician Lord Carlisle belonged to the old Whig school, with quiet yet progressive tendencies to a broader stage of Liberalism. Upright and conscientious in all his views, he gave no heed to an impulsive cry out of doors, and cared not to adopt methods of address *ad captandum vulgus*. He nevertheless stood manfully by the popular cause based on true constitutional principles and honest legislation. From the day he took office as Secretary for Ireland in 1835, when he was made a Privy Councillor with a seat in the Cabinet—honours rarely obtained by so young a Minister—to the hour that his eyes, filled with tears, rested for the last time on Erin's green isle, Lord Carlisle was always found steady to his principles, ever reliable, and ever watchful of the best interests of England. He acted on the Shakespearian sentiment—

> "Perseverance, dear my Lord,
> Keeps honour bright; to have done, is to hang
> Quite out of fashion."

And all this, and more was required to meet the emergencies of his Irish officialism. Coercion had had its day, and arbitrary rule had failed in Ireland; so he followed the bent of his own kind heart, and his love of justice and equality before the law, and won large success as a conciliator of Ireland and a redresser of some of her wrongs. His first official experience was trying enough, for as regularly as an Irish Bill was introduced, the "Rupert of debate" (Lord Stanley) rose and objected to it, and pretty nearly as often denounced the Irish leaders. This led to a regular Irish row, in which O'Connell and Sheil were pitted against Stanley and Sir J. Graham. Curiously enough, as manifesting the good-will of even these fanatically disposed Tories of the hour, not a word of real blame or asperity fell from their lips in condemnation of Lord Morpeth's mode of introducing his Irish measures. The conciliatory tone and graceful exposition of his views seems to have disarmed the Opposition from all uncourteous objections and recriminations; and it is pleasant to note so rare and unequivocal a compliment to his Parliamentary efforts. No state rewards and no popular acclamation could for a moment measure with this gratifying, and, it may be said, unprecedented tribute thus paid his personal worth and high honour.

In May 1850, the Earl of Carlisle was appointed Chancellor of the Duchy of Lancaster, and held this office till the retirement of Lord John Russell and the accession of the Earl of Derby's Ministry, in 1852.

He gave a lecture on the "Poetry of Pope" to the Leeds Institution on December 5, 1850. A noble Lord lecturing to a society of mechanics on a strictly literary theme might well give rise to much public comment; the novelty of the circumstance, however, was less remarkable than the great success attending the effort. The intrinsic merits of the lecture were acknowledged by the press. His Lordship proved his thorough acquaintance with the poet's character and verse; and his quotations and criticism showed his aptitude to please the mixed audience of a manufacturing town.

Lord Carlisle presided at the public dinner given to William Ord, Esq., at Newcastle-on-Tyne, September 8, 1852, and spoke in his usual happy style. After alluding to the crowing of the Tories, then in power, he said he felt convinced that the old-Whig principle was still full of youthful sap and vigour, and that, like the oak on Mount Algidus, it would continue to gather resources and vigour from each descending stroke. He augured well for the march of imperial government under the guidance of his own party, because the opinions and principles they possessed moved in the middle path between opposite extremes; fenced in on one side by respect to property, by the sovereignty of the national law, and by the supremacy of the universal gospel; and on the other side, to the greatest extent of privilege and the widest community of enjoyment which can be conceded to all alike, consistently with these paramount obligations.

On December 14, 1852, he delivered a lecture to the Sheffield Mechanics' Institute "On the Poetical Works of Gray." He treated the English Virgil in the same mode as he had characterized Pope, and with equally pleasant results. He cited the following stanza, because he had known statesmen (and possibly himself) to apply part of it to cheer and sustain themselves in the hours of languor, and under the chill of disappointment—

> "What is grandeur, what is power?
> Heavier toil, superior pain.
> What the bright reward we gain?
> The grateful memory of the good.
> Sweet is the breath of vernal shower,
> The bee's collected treasures sweet,
> Sweet music's melting fall; but sweeter yet
> The still small voice of gratitude."

The installation of the Earl of Carlisle as Lord Rector of the University of Aberdeen took place on March 31, 1853, and on the following day he was honoured with the freedom of the ancient city. His inaugural address to the learned collegiates breathed the true academic flavour; nor was it wanting in happy reference to the spirit that had guided the renowned *literati* of old Aberdeen. Necessarily limited in scope, his address lost nothing of due appropriateness; its pure English diction was heightened by frequent interposition of classic quotation and scholarly criticism. He took one of those Homeric lines which stir us like a war-trumpet, and which he translated—

"Always excel, and tower above the rest,"

and showed its varied application to the interests of the ingenuous youth around him.

In acknowledging the freedom of the city, he spoke of the "Granite City," and hoped a representative of the Athenian Phidias might be found amongst them to turn their famed building materials to good account. In treating of the commerce and statistics of Aberdeen, which showed a marked advancement each decade, he presented the very picture of all others—showing hard lines, it is true, compared with the noble colouring of his academic illustration of the day preceding—to gratify the business habits of the North Countrymen.

On April 4, 1853, Lord Carlisle was made a citizen of Edinburgh, and delivered an excellent speech. On the same evening he attended a very large meeting in the Music Hall on behalf of Dr Guthrie's Ragged Schools, and was extremely well received.

In the summer of 1853, the Earl of Carlisle went abroad. After spending a short time in Germany, he sailed down the Danube, and onwards to Constantinople. From thence he visited Smyrna, Rhodes, and other places of interest in the Eastern Mediterranean, also the Athenian district of Greece, Malta, and the Ionian Islands. He returned home by Venice and Switzerland, in May 1854. The diary of his journeying during those twelve months was published, in an octavo volume, in October 1854—"Diary in Turkish and Greek Waters." The volume is written in his usual pleasant style, and contains much interesting matter relative to the commencement of the Crimean War; the character of the distinguished naval, military, and diplomatic personages he met; and his views of Turkey's position and the miserable Government of Greece. Wandering amid such scenes as Troy and Marathon could not fail to afford him many suitable themes for the display of his fine classical taste. One or two quotations from his diary may be given:—

"We then went to St Sophia. This is the real sight of Constantinople. . . . I was profoundly struck with the general appearance and effect of the building itself—the bold simplicity of plan—the noble span of the wide, low cupola, measuring, in its diameter, 115 feet—the gilded roofs—the mines of marble which encrust the walls,—that porphyry was from the Temple of the Sun at Baalbec,—that verde-antique was from the Temple of Diana at Ephesus. How many different strains have they not echoed? The hymn to the Latoidæ! the chaunt to the Virgin! the Muezzin's call from the minaret! Yes; and how long shall that call continue? Must we always dimly trace in the overlaying fretwork of gold the obliterated features of the Redeemer? This is all assuredly forbidden by copious and cogent, even if by conflicting causes,—by old Greek memories, by young Greek aspirations, by the ambition of states and sovereigns, by the sympathy of Christendom, by the sure word of prophecy."—Pp. 53, 54.

A visit to the Troad, the "most classical and most controverted site in the whole world," induced him to dwell with "comparative minuteness" on the question—"Was there ever any such city as Troy?" His classical quotations from Greek authors may be passed by; but the feeling that possessed his thoughts on surveying the land so rich in historical comment is specially worthy of a place in this volume, as it shows his love of home and canny Cumberland. Thus he writes :—

" I could give any Cumberland borderer the best notion of it, by telling him that it wonderfully resembles the view from the point of the hill just outside the Roman camp at Burdoswald ; both have that series of steep conical hills, with rock enough for wildness, and verdure enough for softness ; both have that bright trail of a river creeping in and out with the most continuous indentations ; the Simois has, in summer at least, more silvery shelves of sand ; on the steep banks still graze the sheep of the breed of Ida, tended by shepherds perhaps not precisely in Phrygian caps, but with most genuine crooks."—Pp. 87, 88.

He read a book of the " Iliad " every day, and might rejoice that, after such long disuse of the Greek, he could get on well without dictionary, note, or translation.

Though in childhood he had been vaccinated by the great Dr Jenner, and once subsequently, he caught small-pox, and was laid up at Rhodes. The attack was not so mild, but luckily he had good quarters at the house of our excellent consul, Mr Newton ; and Dr M'Graith of Smyrna and Dr Sandwith of Constantinople hurried to his bedside—thus affording proofs of their high regard for a nobleman who everywhere made his associates attached friends. Rhodes, in its Pompeian desolation, must have felt astonished at the presence of an invalid who could attract a Constantinople doctor to its shores; even the entombed Knights of St John might have thrown off their cerements to fulfil the duties of their Order by the sick couch of a representative Lord of Britannia. The author of these pages, having gone over much of the same ground as Lord Carlisle, may be permitted to add his testimony to the accuracy of his descriptions of the scenery of the Eastern Archipelago.

On February 7, 1855, he attended at Windsor Castle to receive the investiture of the honourable Order of Knight of the Garter; and on the following month was intrusted by Lord Palmerston with the post of Lord-Lieutenant of Ireland. This office, with the exception of sixteen months of the Earl of Derby's second trial of government, from February 1858 till June 1859, he retained till his health gave way, in the autumn of 1864—but a few months before the end of his earthly career. His highly-successful Secretaryship of upwards of six years, the longest ever held by one person, and his well-known partiality for the Irish, indicated him as the best man on the Whig side for the Viceroyalty; but if any doubt existed on that head, it could not fail to be dispelled by a speech of the most flattering kind from Mr Disraeli, the leader of the Opposition in the Commons, who thus spoke:—

"I sat in this house for ten years with Lord Carlisle, and let me remind the House that those were not ordinary times. This House then reckoned among its members probably a greater number of celebrated men than it ever contained at any other time. At other times, indeed, there may have been individual examples of higher intellectual powers, but a greater number of great men never flourished than during these ten years. Lord Morpeth met them on equal terms; he took a great part in the greatest debates; and he was a man remarkable for his knowledge, his accomplishments, and his eloquence."

On entering upon the duties of Lord-Lieutenant, he was hailed with a true Irish welcome. His exemplary official life in a previous decade was happily as fresh in the minds of the Irish people as the sprigs of shamrock worn by them on the dawn of St Patrick's

Day; and in proof of that remembrance of a nation's gratitude, the old title of "Morpeth" mingled with the cry of "Ireland for the Irish" and "Long life to the Viceroy!" Scarcely any man could have been selected more likely to conciliate the good-will of the Irish than Lord Carlisle, whose name and rank commanded universal respect, while his singular geniality, and the winning gracefulness of his oratory, confirmed that feeling of personal regard, which his well-known liberal views and tolerant spirit had already created.

In accepting the high commission of the Queen's representative in Ireland, and all its heavy responsibilities, he was but following the hereditary instincts of his political House, whose members for many centuries have exhibited a tendency to public affairs, and no small skill in dealing with them. It is a worthy impulse that leads men like Lord Carlisle, born to wealth and ease, to scorn delights, and live laborious days in the sister isle—a land as prolific of grievances as it is of babies and potatoes. To-day, Protestant zealots set the northern heather and Belfast in a blaze; to-morrow, rabid Fenianism stalks over the land like a moral plague; and so the wheel of *mis*fortune turns round and round. *Quousque tandem?*

Lord Carlisle did all that was possible for a viceroy to do to heal the irritable sores of the body politic of Ireland; to lessen the rancour of parties; and to give a better direction to the industrial pursuits of the country. He made no distinction of men, provided they were of good repute and faithful citizens; neither politics nor creed affected his official patronage. He created no jealousy of feeling outside the circle of Orangeism or head-centred demagogism; and for these factions no constitutional Government whatever could be made acceptable—the only mode of treating such types of Irish-Saxon self-will and Celtic *shillelaghism* being a Gulf Stream separation of the antagonists, or a rigid Napoleonic autocracy.

On that disturbing element in Irish life—religion—no English statesman in our times possessed better credentials for governing the country than the Earl of Carlisle. He was a true Protestant, and conscientious in his belief; and his piety was no less exemplary than practical; yet in all things he acted equitably for the beneficial interests of the Catholics; and why?' He had faith, possibly too much, in the principles of Christianity guiding men of every Church; and his charity was not of a kind to deny to others the possession of those virtues which guided his own actions as an Episcopalian. He was justified in hoping for a hearty co-operation of all parties seeking the advancement of the general weal when the Imperial Government had removed every restriction, civic and parliamentary, from the Catholics, and opened the doors of office to men of every creed. If success did not everywhere attend his endeavours, the fault was not his, but sprang from the ingraining of the Irish—their blood or racial elements leading to endless animosity and feuds and fights.*

Lord Carlisle gave ample proofs of his possessing the administrative faculty; without it, his viceroyalty would have run the risk of failure. He was calm and imperturbable under worrying circumstances; and diligent, nay unwearied, in his efforts to please. He

* The author has discussed the Celtic-Irish in his "Life of Knox the Anatomist."

possessed one of the finest tempers in the world, and could bear up against the animadversions of that small yet noisy section of the Irish press that hesitated not to condemn all Government rule for condemnation's sake. His energies were devoted to the great work of pacifying Ireland. During his many years of official life, not a doubt arose as to the motives of his public acts; not a whisper of suspicion was ever heard against his personal honour, or the purity of his private character.

The great body of Roman Catholics were ready to admit that they never had a Viceroy so friendly and cordial, or who held the balance of justice more impartially, or ruled with more gentleness and moderation. Abundant proofs were offered from time to time that he had won and retained the good opinion of every class, from the Irish peer down to the Irish peasant. No wonder he stood well in the eyes of some of our Celtic brethren, whose ideal of authority and regal greatness was in part satisfied by "splendid state and magnificent entertainments" at the Viceregal Lodge. This, however, was but a small claim on the gratitude of the Irish people, compared with his unswerving love of constitutional liberty and religious equality.

Ireland was placed under deep obligations to Lord Carlisle, and its respectable community well knew that in taking upon himself the Viceroyalty he was not seeking political power, nor the privileges of rule and authority, so much as an honourable vocation suited to his culture and high inheritance; nay, more, that everything pertaining to his position had marked him the true English nobleman, imbued with a high behest to do for a sister kingdom all that patriotic Christian zeal could suggest to promote her material interests, her social status, and general prosperity.

His advocacy of Ireland for the Irish was enunciated in different language to that of the demagogic leaders, and assuredly with higher and more patriotic intent; that advocacy had for its text—and none could be more applicable—a well-directed industry and self-reliance. On many public occasions he earnestly appealed to the Irish faculty for work, and sought to call forth the exercise of every individual effort, so that the resources of Ireland might be fairly developed agriculturally and commercially, and the land of Erin become a true home and foster-mother of her children.

Lord Carlisle always spoke sensibly and to the point. His rhetoric showed nothing of the fleeting glare of mere display, but the more steady and sober qualities of good sense conveyed in terms of easy apprehension. The same calmness and gentleness, the same hopeful strain that marked his every-day life, stood him in good need on those trying occasions when he had to address large audiences. Few men of his own, or indeed of any times, were so frequently called upon to take a chief part at the public assemblies of his countrymen. In addition to his many personal engagements, or the demands arising out of his parliamentary or ministerial position, he kindly consented to play many important parts on the world's stage. In conferring degrees and honours at the Universities, in distributing prizes at Royal Societies, in promoting educational boards, Irish academies, medical colleges, and the like, his academic and æsthetic culture was well sustained in the presence of veterans in learning, scientific investigators, technical professors, and scholarly critics.

Lord Carlisle seemed quite at home on all public occasions ;—at convivial gatherings, doing honour to men of worth; at municipal banquets, joining in the civic compliment or commendation of self-governed institutions; at agricultural meetings, discussing the merits of shorthorns and the statistical value of the productions of the soil ; at the inauguration of a statue to an Irish patrician or bard, where it was needful to breathe the fervour of Irish patriotism ; to give colouring to the literary excellence of Goldsmith, or invest the songs of Moore with the warmth of inspiration and love. How beautifully he touched the finest chord of the Irish heart when he instanced the Celtic muse that grew before Tasso enchanted the world !

It was sometimes said that the Earl of Carlisle governed Ireland by speechifying.* If this were true, the mode commended itself not less for the facility of its practice in the hands of a master and governor, than by its pleasantness and general acceptability to the governed people. Could Ireland, by any state process, have been made to emulate the steady bearing of Scotland, whether by rounds of toasts, patriotic sentiments, or palatable doses of blarney, the Viceroy Howard, in addition to his more solid attributes and capabilities of rule, would have succeeded pretty fairly. But not all the blood of all the Howards can change

---

* All his viceregal speeches and addresses were collected and published in 1866 by Mr J. J. Gaskin of Dublin. Some of his electioneering speeches and lectures and poems are also to be found in Mr Gaskin's large volume.

the nature of the true Hibernian Celt, or make him comprehend the meaning of either liberty or constitutional government.

When the first Atlantic telegraphic communication was to be established on the coast of Ireland, on August 4, 1857, a *dejeuner* was given at Valentia, the Knight of Kerry in the chair. In reply to the toast, "The health of the Earl of Carlisle, and prosperity to Ireland," his Lordship spoke in a manner commensurate with the great occasion.

"We are about, either by this sun-down, or by to-morrow's dawn, to establish a new material link between the Old World and the New. Moral links there have been—links of race, links of commerce, links of friendship, links of literature, links of glory: but this our new link, instead of superseding and supplanting the old ones, is to give them a life and an intensity which they never had before. Highly as I value the reputations of those who have conceived and those who have contributed to carry out this bright design, yet I do not compliment them with the idea that they are to efface or dim the glory of that Columbus who, when the large vessels in the harbour of Cork yesterday weighed their anchors, did so just on that very day three hundred and sixty-five years ago—it would have been called in Hebrew writ 'a year of years'—and set sail upon his glorious enterprise of discovery. They, I say, will not dim or efface his glory, but they are now giving the last finish and consummation to his work. Hitherto the inhabitants of the two worlds have associated perhaps in the chilling atmosphere of distance with each other—at a sort of bowing distance ; but now we can be hand in hand, grasp to grasp, pulse to pulse. The link which is now to connect us, like the insect in the immortal couplet of our poet, while

'Exquisitely fine,
Feels at each thread, and lives along the line.'"

The Shakespeare tercentenary and festival banquet was held at Stratford-on-Avon, April 19, 1864, and the Earl of Carlisle occupied the distinguished position of chairman. He had been far from well for some months previously, and his friends would gladly have persuaded him to take no part in the celebration; but his love of Shakespeare, and his desire to see every honour paid the great bard, overcame all obstacles. He surprised the audience by his able and eloquent speech, parts of which are subjoined.

"I heartily approve the idea of this festival. I think the leading events, epochs, and persons of this our earth require their occasional commemoration. Life is stagnant enough, men and women are commonplace enough, to avoid the risk of such disturbances cropping up too frequently. Least of all can the nation which boasts of Shakespeare fear to misplace her homage. . . . But take him in his height, and who may approach him? Presumptuous as the endeavour may appear to classify, there would seem to be a few great tragedies which occupy summits of their own—'Macbeth,' 'Hamlet,' 'Lear,' 'Othello;' I feel we may take our stand within that unassailable quadrilateral, and give our challenge to all the world. I feel indeed tempted to upbraid myself when I think of all the outlying realms of strength and comeliness which I thus seem to leave outside—the stately forms of Roman heroes, the chivalry marshalled around our Plantagenet kings, the wit of Mercutio, Beatrice, and Falstaff, the maiden grace of Imogen and Miranda, Ariel the dainty sprite, Oberon and his elfin court, the memories which people the glades of the Ardennes, the Rialto of Venice, the garden of Verona, giving to each glorious scene and sunny shore a stronger lien upon our associations than is possessed even by their own native land. It is time that I should call upon you, in the right of all the recollections which must throng in your own breasts far more copiously and vividly than I could hope to present them to you—by the thrill you have felt in the crowded theatre, amid all the splendour of dramatic pageantry—by the calmer enjoyment of your closet leisure—by the rising of your soul when the lines which breathe and warm have led you to recognise and adore the Giver of such gifts to men, to join me in drinking, not with the solemn silence which a more recent death might have enjoined, but with the reverential love and the admiring fervour due to the day and the man—'The memory of Shakespeare.'"

Those who, like Archbishop Trench, knew the critical condition of Lord Carlisle's health, could not fail to rejoice that his last public effort was crowned with a great success. Soon afterwards his Lordship returned to Dublin, apparently none the worse for his exertions at Stratford-on-Avon. The respite from ill-health was but short, when signs of cerebral change set in, marked in a very obvious form by paralysis of the right side. Like a brave man he seemed to struggle against this overwhelming condition, as if he still meant to be Her Majesty's representative of Ireland. The Fates ordained otherwise. A vital part of his fine frame had been struck, the more vital that it touched his noble intelligence. That blow was irreparable, nay, mortal. A slight modification of the symptoms enabled him to be moved from Phœnix Park to Kingstown, where a vessel awaited his departure. Accompanied by his truly beloved sister, Lady Elizabeth Grey, whose attentions to her brother were but a part of her natural and highly affectionate disposition, he bade a lasting farewell to the shores of Ireland, the country he loved so dearly. The day of his departure was a day of grief to Ireland, and a day of special mourning to the people of Dublin, for every soul of that large city seemed filled with emotion deep and trying.

He was moved to Castle Howard, Yorkshire. There, as autumn was telling its tale of mellowed leaf and ripened fruit, the decadence and the fall, he was driven through the grounds and foliaged avenue of his ancestors, now looking upon the changing beauties of nature, and ever and anon catching faint glimpses of enjoyment. The season portended his own approaching fate, and on December 5, 1864, he passed away.

His remains were deposited in the ancestral mausoleum in Castle Howard Park, wherein eleven of his predecessors have been interred. The funeral was conducted in the most simple manner. The mourning relatives and friends were deeply affected; nor was this feeling confined to the family of the deceased nobleman. Among the mass of people who had gathered in the park, it is said that none showed more signs of sincere sorrow than the lads from the Castle Howard Reformatory School, for whom, though seldom with them, the deceased Earl had ever a word of kindness and encouragement. About five hundred children of the neighbouring schools were also present.

Miss Martineau, writing in the *Daily News** of the Earl of Carlisle, and his having filled no higher office than Lord-Lieutenant of Ireland, and leaving no enduring work to make him known to future generations, or to illustrate his own time, says:—

"Yet the sorrow, the enthusiasm for the man, the recoil from the thought of his death, which were manifested when he became virtually dead to society, were such as the greatest statesman, and the heads of the noblest households of sons and daughters, might covet. It was his exquisite moral nature, together with the charm of intercourse which grew out of it, which created this warm affection in all who approached him; and through them the rest of the world received the impression of a man of rare virtue being among them—of singular nobleness of spirit, and gentleness of temper, and sympathy as modest as it was

---

* Miss Martineau's contributions to the *Daily News* are published by Macmillan & Co. under the title of "Biographical Sketches." They are worthy of the able pen of this famed authoress.

keen and constant. His function in the world of statesmanship seemed to be to represent and sustain the highest magnanimity, devotedness, and benevolence, properly distinctive of that which is called 'the governing class' in this country. . . . Among those who were personal observers of Lord Carlisle, every one of them would probably say that he was one of the best men they had ever known."

The very Rev. D. Bagot, Dean of Dromore, in his funeral oration, preached in memory of Lord Carlisle, in the Chapel Royal, Dublin Castle, December 18, 1864, by the special desire of His Excellency Lord Wodehouse, said, in allusion to the late Viceroy's eloquence and literary pursuits :—

"But a brighter diadem, and richer far than aristocratic birth and hereditary nobility can confer, encircled and adorned his brow. He was eminently distinguished by great mental activity, by an ardent love for literature, by refined and vigorous scholarship, and by an exquisite power of discerning and appreciating the beautiful, the chastened, and the sublime in every walk and department of classical and historic lore. . . . All his productions show that he was deeply impressed with a conviction that education should not only be scientific, and religious, and moral, and practical, but eminently æsthetic—that it should impart knowledge calculated to ennoble, to dignify, and to refine the affections of the heart, to develop our instinctive tastes for order and harmony in creation, and for admiring 'whatsoever things are lovely' in the works of nature and of art, as well as to convey instruction to the mind."

The *Carlisle Journal*, writing of Lord Carlisle's death, and giving expression to Cumberland feeling, said :—

"It was no wonder that the loss of one possessing so many noble virtues should be deplored. He was truly a man free from all guile, and perhaps few have carried with them to the grave so much real public affection. In the various walks of his public life—as a thoughtful and accomplished writer, as a graceful and eloquent orator, as a painstaking politician—Lord

Carlisle was always true to his character as an amiable and benevolent man. As an ornament to his class, and an unobtrusive benefactor of his race, his loss will be widely felt, and as widely lamented."

In the newspapers of Yorkshire and throughout the northern counties similar expressions of exalted regard for Lord Carlisle's character were conveyed; the metropolitan press was equally laudatory of the public services and personal worth of the deceased statesman.

The Irish people, wishing to commemorate the noble character of their late Viceroy, whose long term of office had endeared him so much to their hearts, decided on erecting a memorial statue of bronze to the good Earl: the distinguished Irish sculptor Mr J. H. Foley, R.A., was authorised to do the work.

On May 2, 1870, Mr Foley's noble statue of the late Earl of Carlisle was unveiled in the Phœnix Park, Dublin, in the presence of the Lord-Lieutenant of Ireland and the Countess Spencer, the Lord Chancellor, the Dukes of Devonshire and Leinster, and a great number of noblemen and ladies, men eminent in science and literature, and others of high position.

"In excellent taste," says the *Dublin Express*, "all inaugural ceremonial was dispensed with. It was felt that amid this Irish people, whom he loved so well, Lord Carlisle needed neither pageant nor eulogium. The statue itself, recalling vividly the genial expression, the benevolence, and the intellectual thought of Lord Carlisle, will speak more touchingly to the heart of every passer-by than any word of eloquence. Each one who looked in mournful recollection on Foley's admirable impersonation experienced a relief that the conventional speech was decreed superfluous. The good Earl was emphatically the people's friend, and here, in the people's garden, which he himself created, his statue, appropriately placed, will attract many a kindly glance, and revive many an affectionate remembrance. It will restore to us, who knew him, and familiarise to future generations, the face and form of one who combined with high lineage, brilliant talents, and universal philanthropy, a heart devoted, honestly and warmly, to the welfare and happiness of Ireland."

This statue of Lord Carlisle represents him in his full robes as Grand Master of the Order of St Patrick. It is eight feet three inches in height, and stands on a pedestal of pretty nearly the same elevation. The following inscription appears on the entablature :—

"GEORGE WILLIAM FREDERICK,
SEVENTH EARL OF CARLISLE, K.G.,
CHIEF SECRETARY FOR IRELAND 1835-41,
LORD-LIEUTENANT OF IRELAND 1855-58 ; 1859-64.
BORN 1802, DIED 1864."

On the opposite side are the words—

"ERECTED BY PUBLIC SUBSCRIPTION, 1870."

An influential and numerous assembly of the nobility and gentry of Yorkshire was held at York in November 1865, to concert measures for commemorating the public and private virtues of the late Earl of Carlisle. Earl Fitzwilliam presided, and he was supported by the Earl of Zetland, Earl Cathcart, and other leading noblemen in Yorkshire. The Archbishop of York, who proposed the second resolution, said, *inter alia:*—

"To hand down the example of Lord Carlisle to posterity was a good thing. They would find few like him. He was a man of such a high and pure temper, so incapable of resentment, so full of refinement of mind, and such intense necessitude for loving, that perhaps there would not be one man in a century that should come near him. And therefore it was a good thing that the noblemen and gentlemen of the country should meet to commemorate one that was indeed noble and gentle in the truest and highest sense of the words."

The result of this meeting was the erection of "The Carlisle Memorial Column" upon Bulmer Hill, at the edge of the Castle Howard estate, about two miles and a half from the castle, and facing the magnificent avenue which traverses the park, and about twelve miles from York. The total height of the monument, from the foot of the steps to the top of the gilt urn, is 110 feet, and the diameter of the column 7 feet 4 inches. The four pedestals at the corners of the platform are surrounded by knightly helmets, and carry on one face a sword and shield, bearing alternately the arms of the Howard family and the royal arms, in allusion to the viceregal dignity of the late Earl. The total cost of the monument was £2061.

The men of Cumberland felt equally desirous with those of Yorkshire and Morpeth in England to show their sincere appreciation of the character of a nobleman who never moved amongst them without exciting their admiration and hearty reverence. A county meeting was called at Carlisle, and subscriptions obtained from both political parties in Cumberland, and specially from the men of Brampton and the barony of Gillesland, tenants of Naworth. Knowing the feeling of the late Earl, it was decided to erect a statue on the Moat—the high elevation on the east side of the town, and on a spot often much admired by him whose virtues they sought to commemorate. Mr Foley was intrusted with the work, and happily satisfied everybody; the excellence of the portrait-statue, executed in bronze, cannot be exaggerated; it is worthy of the good Earl; it is no less worthy of the artist himself. His Lordship is exhibited in the robes and insignia of the Order of the Garter, in a standing position, one hand resting on a book, the latter being introduced as suggestive of his taste for literary pursuits. The statue fulfils every indication, and Cumberland may well be proud of the work.

On August 9, 1870, the inauguration of the statue took place, and was attended by thousands of people. The subscribers marched in a body from Brampton, headed by Oddfellows, Foresters, and the "Belted Will" Rifle Volunteer corps, bands of music and banners. No such open-air meeting was ever witnessed in Cumberland. Many Cumbrians in London and other large towns of England, as well as the agricultural districts, made it their special business to attend the ceremonial; and not a few wept as they looked upon the sculptured features of a nobleman whom they so truly esteemed.

The statue, larger than life-size, is placed on a pedestal of nearly eight feet in height, and bears the following inscription :—

"ERECTED BY THE PEOPLE OF CUMBERLAND TO COMMEMORATE
THE PUBLIC SERVICES AND PERSONAL WORTH OF
GEORGE WILLIAM FREDERICK HOWARD,
SEVENTH EARL OF CARLISLE, K.G.
BORN APRIL 18, 1802. DIED DEC. 5, 1864."

After the unveiling of the statue by T. H. Graham, Esq., of Edmond Castle, Sir George Grey offered a just tribute to the memory of his friend, the Earl of Carlisle, by referring to " his Christian philanthropy, his warm and unceasing sympathy with everything good, charitable, and benevolent, his generous large-heartedness, and his energetic co-operation in everything that tended to lessen human ignorance, to mitigate human suffering, and to promote the social, moral, and religious welfare of his fellow-men, irrespective of country, of creed, or of colour."

Mr W. W. Story, the American sculptor, and author of "Roba di Roma," followed with a vigorous and sympathetic speech, saying,—" Among the dead of England of these latter days, it would be difficult to mention one who was more worthy to be blest in the memory of man—one of a broader and larger nature, of a nobler and higher character, of loftier inspirations, of a more spotless life, than Lord Carlisle."

The Marquis of Lorne also delivered a short yet effective address, and expressed his belief that " the Lord Carlisle, who made the Irish people love him, did more to preserve the peace of the empire than many of the old lords of keeps and Wardens of Marches."

At the conclusion of the ceremony, three hundred and fifty ladies and gentlemen sat down to luncheon in the great hall of Naworth Castle. The Hon. Charles Howard, M.P., presided, and was supported right and left by the distinguished guests who had taken part in the proceedings on the Moat.

The very pleasant relations of the Howard family with the borough of Morpeth, dating as far back as 1604, when "Belted Will Howard" presented the corporation with a silver mace, unique of its kind in bearing the arms of James I. and of the several families whose inheritance had centred in the noble donor, naturally called forth an expression of grateful remembrance for the much-cherished representative of a family so long endeared to the barony. Nowhere more than in Morpeth and the neighbourhood was the late Earl of Carlisle better esteemed. To them he had addressed his first political declaration in 1826, one sentence of which is worth quoting here:—" The principles which shall ever regulate my conduct are loyalty to the King, a sincere attachment to our free and equal constitution, an earnest desire to secure the welfare of every class of my fellow-subjects, and an ardent love of that freedom which has made us the proud and happy people it is our boast to be." The sum of £400, subscribed by the inhabitants of Morpeth and neighbourhood, was spent on a bust of the late Earl of Carlisle, executed by Foley, and the formation of a library containing the Earl's published works and speeches—a most appropriate mode of commemorating a nobleman whose literary tastes* formed a chief feature of his character. At the ceremony of opening the library and placing the bust in the Town Hall of Morpeth, a very goodly company of Northumbrian gentry, including the Mayor and other officials of Newcastle, assembled. Earl Grey, Sir George Grey, and others spoke on the occasion, and dwelt with much feeling on the historical qualities of the Earl of Carlisle, whom the citizens of Morpeth had always held in the highest regard.

In an address conveyed to the reigning representative of the Carlisle family, the people of Morpeth spoke of the deceased Earl of Carlisle in terms very befitting the conclusion of this brief memoir:—

" In every relation of life, in every society, in every

---

* Some of Lord Carlisle's poetical efforts were published by Moxon in 1869, under the title:—" Poems by George Howard, Earl of Carlisle, selected by his Sisters. *In memoriam matris.*" With the appropriate motto on the title-page:—
"Not wholly lost! thy letter'd fame shall tell
A part of what thou wast,—Farewell! farewell!"

country, he called forth the admiration and respect of all, and has left only pleasant memories; these must pass away with the living, but his eminent public services, and their grateful recognition by those best able to estimate them, will be unmistakably handed down to future generations, so long as the Irish Roll and the Yorkshire Vase shall remain in the library of Castle Howard."

REV. RICHARD MATTHEWS, M.A.,

OF WIGTON HALL.

"Of lettered science and patriotic zeal."

THE Rev. Richard Matthews, M.A., was born at Wigton Hall, Cumberland, on December 17, 1771. His school-days were passed at St Bees, after which he was entered at St Catherine's Hall, Cambridge, of which college his uncle, Dr Lowther Yates, was master. He graduated at Cambridge, and was ordained to a curacy in the neighbourhood, which he held for two years. On his father's death, in 1798 or 1799, he came home and took possession of his fine property, and then relinquished the calling of a clergyman, excepting on rare occasions, to supply the place of the Vicar of Wigton. He was seldom spoken of as "The Reverend," but as Mr Matthews of "The Hall" (Wigton), the ancient family mansion, and his own residence from 1799 till his death on March 20, 1846.

Owing to his delicacy of health, and frequent liability to headaches of a severe nature, inducing him to stay a good deal at home, he was but little known to the general public of Cumberland; though it is not too much to say that no man in the county was more highly esteemed by his intellectual contemporaries, and by the generation that immediately bordered upon his own.

Mr Matthews had two sisters. Mary, a genial, kind-hearted, and pleasant person, married Major Aglionby of Nunnery in February 1813; his other sister, Jane, remained a spinster, and looked after his domestic comforts. He was a bachelor. For many reasons affecting himself, and his more free intercourse with society, to say nothing of posterity, which seems to stand more and more in need of a better infusion of blood, it would have been well if he had chosen for wife one of Cumbria's fair daughters, to one of whom he was deeply attached. His domesticated character and fondness of children increased the regret his friends felt that he did not marry and become *paterfamilias*. Nothing gave him greater delight than playing with his three nieces,[*] the bright-eyed children of Major and Mrs Aglionby; and as they grew in understanding he read much to them on natural history, and by a happy exposition of the facts laid before them, secured their ready attention to the general principles of natural science.

After passing his meridian, his partiality for study and home quietude prevailed with him much more than general society. To his attached friends, however, he showed no difference. The same hearty

---

[*] His nieces, Miss Aglionby, Mrs Porteous of Eden Hall Vicarage, and Mrs Charles Fetherstonhaugh of Staffield Hall, are now living—each and all of whom cherish with grateful feelings the memory of their ever kind and most indulgent Uncle Matthews.

welcome awaited them at the Hall, and the same free interchange of opinion existed between them. Even the casual visitor of his house was received with an urbanity characteristic of the true English gentleman in the higher walks of social life.

His habits were nearly as regular as time itself. He rose and breakfasted at the same hour all the year round; at noon, he mounted his horse and rode leisurely along the roads, and returned to a minute for his three-o'clock dinner. Indeed, he was systematic in everything he did, and never in a hurry either as to decision or action. He rode his bay pony at walking pace, and was followed by his groom. His dress, or what Wigton folk called his "top-gear," could not be mistaken on the road. He wore a broad-brimmed drab-coloured hat, a red tartan cloak, a loose and large white neckcloth, and grey-coloured trousers.

The Hall partook of the old-fashioned English manor-house in its plentifulness, its warmth, and its substantial comforts; but its owner lived on the simplest of fare, taking scanty supplies of solid food, and indulging largely in the use of milk and tea. His dinner consisted of a bowl of good milk, a slice of bread, and two hard-boiled eggs. He took no wine and no stimulants. Probably he ate too sparingly, and his habits assumed too uniform a phase for the ordinary usages of the world. A glass of his fine madeira or of wholesome port would have helped his thin blood to a higher oxidation and power, and fitted him for larger intellectual endeavours, and a more active part in county affairs, for which he was so eminently qualified.

In point of height Mr Matthews was about the middle stature, well built, and possessed of a mixed temperament. His head was well formed, and his countenance open, mild, and benignant in expression. His temper and feelings were placid; he never seemed too highly exalted or too lowly depressed. If he had a less robust frame, he had a fine intelligence—a grand possession to any man, and especially to one who could live at home at ease, and view the world outside with complacency as a diorama of humanities struggling with life's *inertia* and nature's imperative behests.

Tolerant and wise in small things as well as in great, he knew that if milk and eggs sufficed his bodily wants, beef and beer might be needful to sustain the frame of the artisan daily deteriorated in functions by labour, depression, and fatigue. Had he lived till now, when the world is full of schemes of reformation and panaceas for all the ills that flesh is heir to, proclaimed by peripatetic pedants, lay and clerical, and with much platform drumming, he would have smiled at the vain attempts to arrange universal man under paper pledges and untenable restraints.

Exempt from "the cure of souls," and free from the petty cares incident to domestic and connubial life, he devoted his leisure hours to various pursuits becoming a man of property and of superior mind and education. Biography, political economy, history, and collateral subjects, occupied his thoughtful hours. He perused the new statutes, the driest of all dry reading, with the care of a lawyer actuated by zeal in the cause of a client. He considered it imperative to be a just exponent of the law, and to have a full knowledge of his judicial functions. He got the credit of being the only man of his time in Cumberland who could really unravel the depths, and, it may be added, the doubts of an Act of Parliament. Accurate and concise, he discharged his magisterial duties with peculiar gravity, and with a faithful reference to the public interests. It was said that his legal knowledge enabled him to dispense with the opinion of the magistrate's clerk. If so, he enjoyed a very enviable position among the Justices of the Peace in Cumberland.* He was highly appreciated by his contemporaries on the bench. It was therefore a matter of general regret that he would not allow himself to be nominated to the Chairmanship of Quarter Sessions, —an office that he would have filled with so much dignity and honour. He preferred the study of entomology, botany, meteorology, and other kindred pursuits, to the more responsible position of the county magnate. As a botanist he explored the flora of the Wigton district, and probably was only second to Thomas Heysham of Carlisle on matters entomological. In meteorology, he took special pains to register every phenomenon bearing upon its elucidation: he apparently took up this inquiry at the dawn of the century. Such studies were far from fashionable, but things are greatly altered since he first gauged the rain-fall at Wigton Hall, and studied

* The administration of the law in "Petty Sessions," in the majority of instances, in Cumberland, would be little better than a farcical exhibition, without the intervention of the attorney on duty ; and even with him at elbow it is not always free from the ludicrous and "Justice Shallow's" style. The political genesis of the magisterial body, without reference to mental acquirements or fitness, has made all sensible men long for stipendiary and qualified magistrates.

the philosophic observations of Dr Dalton,—observations, it may be noted, framed by a Cumberland man, and derived from the Lake District, that exhibits the most pluviose atmosphere in the kingdom. Even as late as 1826, those who, like Mr Matthews, observed atmospheric phenomena with a view to scientific data, were laughed at for their new-fangled notions.

In 1866, the world was startled by a suggestion no less marvellous than that the manufacturing towns of Yorkshire and Lancashire, if not the great metropolis itself, should be supplied with water collected amongst the mountains of Cumberland and Westmoreland. The pioneers of this grand scheme—a scheme rivalling, nay, far surpassing, the Roman system of aqueducts stretching across the Campagna from the Sabine Hills to the Capitol—were not engineers, but scientific observers, like John Dalton the chemist, Ottley and John Miller in the Lake District; Mr Matthews; Mr Pitt of Carlisle, and others. To-day the writer's intellectual friend, Isaac Fletcher, M.P. for Cockermouth, stands pre-eminent for his services in ascertaining the rain-fall amid the mountains and lakes, and over a wide district of Cumberland. As nature's supply of water from the clouds is the most pure, so is it by far the most abundant in quantity in these northern parts of England; and the fact of such a scheme being propounded as the one mentioned above is another apt illustration of the value of scientific observation in furtherance of man's interests, nay, his life, longevity, and daily comforts.

As showing the bent of his mind on these matters, he was wishful to see an instrument invented for measuring the force of the wind, and there is reason to think that he made some designs for the practical carrying out of his views.

Nothing could be more consonant with Mr Matthews' out-door enjoyments, as well as in-door studies, than the investigations of natural history. He had shown a predilection for it in his youth, when the pages of Buffon and Goldsmith were the only standard sources,—pages no less redolent of fancy than of fact, but well chosen to amuse and instruct the inquiring mind. As he grew in knowledge, he became conversant with the botanical discoveries of Linnæus, the discussions of Hutton and Werner on the earth's genesis, the researches of Cuvier, and the new science that sprang from the study of the organic remains of the geological epochs, the chemistry of physics, and the dawn of meteorology in Dalton's hands, the views of R. Brown and Decandolle, and the "natural system" of Jussieu, and of many smaller lights on the horizon of discovery, giving form and perspicuity to the study of living nature. Within the period of Mr Matthews' life, it may almost be said that natural science had its birth and development, arising as it did from the chaos of conjecture and crude analysis,— showing little advance from the era of the "Historia Animalium," onwards for centuries,—to a record of actual facts, observations, and phenomena, and a history of descriptive forms, generic and special, the only data upon which a true science could be established. He was a great man for facts and accurate data, and showed his partiality for the Baconian method. The progress of discovery could not fail to interest a person of such general attainments as Mr Matthews; and he used to dwell upon the gradual enlightenment of humanity by study, experiment, and discovery, and the happy order of things that prevailed in the world of nature.

He had a great penchant for the study of anatomy and medicine; and had he not found the anatomical rooms so highly objectionable at Cambridge, would doubtless have taken to physic rather than divinity. No book pleased him more than his old friend Dr Paley's "Natural Theology," which he used to read to his nieces, the Misses Aglionby, on winter evenings.

At one time he gave considerable attention to archæology, and to enable himself the better to carry out his hobby, purchased the site of "Old Carlisle," a mile south of Wigton, and for long one of the chief Roman stations in the county. The fort itself was of an oblong figure, 500 feet by 400, and the foundations of the buildings around it were so plain in the time of Stukeley (1720) that a plan might have been formed of the streets. Here Dalmatians and Moors were long quartered, and probably fifteen hundred years have not entirely effaced the blood of these bold defenders of Roman territory. Amid these Roman ruins Mr Matthews found altars, bronze lamps, sandals, &c. He also deciphered many inscriptions. See Lyson's "Cumberland," pp. cxliii., clxxxiii., and clxxxvi.; also *Gentleman's Magazine* for 1756, for additional information on discoveries made previous to Mr Matthews' time.

Though so retiring in disposition, and mingling with so few men of his own epoch, he possessed a very large influence in the old Whig circles of Cumberland from the Peace of 1815 to the passing of the Reform Bill in 1832. He was also held in high esteem by men of the opposite party for his moderation, scholarly acquirements, and excellent judgment. The central position of Wigton Hall favoured Mr Matthews' residence as a rendezvous for the leading men of the county, but much more was owing to the well-endowed mind, good talk, and mature judgment of "mine host." Mr Matthews shone best at his own fireside, round which J. C. Curwen, his senior; Major Aglionby, and John Rooke, his contemporaries; Sir James Graham, William Blamire, Thomas Spedding of Mirehouse, and others, his juniors, were wont to gather from time to time to listen to his instructive conversation, and to benefit by his able counsel and clear expression of opinion on matters engaging the attention of the country. He delighted in the society of these gentlemen, particularly Sir James and Mr Blamire, both of whom had rooms at the Hall whenever they chose to occupy them. He was truly the guide, philosopher, and friend to these young politicians, and no man in Cumberland enjoyed more hearty pleasure than Mr Matthews in seeing his two political *protegés* returned to Parliament as knights of the shire in 1831. His knowledge of men and events, his political experience and equanimity, fitted him for the high distinction of mentor of the Whigs in Cumberland. Averse to extreme measures and too hasty legislation, he was for the moderation that tempered liberty of speech and political functions with social order and respect for the laws as guiding principles to our countrymen; these principles will ever find support with the true citizens of every nation, as they assuredly gain in credit and in strength in every cycle of human history. The noise and clamour of popularity-hunting partisans in any cause received no favour at his hands.

Possessing a marked individuality of character, scholarly habits, liberal and generous views, untainted by the slightest ambition, and bound by no ties but the pleasant amenities of life, Mr Matthews might well shine with superior light among the bucolic gentry of Cumberland. The cool head, placid manners, and persuasive tone gave force to his statements, and carried conviction to the mind when differences of opinion arose among friends in the discussion of political questions. After the struggle of parties had settled down, by the Tories usurping the West, and the Whigs becoming masters of East Cumberland, Wigton Hall was no longer quickened by the presence of political suitors appealing to the faithful oracle for counsel; and its social surroundings naturally became the reflex of a gradual decadence that marked the owner in his approaching trials of threescore and ten years of age.

He was active in his benevolence, and sympathised with the distressed, the more so when he perceived a leaven of legislative injustice as the proximate cause of the poverty and dissatisfaction prevailing in the country. His clerical character was never made visible; his religious views, like his catholic spirit, were based on grounds of charity and large toleration to all men of honest convictions. He was vastly superior to the Episcopal order reigning in Cumberland, and though averse to the High Oxonian views developed in 1839, he would never have been a party to the introduction of stupid shop-lads and bankers' clerks to the pulpits of an English Protestant Church

—a practice too long followed by the late Bishops Villiers and Waldegrave, and likely to be productive of a lasting deterioration in the Establishment.

Sir James Graham had a thorough love for his political counsellor at Wigton Hall, and often invited himself there to discuss the graver questions of State policy with the friend of his youth, whose historical knowledge of the times, past and present, surpassed most men of the day. Mr Matthews, admiring the keen perception of the Netherby Baronet, his clear insight into public matters, and the soundness of his principles, counted upon his becoming the representative of the Liberal interests of Cumberland. The championship of the Blue cause had long been in Curwen's hand, and as time waned with him, it was no small gratification to Mr Matthews that the belt of honour, so long encircling his old friend, would be handed over to the most able of his disciples, the young Baronet of Netherby Hall. Nor was Mr Matthews less slow to recognise the high claims of his friend William Blamire of Thackwood. Both his *protegés* did him honour, and ever showed him the most affectionate regard.

John Rooke, whose character is presently to be discussed, was glad to avail himself of the library of "The Hall," and the learning of his friend Mr Matthews. Though Mr Rooke was a Tory, the political sway of the two men in no wise interfered with their pleasant relations. Geology and political economy were more agreeable themes than party polemics to both men. It has been said that Mr Matthews was the only person who really understood Rooke's thesis on the formation of the earth's surface, whilst to the rest of the neighbourhood the Akehead philosopher appeared little more than a dealer in moonshine. Of the Speddings of Mirehouse, the Lawsons of Brayton, and others who frequented "The Hall," it is impossible in this limited notice to speak.

Late in the autumn of 1845 the health of Mr Matthews seemed deeply affected. Seeing that his medical advisers did not exactly agree in opinion, he remarked, with his usual tenderness of expression, and very philosophically, "Well, my friends, I see there is a little difference in your diagnoses, which time will enable you to settle, as my days cannot be very long here." On the 10th March 1846, he saw that death was approaching, and on the early morning of the 20th March he passed away. In accordance with his own wishes, a *post-mortem* was made, and revealed an immense liver, affected with cancer. On the 24th he was interred in Wigton Churchyard. The spot is marked by a white stone cross above a basement slab, upon which is recorded both Mr and Miss Matthews' interment. Inside the church is a memorial slab of more elaborate workmanship, with floral scroll inscribed to them; and flanking this are slabs dedicated to the memory of their father and mother, and "Uncle Yates" of Cambridge, who seems to have died at Wigton Hall.

John Rooke

JOHN ROOKE,

POLITICAL ECONOMIST AND GEOLOGIST.

---

*"He did look far
Into the service of the time, and was
Discipled of the bravest."*
—SHAKESPEARE.

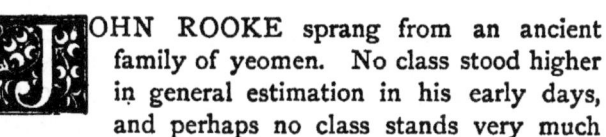

JOHN ROOKE sprang from an ancient family of yeomen. No class stood higher in general estimation in his early days, and perhaps no class stands very much higher now in Cumberland. The term "yeoman" is here applied to a person who occupies and cultivates his own land, leasehold or freehold. In Cumberland, the yeomen are designated "states-men" by old-fashioned folk, as well as the agricultural community; that is, men having an estate of land. "An able and honest states-man" is one of the proudest of titles in Cumberland and Westmoreland. These "states-men," or yeomen, are not so rich in the world's goods as the small landed gentry, the class immediately above them in society; but they are richer in proportion to their wants, and often richer in healthful contentment. They seldom pretend to anything more than what they really are in the eyes of the world. They live and labour as farmers, and appear as such in social life; but in possessing their own freeholds or lands, they can step beyond the tenant-farmers in various ways, and notably in the education of their children, and in placing them in commercial walks or professional positions. They constitute a landed middle class, and at one time were very numerous, and not less politically influential, in Cumberland. The incomes of the yeomen necessarily vary, and to a great extent, between the extreme points in the scale of a forty-shilling freehold, with dwelling attached, to £300 or £400 a year and upwards. An average would be difficult to estimate, but it may be taken roughly at £150 a year.

The small holdings of "toft and croft" sprang from the feudal ages, and were among the first indications of an enfranchisement of villeins, when the barons and squires sought to increase the number of their retainers, to be used as fighting men in the Border service. Some of these very "sma' states-men" appear as the dying remnants of the "coterels" of the mediæval parishes, who possessed curtilage or huts, with small parcels of land annexed, or virgates of land merely. To-day they are viewed as cottars, having garden or garth, and whose subsistence depends on other means and employment than their own scanty holdings in land. Ascending much higher in the scale than these garth-holders, many of the yeomen ranked with, and often fared worse than, tenant-farmers, owing to their reliance on the yield of their lands, imperfectly cultivated, rather than a well-directed industry. Yet they prided themselves on being landowners, however limited their acreage; and over their cups, with John Barleycorn as their emphatic oracle, became pretty demonstrative and swaggering.

The yeomanry offer no division of classes; they all appear alike at fair or market, church or roadside public. Whatever distinction exists is to be found at home, and mainly with the character of the family, and their aspirations to a higher status or position in life. The slow and inert yeomen not seldom fell away to the position of farmers and something worse; on the other hand, the better class of yeomen kept supplying the towns with enterprising lads, the church with honest pastors, and the distant colonies with worthy emigrants and good English blood. With the former class the estate of land, after one or two mortgages, dwindled away; while among the enterprising folk it was maintained intact, or even considerably enlarged by each generation being solicitous for the family name and its claims to respectability. Instances not a few occurred, and unfortunately do still occur, of men who sunk into slovenly and intemperate habits and debt, and died out as landowners, to the advantage of their more decent neighbours, and not less well for the interests of the soil they had so long impoverished.

The "states-men," who constituted so large a body in Cumberland at the passing of the Reform Bill in 1832, are fast diminishing in numbers, owing in part to the pressure of the times requiring energy and business habits, and in part to the tendency of their families to gravitate to their own homesteads in all the vicissitudes of life, till the old hive became filled with drones, and the land burthened beyond its capabilities. The patriarchal system of living and farming is gone by, and can never return; but too many of the yeomen in isolated districts would not see this, but hugged as closely to their grandsires' methods as a Hindoo would swear by his fetichism. This clinging to the "old place," without attempting to prop up its timbers, brought many a roof-tree to the ground, with ruin of fortune and ruin of character to all concerned in its fall.

The education of the yeomanry was almost invariably defective, highly so, even to a late date. The three R's, or reading, writing, and arithmetic, were barely accomplished at the village schools, along with Bible history and other commonplace dull reading. The memory of the boys was taxed just as wrongly as their backs were whipped, but there was neither teaching nor training, much less education of the mind. There was a kind of humdrum reading of humdrum books, but real enlightenment, the greatest desideratum of all, was almost an unknown quantity in the school formula. There were some exceptions, and notably in the old grammar-schools, occasionally found in the market-town or parish "foundation," where an improved system of things prevailed; but even these were seldom worthy of commendation. There was little taste for reading, and that got crushed by a perpetual Bible-thumbing and spelling of Nebuchadnezzar-isms. No opportunities for mental improvement existed at home. The few books to be found on the shelf in the ingle-nook could be counted on the fingers. Bunyan and Defoe ("Pilgrim's Progress" and "Robinson Crusoe") were perhaps the most constant authors, a volume of sermons, an odd number of the "Spectator" or "Tatler," a quaint herbalist or book on witchcraft or superstition, a few half-torn almanacs and pamphlets, mixed up with fly-sheets of ballads from "Chevy Chase" to "Caldbeck Wedding," were the main constituents of a fragmentary assortment of prose and fiction,—solid works of any kind being seldom seen, except the big Bible, with its registry of family births, marriages, and deaths. The pride of the young "states-man" lay in other directions than mental culture. A gun with "a good shot in her," a trotting nag that could keep its place in a run with the hounds, rural sports, "merry neets," fairs, dancing-lofts,* and "Carel" races, were the *beau ideal* of his enjoyments. The winter evenings were trifled away in the farm-kitchen, or in a "gude crack" at the "smiddy" and "public," discussing the tittle-tattle of the country-side, its gossip and slander, and puerile nothingness. The women folk, mistress and maids, were at home engaged in their needlework, darning, or spinning. No wonder that generation after generation followed each other in the exercise of manual labour and the routine plodding of the farm. The

* Dancing *was* dancing in those days, and the "loft-boards" shook under the emphatic stamp and vivacious shuffle of lads and lasses blithe and buxom. Nothing could be more exhilarating than—

> "Scrape it, fiddlers! foot it, dancers!
> See how heel to fiddle answers!
> Foot it, shuffling, shifting places,
> Down the avenue of faces;
> Shifting, shuffling in and out,
> Up and down, and round about;
> Whirling skirts of ribbons streaming,
> Neat-laced ankles trimly gleaming,
> Corduroys all shaking, reeling,
> Hobnailed boot-soles toeing, heeling;
> Stamping, shuffling, all in line,
> Treading out the time like wine."

little holding supplied the wants of life, and bucolic contentment rested there—

> " Wi' sma' to sell, and less to buy,
> Aboon distress, below envy;
> O wha wad leave this humble state,
> For a' the pride of a' the great?"

The sons of yeomen, growing up with all the prejudices that ignorance and isolation bring in their train, were apt to continue in the paternal groove, unless one of the family, gifted with tact or brain-power, stepped out of the ranks of his brethren, and turned the tide of family affairs. It was only in these instances, where younger sons sought other vocations, or the virgin soil of the Far West, where self-dependence was the law of life, that the humbler yeomen, with redundant families, had a chance of holding by their own hearth-stone. One active-minded lad was often the saving of a family, and his return from London with new ideas, his personal appearance, talk, and example, were encouraging facts, and often paved the way to the well-doing of a whole neighbourhood.

A noble spirit, and a not less noble sacrifice of home comforts, must have governed those yeomen who, with limited incomes, reared large families, and sent some of their sons to higher-class grammar-schools, and even colleges, to afford them the opportunities of rising in the world. Like Goldsmith's village preacher, they seemed passing rich on forty pounds a year. Frugality, industry, thrift, and foresight were essential in their domestic economy. Their food consisted mainly of oatmeal porridge and milk night and morning, coarse bread of the seconds of wheat flour, with barley and rye, bacon and potatoes, or peas and beans, all which were derived from the produce of the farm, and all staunch feeders. In this respect, what could surpass the "cow'd-lword," a pudding of oatmeal and suet, and apple-dumplings, along with a bountiful supply of good milk? Tea and coffee were very much for Sundays, along with the ribboned bonnet and best "bib and tocher;" and these town's luxuries had oft been obtained by the sale of surplus eggs, poultry, and orchard produce, special perquisites of the women-folk. They had barn-fowls in the yard, bacon of their own curing, cloth of their own spinning, and coats and petticoats of their own making; and home work counted as nothing in the balance-sheet of expenditure. The women of the household wore linsey-wolsey under-clothing and print "bed-gowns" for six days in the week,—as they do still by the Fell-sides; and a Sunday's dress had to continue long in fashion. The men and lads trusted mainly to their grey coats of rough-spun wool, home made, and fustian; hence this class came to be distinguished as the "grey coats" of Cumberland. Clogs, or wooden shoes iron-plated, served both sexes on the farm-stead; wooden bowls, pewter plates, and horn spoons graced the kitchen dresser; deal tables, chairs, and settle (a kind of wooden couch), chaff-beds, and simple furniture, were consonant with the living and appearances of these country-folk,—farmers or yeomanry. But with all this frugality on the part of these hard-fisted people, it is marvellous how they held their heads above water, and accomplished so much in the promotion of their children's interests. Amongst the "*two-or-three-hundred-a-year lairds*," who had tea and toast, capon, and possibly cauliflower and surroundings to match, there was less difficulty in giving their families a fair chance of success by higher education and other purchasable advantages, provided the family was not too large and not too expensive in their notions.

It is well known that the towns of Cumberland, commercially and socially, have derived their best blood from the spirited sons of the farmers and yeomanry; that the professions are supplied from the same source which has also furnished the Church with sympathising earnest clergymen. As long as the youth who has been well or even partially educated, and home-nurtured under happy maternal influences, remains true to his Cumberland feeling as a yeoman's son, with character to sustain and family to uphold, he pushes his way manfully in the world; and in London and other centres of industry the Cumbrian is not the last in the race, but is more likely at the head of commercial establishments, or adorning by his steady worth other respectable walks of life.

The great feature of these Cumberland "statesmen" was their independence, and this they occasionally exercised in a sturdy pertinacious fashion. They thought and acted for themselves, or followed the leading wishes of some noted member of their own body; for nearly every parish had its chief counsellor or authoritative man, who guided the less confident, headed the vestry, and occasionally snubbed the parson and schoolmaster. The yeoman was much less influenced by the sentiments of the squire or the preaching of the rector than might be supposed, unless both accorded to him a thoughtful consideration. He was not at the beck of manorial lords, and not easily cajoled by hustings' promises, or the "bows and scrapes" of political candidates seeking his suffrages. In short, he somewhat resembled the old cock-sparrows nestling under the farm-house eaves, in being not easily caught with chaff. Preferring the corn of honest sentiment to much verbiage and profession, the farming class voted for the knights of the shire as men having opinions of their own, and thus were regarded as the only true type of the free and independent electors.* They were the mainstay of Curwen and Blamire, and held by Sir James Graham as long as he held by his first love—Whiggism; but when he joined the Peel party, they drove him somewhat unmercifully from the county. Diffident and retired with strangers, curt in speech, and somewhat unpolished, the yeomen generally have had the credit of being decent neighbours, hard and tolerably fair dealers, except in "horse-couping;" partisans in friendship, shrewd and calculating; impartial jurors at the Sessions or the Assizes, though vastly more happy in their decisions when guided by the Court than when left to their own unaided judgment. They are peaceful and decorous in their fashion, and though far short of what they might be, ever loyal supporters

* Many of the so-called independent electors are led by other circumstances than party colours, and not the least by self-interest or personal aggrandisement. At the election for East Cumberland in 1837, when Sir J. Graham was defeated, a Mr T. T. of —— Hall took a very active part in his own district. One of the electors of the said district being asked how he voted, at once replied, "Oh, for T. T., to be sure; he buys aw my bacon and butter—whae sae likely to get my vote?"

Since the introduction of penny papers, this mode of selecting a knight of the shire may have been changed; but, to the writer's view, very much requires to be done in Cumberland to enlighten the bucolic mind on matters political.

of the Crown. They are decent folk, but not without their failings. Their pride of independence often glides towards wilful stubbornness of opinion, occasionally merging into an offensive and overbearing attitude to others that does not eventually benefit their own interests. The straightening of a hedge or the clearing of a watercourse between two fields, where both the owners concerned would derive equal benefit, cannot always be accomplished without much trouble. Sometimes the arbitrament stands still, and generates animosity, unless some equivalent beyond the mere act of obligingness can be thrown into the scale by the person who first suggests the improvement. This arises from the suspicion of his neighbour running him within the post. So proud of their land, and so tenacious of what they call their rights, that rather than meet a neighbour half way in a matter of dispute, numbers of them would go to law, and spend some years' income over a trifling issue. It was the litigious spirit of the yeomen, who were apt—

"To wrangle
About the slightest fingle-fangle,"

and the disputes arising out of fishery rights, that made the Northern Circuit so attractive to aspiring barristers in days gone by.* John Scott (Lord Eldon), Scarlett (Lord Thesiger), and Harry (Lord) Brougham,

---

* The unsophisticated Cumbrian overlooked the fact that—

"Lawyers hire out their tongues,
And make their best advantages
Of others' quarrels."

Brougham and Scarlett were called the champions of these litigants; and a sharply-fought trial at the Assizes appeared to the bucolic lookers-on as of equal interest with a day's cock-fighting, or the Carlisle races with a grand wrestling competition.

made their fame and fortunes at the expense of litigious lairds; and now and then these wigged pugilists appeared to fight as valiantly over the suits of the yeomen as the yeomen themselves had done out of court.

Whether the failings or the virtues of humanity prevail most with yeomen, there is one thing manifest in their history, and that is, their gradual decadence, —particularly seen during the last thirty years. Many a "canny house" or "stately hall," or by whatever name the residences were known, where yeomen had for centuries kept their Yule, taught their sons and grandsons the traditions of their home, narrated the ups and downs of ancestral life, and all the cherished topics of auld langsyne, no longer shelter the "weel-kent folk o' ither days;" even the names of their founders are forgotten. This disappearance of names, if not of habitations, in many rural districts, brings about reflections of by no means an agreeable kind. Among many changes affecting both men and interests in these northern counties, there is no change more marked than that arising from the purchasing of real estates, and the further absorption of small holdings of a few fertile fields or share of pasturage— once the pride of decent folk content in their clay bields and cloyless life—by large landed proprietors. Should this mode of adding house to house and land to land continue to be acted upon at the same rate as during the last ten years, the grey-coated lairds or "states-men" of Canny Cumberland will be little heard of beyond the present century. They are best seen in their primitive, semi-patriarchal state by the "fell sides," or the retired dales (especially in Westmoreland), and in out-of-the-way districts, where the arterial current of active humanity reaches not; and there, if anywhere in English life, you realise the easy conditions upon which contentment is made to rest—few wants, fewer aspirations, and, above all, the fewest heart-burnings. It is to be hoped that the isolated nooks in which these yeomen reside, mainly on pastoral land; and their less attractive surroundings, will forbid the approach of the territorially aggrandising lord, or squire, or "Manchester man," coveting investments which would lead to further changes damaging to the old lairds and the old traditions; and all that remains of the British agriculture of the olden time.*

The life of the yeoman was monotonous to a degree. The market, the fair, and church-going were the only diversions to a vapid yet tolerably satisfied existence. The mental powers laid dormant, the social faculty was but little exercised without some rare and impulsive effort. A decorous dulness prevailed at home; there was no exchange of ideas beyond farm operations, and but little expanse of thought in any direction. Life and morals were tolerably respectable, unless the cozy parlour of the "King's Arms" became more fascinating than family and home influences; then affairs went from bad to worse—drunkenness being the highroad to destruction. Reading was confined to the local weekly paper, and this was obtained at the fourth or even sixth

---

* Whilst the author expresses his regret at the dying out of the old types of bucolic simplicity, he is well aware, and has, in a previous page, spoken of the greater advantages accruing to agriculture from the management of large holdings of land by active tenant-farmers, than under the old jog-trot system prevailing among lazy and slovenly "states-men."

hand in those days of eightpenny newspapers. The Sundays were not enlivening, nay, rather tiresome; there was a longer afternoon's nap, an extra yawn over the fire after church; that is, if the church was attended, for the majority of folk required a greater stimulus than the musty fodder of a Low Church sermon; and this they occasionally found in the announcement of a sale at the church door.*

" Last Sunday forenoon, after sarvice,
I' th' kurk-garth, the clerk caw'd a seale."

The farming class of the northern counties are generally tall in stature, and present thick-set forms of humanity. They are big-boned and fleshy, and well capable of vying with the physical obstacles besetting a life of real labour and hardship. They have endurable skins, and hard, leathery fists; their joints are broad and well knit together; and their whole *physique* indicates adaptation to the wants of their

* Without an explanation being offered of this extraordinary custom, the Southern reader will fancy some gross error has crept into the text. About forty years ago, the writer, then a boy, attended Wetheral Church, and wondered why the clerk should leave his desk and hasten out before any one else. He soon discovered the reason. Around the door of the church the male portion of the congregation were standing, whilst "Amen," as the clerk was generally called, took his position on the highest grave, and cried out—"Oyez! Oyez! this is to give notice that a sale of stock and crop and farming utensils, &c., will take place on Wednesday next, at the house of Mr John *Blank* of *Blank* Hall." He then read the list of things to be disposed of, and ended with his own vernacular—" The *seale* begins at nuin. I wad advise ye to be there in guid time for bread and cheese and yell." This was the usual mode of announcing sales, as advertising was held to be too expensive; moreover, few newspapers were read, and therefore they were valueless for publicity; whereas a *" kurk duir telling"* reached far and near within a few hours—the congregation being glad of some news to convey to their neighbours. Wetheral was and is one of the most respectable churches in Cumberland.

employment—exhibiting a natural selective force or Darwinism in full operation. Their feet, like their hands, are of big breadth, and move in sweeping lines, and whilst carrying off the morning dew, level the finer grasses to the earth's surface. They want agility and suppleness; they show unacquaintance with the gymnasium and the training of the drill-master; they have no *esprit de corps*, and few or none of the graceful attributes of educated mortals. In complexion they show more of the dark than the fair race. The colour of their hair varies from light brown to raven black; a few are red and carroty, but not a third are of the fairer complexion attributed to the Saxon; yet their moral nature has but little of the Celt, and their physical form generally has no affinity with this specially-marked race. The ethnology of the class is, however, too large a subject to be discussed in these pages.

The yeomen practised early hours; they had their servants up at five o'clock for the greater part of the year, and during the old days of scythe-mowing of grass, as early as four. The breakfast, of porridge and milk, and bread and "whillimer," or skim-milk cheese, was over before seven o'clock. They dined at noon,*

---

* The Cumberland ballad-maker, deploring the introduction of fresh customs fifty years ago, by which the country was "puzzen'd round wi' preyde," goes on to say:—

"We us'd to gan to bed at dark,
   And rose agean at four or five;
The mworn's the only time for wark,
   If fwok are only healthy and wad thrive.
Now we get up—nay, God kens when!
   And nuin's owre suin for us to deyne;
I 'se hungry or the pot 's hawf boil'd,
   And wish for teymes leyke auld langsyne."

off broth and beef twice a week, or potato-pot, made up of the scraps, and bacon for the majority of days, not forgetting the different dumplings of gooseberries or apples or plain suet, which occasionally constituted a dinner of themselves with milk. The supper came off between six and seven, and consisted of the same food as breakfast. The heads of the family sat down occasionally with the servants; if not, they had tea and toast night and morning, and a tit-bit of fowl or mutton for their one-o'clock dinner. The family was in bed before ten o'clock, and the servants more frequently at nine.

The living was simple and substantial, and the hours of labour and rest pretty fairly divided; but then there was no variety in the operations of the human mill; it had to grind away all the day, all the week, all the month, nay, all the year round. The pure animal functions were kept oiled and smooth, and ever in working gear; but what of the higher feelings? The ethical standard could hardly get raised; and of the true intellectual there were but small indications; whilst modesty and refinement had a hard struggle where there was so much of Audrey's calling and Touchstone's plain speaking on matters relating to the sexes. Their holidays were few and far between, and mainly bestowed on cock-fighting, races, and shooting-matches, ending too often in drink. In those days intercourse with towns was confined to mere buying and selling; libraries were unsought for, and but little known. With all these drawbacks, however, the yeomanry of Cumberland maintained a respected position, not owing to their faultless character or virtues, but rather from healthful comparison with the denizens of towns, more liable to temptation and vice. Much more might be written on this subject,—describing the domiciles and old-fashioned clay bields of the yeomen, with their big hearth-places and curious open chimneys, in which bacon-flitches, and hams, and legs of mutton hung, and dried and smoked; the Swiss-like arrangement of many of the interiors; the family gatherings by the ingle-neuk in the winter evenings, and other special features in their social life; their market-going and habits in the market-towns; their celebration of births and marriages, and the objectionable modes of conducting country funerals; also their habits of thought, their superstitions, and many other circumstances affecting their lives and history; but the foregoing sketch may suffice to show the characteristic features of the yeomanry of Cumberland.

ANCESTRY, SCHOOLING, AND FARMING.

About a mile and a half northwards of the market-town of Wigton, in Cumberland, is the hamlet of Akehead, where the respectable family of Rooke have had a habitation and a name since the days of Oliver Cromwell. John Rooke, born 22d April 1750, was the representative of the family for about sixty years, and his death took place in September 1817. In addition to occupying his own estate of 100 acres, he held the office of Surveyor of Roads and Bridges under the Enclosure Commissioners for the parishes of Wigton, Aspatria, and Westward. About 1779, he married Peggy Barnes of Little Bampton, whose mother was one of the Liddells of Boustead Hill, and had issue four sons and four daughters:—*John*, born August 29, 1780, the subject of this memoir;—*Jane*, born April 6, 1782, married Francis Sibson of Crosscannoby, by whom she had six sons; the only surviving one is the distinguished London physician, Dr Francis Sibson;—*Ann*, born March 17, 1784, married Samuel Rigg, banker, of Wigton, and had three sons;—*Robert*, born December 6, 1786, married Mary Sterndale of Manchester, and had issue one daughter;—*Thomas*, born January 21, 1789, died in 1792;—*Edward*, born September 9, 1792, and died unmarried March 27, 1829;—*Thomas*, born October 12, 1794, now living at Gretton, near Uppingham, married Margaret Rigg of Abbey House, and has issue two sons and two daughters;—*Peggy*, born May 19, 1798, married Harry Brierly of Brincklow, Warwickshire, and left issue two sons;—*Mary*, born July 21, 1801, married John Ferguson, and died without issue.

John Rooke was sent to the village-school of Standing Stone, a mile or so from his home. Mr Ewan Clarke, the pastoral poet, and brother to the Vicar of Wigton, was the master, who might have parts, but had no great opportunities of displaying them, as the guardians of his boys only sought a very plain English education at his hands. John was afterwards placed at Akebank School, under the tuition of a namesake, Joseph Rooke*—a self-taught man, who began life as a weaver, and made himself pro-

---

* Schoolmaster Rooke saved money and bought land; and in after years, when his pupil John Rooke had become an agricultural authority, went to Akehead to consult him about his land being in "such a tough bad way as to grow nothing," John's advice to his old schoolmaster was pointed enough—"Manure thy land well, and that will open it."

ficient in various walks of learning, and in music and the fine arts. John's schooling was of the old-fashioned country sort, and by no means elevating in character. When he was a boy, the villagers of Akehead took a weekly paper amongst them, which was sent to the several subscribers' houses in turn, and was there read aloud in the evening to the assembled party, and afterwards discussed for an hour or two. John took especial delight in being present with his father at the readings and discussions of the weekly paper, and it is not improbable that such discussions gave a bent to his thoughts on political questions; for in those days a man who could " argue well," or had a gift of talk over his fellows, was held to be worthy of popular regard; indeed, he often became the representative man of the yeomanry and farmers, and a kind of oracle to the parish. All that he ever knew worth the knowing was acquired by his own exertions after the age of thirty. The want of proper instruction placed him at a great disadvantage as a writer, and this he felt keenly when his pen could so inadequately express the ideas daily floating in his prolific brain.

John Rooke would follow his father's footsteps, and become a farmer. He commenced the art in his early teens, and equipped himself thoroughly for the work assigned him. It has been supposed that John only talked about farming, leaving the real labour of the farm to his younger brothers. This is a mistake. He planted and sowed, reaped and mowed, and took his part at markets and fairs. He was a good plougher, but neither constant nor systematic in its pursuit. He had his own pair of horses; but when the philosophical humour seized him in a morning, he took to his pen and books, and forgot his outdoor engagements. On the family assembling to their noon-dinner, John was reminded that his nags had been in the stable all morning! This set him off at once to his work. His ploughing was guided by mathematical principles, and no one in the district took more interest in the form of ploughs than he did; and wherever he saw a bit of good ploughing, he examined the implement, and the mode of using it. In his latter days he suggested the propriety of instituting a Ploughing Society, and offered his farm for the testing of the workmen. He was also instrumental in getting up the Wigton Agricultural Show, now so successful and well supported. Whilst ploughing, he used to talk to himself, apparently going over the philosophical arguments that had engaged him on the previous evening; and sometimes he went beyond the talk, and manifested as much energy as the orator on his platform.

Up to the age of thirty years, John Rooke was simply a farmer, and nothing more. His position as a yeoman's son was highly respectable, but his education and surroundings afford not the slightest clue to those abstract studies of his riper years. He saw nothing but bucolic life. Wigton, the neighbouring market-town, was exceedingly slow,* and without

* The trade of Wigton in Rooke's early days will be best illustrated by the following story, the correctness of which is undoubted. There were three small drapers' shops in the town. One market-day, Isaac Bowes, from the Abbey Holme, walked into Thomas Addison's shop, and asked for "stuff for a pair of breeks." The goods were shown, and the price fixed, when Isaac coolly remarked, "This is the first shop I have been in, I'll gan round to t'others, and see what I like best." "All right, Isaac," said Addison, who watched his customer's movements, and then apprised his brother drapers of Isaac's transaction. The two drapers entered into the joke, and agreed "to fettle the well-known

library or any other source of intellectual improvement. The only person of superior position in the place was the Rev. R. Matthews of Wigton Hall, whose acquaintance Rooke was slow to make. It is true that Rooke lived in highly exciting times. His school-days had scarcely closed when the French Revolution was at its furious height, and the political affairs of England were becoming imminent; so that, if his mind could be awakened by current events, there was scope and verge enough for thoughtful meditation. Peace did not slacken the force pressing strongly on the national interests, but rather added to the gravamen of the situation. The agricultural ship, in which John was a partner, had for years been sailing under the most favouring zephyrs; but with the downfall of Napoleon came an eddy-wind, swaying the vessel towards rocky coasts; and apparently there was no pilot at hand to direct her course or save her timbers. As a cycle of prosperous years was attributed to the French war, the cyclone of adversity that followed seemed naturally to arise from the establishment of peace.

Men of capacity began to ponder over the grave position of public affairs, and those who had the power lost no opportunity of making their opinions known. The newspapers teemed with advice; pamphlets were

Isaac this time;" so when he called, they asked an exorbitant price for their cloth, and of course drove him back to Addison's shop. It was now afternoon, and Addison, tired by his market-day exertions, had stretched himself on one of his counters for a nap! Isaac returned, and said he would take the "breek stuff" at the price. Addison, partly raising his head, said—"O Isaac! is that thee? thou sees I 'se teking my nuin's rest, and wad rather nit get up; but thou'll be coming in next week, and then thou'll get thy breeks. Good day, Isaac!"

issued in hot haste from the press, and oft stamped with hotter prejudices; the Parliament was deluged with the dogmas of would-be State doctors—each dogma being held up as a specific for the cure of "the body politic" with as much assurance as the polemic parson would maintain his "doxy" to be the only soul's comfort, or the itinerant quack his universal panacea for the ills of the flesh. In the midst of this chaos John Rooke, having sufficient leisure, and a good many notions floating in his brain, would also try his hand at soldering the British Constitution.

There was no local magnate likely to influence his reading or his thoughts. The most prominent man of his adolescent days in Cumberland was John Christian Curwen, M.P., of great agricultural repute in the North of England, and of no small distinction in Parliament. John attended the Workington Shows on the Schoose farm, saw the notabilities assembled there, and heard the "old Squire" and all the leading men of the northern counties discuss agricultural topics. Such a company of "big-wigs" and talkers could hardly fail to inspire a man of intellectual cravings like John Rooke. At any rate, he always spoke in high terms of Curwen's patriotism and promotion of the agricultural interests, adding, that without Curwen there would have been no Agricultural Societies in the county. These two distinguished Cumbrians used to meet at the Abbey Holme gatherings; and Rooke always returned home from his intercourse with Curwen with fresh ideas and fresh talk about farming operations.

Nearer home there was but little to attract. Wigton, as already stated, was dull and vapid; its trade was limited, its society shopocratic and mediocre. It is worthy of note, however, that Wigton brought forth Smirke the painter;* and at least one truly patriotic son who went to London, expecting to cut a figure there, but tired in a short time of the metropolis, and returned to his native place, which he vaunted as "aboon Lunnan and aw other places; ay," said he, "Wigton is the throstle-nest of aw England."

About 1809, John persuaded his father to drain a nine-acre meadow with quarry-stones, and grass sods on the top. There were no drain tiles in Cumberland till 1821. Before draining, it was the wettest piece of land in the parish, nay, so boggy, as hardly to be safe for cattle to graze upon part of the year. The drainage caused so great a change, that all the neighbours and "country-side" talked of Mr Rooke's meadow and its luxuriant green growth. Sir James Graham, on one of his earliest visits to Wigton Hall, rode over with the Rev. R. Matthews to Akehead to see the

---

* Smirke, after attaining fame as an artist in London, offered, on one of his home visits, to paint gratuitously the east window of the parish church, to show his regard for the town in which he was born, and the church he attended in his youth. To carry out his plans, it was needful to make some trifling alteration in the stone-work. When the vestry met to discuss Smirke's highly liberal proposal, one of the members objected to its acceptance. "Surely," said the chairman, "you would like to see a fine window in our old church!" "Ay," rejoined the other; "but what about the expense?" It was explained that the artist offered his services gratuitously, and nothing could be cheaper; however, the cheese-parer, a half Quaker, maintained that if Smirke would paint, he also should make the other alterations—likely to cost £20—and actually carried the vestry with him! On hearing of this shabby procedure, it is said that the renowned Royal Academician cast the dust of Wigton from his feet, and never returned to his native place.

said meadow; and this was his first introduction to John Rooke. The improved condition of the meadow was no doubt remarkable, but Sir James, in listening to the young laird of Akehead discussing more recondite matters than farming operations, made the more pleasing discovery of recognising in him a learned political economist. This almost incidental meeting led to a singular intimacy, a close friendship, and a confidential political correspondence between Sir James Graham and Mr Rooke of nearly forty years' duration. The same meadow attracted William Blamire—a man whom Rooke admired exceedingly for his affability and thoroughly practical knowledge of agriculture. Rooke's initiative draining effort, therefore, brought about happy results; it made a poor meadow good; it set a capital example to the neighbourhood, and paved the way to the adoption of a regular tile-draining in the district; and, above all, it brought him in personal contact with the Rev. R. Matthews of Wigton Hall, Sir James Graham of Netherby, and William Blamire of Thackwood. When news reached Akehead of a drain-tile manufactory at Drawdykes, or rather the Grove, two and a half miles east of Carlisle, Rooke was among the first to patronise the tilery.

A notice of tile-draining and its rise in Cumberland is discussed in the "Life of Sir James Graham" (pp. 38–40). It so happened that Robert Lucock, tile-maker and well-known drainer, seeing carts all the way from Akehead (fifteen miles), and knowing Mr Rooke's wish to promote draining, walked over to Akehead to ask his aid in establishing similar tileworks in the west. Mr Rooke heartily responded, and off they started in search of a suitable field; and that morning's search led to the great tile-works founded at Aspatria by Robert Lucock, who extended his operations to other parts of Cumberland, with great benefit to the landed interest and his own prosperity. He was succeeded by his son Joseph, whose premature death a few months ago caused a general feeling of regret in the west of Cumberland.

John Rooke began early in the century to devote his thoughts to historical subjects, and the more special relations of political economy. He read much, and pondered more; he compared the opinions of the great men of the time, and weighed them in the Akehead balance; and as he digested the meaning of his authors, he made copious extracts from their pages. The plodding industry of the man went on from month to month, from year to year, with no extrinsic aid, and no friendly encouragement to support him. His own folk-circle, far from being alive to the nature of his studies, could hardly be expected to give a willing ear to his philosophizings. This indifference, which has been found sad and painful enough to bear by others as well as Rooke, found some excuse in the general ignorance that prevailed on matters of political economy; indeed, the very meaning of the word had hardly reached the middle-class minds of England till the third or fourth decade of this century. Being looked upon as a visionary, or dreamy talker, he had but the consciousness of doing right to comfort him. In the midst of this disheartening he was thoroughly patriotic and unselfish, and the desire to benefit his country, raging like a strong instinctive force, impelled him to go forward in a career of investigation that few Englishmen have cared to follow, and still fewer have had the happiness to succeed in.

He now began to experience the defectiveness of his education, and that he had to acquire, after the turn of *the thirties*, what should have been in his possession before the expiration of his *teens*. His ideas were abundant and often original, but the words to convey them, or the trite exposition, were wanting. Had he been taught mathematics, or gained the smallest classical culture in youth, he would have stood on vantage-ground. As it was, he had precious hard work to get a logical footing as a propounder of new and abstract theories. Possessed of a buoyant energy, he continued his mental tasks, and, by the help of editorial arrangement and pruning, improved his style of writing; and in time rose to a fuller comprehension of the language. To the last years of his life, however, he had to contend against the deficiencies of his youthful training; and however clearly he saw the argument himself, he wanted the lucidity and conciseness imperative to a full setting forth of his political philosophy.

His heart was in the cause of cheap and free government, and the promotion of the national interests, independent of party direction. He found fault with both Whigs and Tories, who appeared to him to be more anxious for the shibboleth of party than the general interests of the country. With the passing of the Reform Bill of 1832, public opinion became more enlightened, and much more felt in the State. But in his earlier days it was difficult for a man of his position to get a hearing, unless some able editor or "parliamentary man" could lend a patronising hand. No such support was extended to Rooke; but he obtained publicity for his views in the *Farmer's Journal*. Here is all that has come into the writer's hands that can be construed as autobiographic. It formed part of a letter addressed to E. H. Davenport (May 13, 1825), and in claim of certain new principles in political economy—"that the annual price of agricultural labour is the best criterion by which we can ascertain the value of money in different periods of time;" and that "the average price of corn is regulated by the cost of producing it on the worst class of soils which the demand brings under tillage." Rooke says—"the political events of the years 1811 and 1812 first led me to study very closely the nature of the economical structure upon which our very existence as a people seemed to rest." In order to test the correctness of his opinions by public discussion—

"I commenced, in the *Farmer's Journal*, in July 1814, a course of essays immediately connected with questions on political economy. These essays are upwards of fifty in number, and contain the substance of my work on 'National Wealth;' many of them occupy more than a page of closely-printed matter in that Journal, in some instances as much as two pages, and all of them bearing the impress of those views which I have recently published in a more arranged and connected form. The first of these essays, published July 4, 1814, entitled, 'An Examination of the Cause of the Rise in the Price of Corn,' was intended to show that the price of agricultural labour is ultimately regulated by the rate at which foreign trade brings money into the country, and that the expenses incurred in the various processes of raising corn (and which constitute the cost of production), ultimately regulate the price of that corn. The second and third essays are a further illustration of this doctrine; and the latter of them, written in October 1814, published February 13, 1815, contains a laborious table, by which I attempted to prove this part of my subject, by showing that the price of labour and that of corn, on an average of years, usually bear a proportionate rate to each other. The fourth essay, written in November 1814, published February 20, and (in continuation) March 20 following, contains the outline of the doctrine on rent, in which I described 'rental as the overplus produce, after deducting the expenses of husbandry, and a due return for the employment of capital.' This proposition, however, is somewhat modified, and more fully examined in my late work. In this essay it is also said, 'that population, and our limited supply of land, require that soils should be cultivated which are capable only of returning the expense of cultivation and the remuneration of capital.' The fifth essay, addressed to Arthur Young, Esq., proposed agricultural labour as the most correct and fair standard by which the annual rent of land could be regulated,—entering in full into all the matter of that doctrine, which was expounded eight years afterwards by Mr Malthus in his ingenious pamphlet 'On the Measure of Value.' Having had these essays inserted in the newspaper already alluded to, without interruption, I proceeded to enter upon other topics of more general inquiry, and took part in various controversies then carried on; and, finally, in these essays, left scarcely any point contained in my work on 'National Wealth' unexamined. My work was published October 1, 1824, and a copy of it was transmitted to Mr M'Culloch in Edinburgh, without loss of time."

Mr Rooke was of the English school of political economists headed by Dr Adam Smith, who kept mainly in view the connection between the demand for the necessaries and luxuries of life, and the labour and means of supplying them. Whilst this school of political economists seem content with the consideration of material interests only, the French and Italians looked beyond these to the polity or general government of the State. He was evidently unaware of Custodi's learned work, from which he might have derived much information. Nor is it likely that he had any knowledge of the "Economistes" of France, so nobly headed by Quesnay, a medical man, ably extended by Count Mirabeau (senior), Condorcet, and Necker. The French Encyclopædists had a bad name with us, and political bias ran strongly in England against all French doctrines, economic or republican. Mr Rooke was well aware of the import of political economy, and that though the elements of the science be few, the constant vacillation of the premises upon which it is based, their abstract and relative properties demand a cautious and philosophical examination.

ON THE NATURE AND OPERATION OF MONEY.

Having got his pen into working order by his contributions to the *Farmer's Journal*, and some shorter articles in the *Carlisle Patriot*, he would venture further, and issue a pamphlet entitled " Remarks on the Nature and Operation of Money, with a view to elucidate the effects of the present Circulating Medium of Great Britain; intended to prove that the National Distresses are attributable to our Money System." By Cumbriensis. (Baldwin, Cradock, and Joy, Paternoster Row, London. 1819.)

One of his earliest, as it was among his latest, opinions, referred to the price of farm-labour as a standard of real value in money, and subject to no fluctuations. He framed a table showing the price of wheat in England, and the price of farm-labour in the county of Cumberland, from 1730 on to 1818; and looked upon these prices as coincident with the actual depreciation of the real value of the current pound sterling. If his data be correct, the wages of farm-servants per week in Cumberland was below 5s. in 1753, 6s. in 1765, 7s. in 1776, 8s. in 1794, 9s. in 1797;

the increase then becoming rapid compared with the sixty years previously, till wages reached 15s. in 1806. They were stationary at 15s. 6d. from 1807 to 1810, after which they fell gradually to 10s. in 1818. He gave the wages in quantity of wheat per week in each year, and dwelt particularly on this, as the cost of tilling the soil determined the natural price of farm produce. He took into account the board and lodging of the farm-servant, and calculated these expenses as pretty nearly two-fifths of the cost of labour. He was fully alive to the cogency of his arguments, drawn from a county like Cumberland, in which commerce, manufactures, and agriculture were so nearly balanced as to constitute a more complete specimen of a nation in miniature than any other county in England.

He had a great opinion of Sir R. Walpole, Lord Chatham, and Mr Pitt, whom he looked upon as masters of the principle and influence of money, and as having successfully practised the art of causing foreign commerce to reflect its invigorating beams upon the general wealth of the country.

He maintained that, after the adoption of coined money, every state in the world had been under the necessity of depreciating its value; but the productiveness of gold and silver mines was insufficient to account for the fluctuations which have taken place in the value of money, particularly mentioning the years from 1776 to 1788, when the price of farm-labour remained steady, though the precious metals were more readily obtained.

His sixth chapter or section was "On the Equity of Debasing the Current Coin of the Realm." He looked upon the Bank Restriction Act of 1797 as saving England, but could not reconcile the policy of that Act with the Resumption Act of 1819. He apostrophises the heaven-born Minister thus:—"Pitt! we want thy genius, eloquence, and patriotism to guide with an unerring hand the vehicle of public wealth, and to secure to the labouring classes that plenty which they enjoyed under thy auspicious administration." Rooke, in his exaltation about money, seems to have forgotten who commenced the absurd policy of waging war with Napoleon, that eventually saddled Englishmen with nine hundred millions of national debt. At that time he thought, that "nothing but the debasement of the current coin of the realm, an act of political justice as well as of necessity, can restore the due balance in distribution of property."

This pamphlet, of 75 pages, published in July, was followed by a supplement of 103 pages in November, to which he attached his own name along with "Cumbriensis."

He entered into the circumstances affecting the money market during the early period, and indeed throughout the whole of the French war, and weighed all the *pros* and *cons* of paper issue and the circulation of the precious metals; the position of our commerce whilst Germany was free; the change produced when she was ruled by a French despotism; our Bank Restriction Act; and all the leading influences, both at home and abroad, that were calculated to affect money.

He objected to gold as a standard of value, and instead of reckoning an ounce of gold at £3, 17s. 10½d., he proposed to make 14s. per week to farm labourers annually the fixed standard. He was in favour of a paper currency, and making gold a commodity the holder of which would be subject to its profit and loss the same as any other marketable article.

In concluding his remarks, he calls upon Parliament to repeal the corn laws, and then they would see the necessity of shaping a new course.

The year 1819, when Mr Rooke issued his first *brochure*, was a year of great excitement, politically and socially. In all the manufacturing towns there was much disturbed feeling. This was the year of Cobbett's great success with his *Political Register*, headed as it was by the emblem of a gridiron, upon which, or rather upon one large enough to receive a six-feet carcase, Cobbett was prepared to be broiled if Peel's cash-payment bill of that year should be carried. His words were, "I, William Cobbett, assert that to carry their (Tory) bill into effect is impossible; and I say that if the bill be carried into full effect, I will give Castlereagh leave to lay me on a gridiron and broil me alive, while Sidmouth may stir the coals, and Canning stand by and laugh at my groans."

NATIONAL DEBT AND FUNDING SYSTEM.

On March 17, 1822, he published "An Essay on the National Debt, showing the Use and Abuse of the Funding System." It contained 45 pages, and was intended rather as an introduction to a greater work on political economy. He looked upon a national debt to the State in the same light as a cancer to the human frame, and of course wished it wholly eradicated. The principles which he advocated seem to approximate very much to those now guiding the Government of the United States of America; but they seem to have made no impression on the finance authorities of England.

THE PRINCIPLES OF NATIONAL WEALTH.

"The demands for the produce of agriculture are uniform; they are not under the influence of fashion, prejudice, nor caprice. To sustain human life food is necessary; and the demand must continue in all ages and in all countries."—RICARDO.

Mr Rooke's first work of importance was "An Inquiry into the Principles of National Wealth, illustrated by the Political Economy of the British Empire," which he published in 1824. In his dedication to the merchants and manufacturers of Great Britain he remarks:—"Commerce is the parent of industry, of the arts of peace, and of the comfort and happiness of our species; it is the surest preparative towards the universal introduction of civilization, of good government, and personal liberty into all nations, since it everywhere enhances the value of labour, and gives it greater powers of production." The work is a large octavo volume, containing upwards of 400 pages of text, and extensive notes, making 100 more. It is divided into four parts, each part containing chapters and subdivisions as sections, and is truly an elaborate literary production, fit for the study of the Gladstones and the Mills as an authoritative record, and a text-book for all financial inquirers and economists.

Mr Rooke starts with "general principles," and,

under "the influence of physical causes considered," treats of the requisite supply of the necessaries of life, population, labour, and the physical relations upon which political economy is based. He remarks on the rude state of society in mediæval times, and the low condition of the Germans, whom he considers our ancestors; but colonization, commerce, and civil liberty laid the foundation of that progressive change which marks the almost incredible history of the people of the British empire; and illustrative of which "the necessaries of life which might have formerly satisfied a German chieftain would now be starvation to an English pauper."

Treating of "value," he is strong in urging that the annual market-price of able-bodied farm labourers is the correct rule by which the immediate value of the money unit can be ascertained. He had Dr Adam Smith ("Wealth of Nations") on his side, but was at issue with Malthus and Ricardo on this—an almost *basic* question with Rooke in political economy. The tables he adduces in proof of his theory go far to support him; at the same time they reveal some curious facts. Thus, in the year of grace 1150, the price of labour in England was *one shilling* per *week*, and in 1810 it had risen to *fifteen shillings and sixpence* per week; again, in 1150, the sum of £9 (fractions omitted) would command equal means of living with £140 in 1810; the total value of the produce of a hundred acres of land was £37 only in 1150, and this had increased to £577 in 1810.

His chapter on the application of capital to the cultivation of land, and on the profits of capital and the interest of money, contain a great deal of information; whilst a more extended survey of the rent of land, and the relations of rent to profits and wages, occupies a considerable number of pages. He considers rent among pastoral nations, and rent after land had been subjected to husbandry. "On the principles which regulate the cultivation of land" he institutes comparisons between beef and corn, natural pasturage and cultivated crops, and brings a great array of facts to bear upon the elucidation of the subject—not overlooking the views of Cleghorn, Ricardo, Arthur Young, and others. In discussing "the means the people of the British empire possess of investing a new capital profitably," he points out what might be done by more perfect systems of husbandry in raising an additional supply of provisions. In proof of his views, and of what might be done, he cites the operations upon the management of a bad soil by J. C. Curwen, M.P., at the Schoose farms.

In his chapter on the accumulation of wealth, he takes cognizance of free trade, commerce, navigation, and manufactures; and would appear to be as much at home on these subjects as with agricultural facts and figures. Many of his views were prophetic of what is now in force in reference to trade and the distribution of population. He institutes a comparison between the towns of Glasgow, Manchester, and Carlisle, starting alike in 1766; and shows how much their onward march was influenced by the greater facilities for carriage, and the presence of coal, &c., and evidently hits Carlisle for lagging in the race, when she might, by a canal* connecting the east and

* A canal between Newcastle and the Solway Frith was suggested as long ago as 1795; and a rough survey of the district west of Carlisle,

west seas, have been on an equality with the two great marts named with the Border city.

He looked upon the annual price of farm labour as infinitely less objectionable as the basis of a well-regulated currency than any other commodity or set of commodities, and that neither its supply nor its demand was subject to temporary accidents. The annual money-earnings of the farm labourer never fell from 1750 to 1807, and then kept regularly falling from 1810 to 1823. In 1824, they again advanced in accordance with the prosperity of our foreign trade. In another place, he argued that the true policy of the Legislature in 1824 was to free trade, force bank paper into circulation so long as gold does not rise above £3, 17s. 10½d. an ounce, and fix the price at which annual farm labour skill shall in future regulate the value of our current metallic and paper money.

He was strong in his condemnation of tithes, as they oppressed and fettered down industry; and like all men who had given attention to the matter, urged the necessity of commutation. He viewed the tithes as a foul stain imprinted on the official character of clergymen, and behoved them to try and wipe it off. He had a great aversion to tithes and poor-rates—viewing them as more destructive of national prosperity, and more powerful obstacles in the way of productive industry, than the whole of the Government taxes put together. He contrasts Scotland free (at that time) from both these imposts, with England

by Dalston and Cardew mires towards Mayport, was then made. Either lack of enterprise or lack of money, or probably both, stood in the way of the work being accomplished.

shackled, and then with Ireland in the very depth of misery, and not less a burden to England.

It is curious to note, in his "Considerations on the Financial and Political Policy of Great Britain," expressions of opinion, in 1824, so thoroughly in accordance with the Gladstone policy of 1864. "Surely," says he, "the days of our infatuation are past; and the time is fast approaching when we shall convince the nations of the earth that liberality is the only sure foundation of State policy; that restrictive systems of commerce are founded in the grossest ignorance. . . . France, indeed, may display some obstinacy, but we have full means of forcing her, whether she will or not, into the universal compact of nations, and the reciprocity of commercial interchange; by buying her own produce liberally we ought to reduce to a low rate the extravagant duties we levy upon her wines and her brandies, &c."

His views on the "poor-laws" and "public charities" might still be cited with advantage, though the circumstances are greatly changed since he wrote his book. There is a great temptation to quote some of the striking passages bearing on the improvidence of the poor, the misapplication of the poor-rates, and the danger of indiscriminate charity, &c., were it only to show that the education of the world, whether by political economists or ethical teachers, is demonstrable in a series of cycles—the present epoch being but a repetition or reflex of a preceding one—old ideas coming to the surface like so many fresh conceptions and discoveries.

In 1820, Mr Rooke endeavoured to teach sound principles of social and political economy, by which industry, human life, and comforts may be increased; and, at the same time, having a due regard for the aged, the orphan, and the indigent poor, pointed out the great risk of destroying the independence of the working classes, and the not less danger of abusing the public charities. In 1840, the British Association met in Glasgow, and the Statistical Section offered a special attraction for the purpose of hearing a discussion between Professor Alison and Dr Chalmers upon the propriety of introducing poor-laws into Scotland. Dr Alison, whose private benevolence and public philanthropy knew no bounds, wished the Government to be liberal-minded, and to institute a poor-law for Scotland on the English basis; the arguments of Chalmers the divine, on the other hand, were against any interference with the poor that would be likely to destroy their independence—a principle of much power in the Scottish heart generally. Dr Chalmers' opinions were but a modified expansion of the political principles laid down twenty years previously by John Rooke of Akehead. But then Rooke lived in a hamlet, unknown, and his book had scarcely reached the units, let alone the thousands of society; Chalmers occupied a public position of high eminence, from which his thoughts could be sown broadcast over the United Kingdom. The voice of Chalmers was grandly impressive to his countrymen—the pen of Rooke might have been compared to an old-fashioned timepiece, credited for a clacking accuracy only in the parish where it stood.* Had the great divine

* The similarity of sentiment in Dr Chalmers' speech—a speech full of that marvellous power that characterised this able divine—and Mr Rooke's writings, is the more striking that, after the lapse of thirty

read Rooke's book on "National Wealth," he would doubtless have quoted it in support of his views; and with the more readiness that Rooke's opinions were English, derived from experience of an English poor-law.

Mr Rooke's last chapter is on the application of political economy, and fully sustains the character prevailing throughout the work for depth of reasoning, as well as multitude of facts; it also summarises the preceding portions in the volume. One or two sentences may be appropriately quoted :—

"However wisely the social fabric of the British empire may be constructed, and whatever energy it may impart to industry, the happiness of the State is not more highly indebted to our civil institutions than to the division of the several ranks of the people into landlords, capitalists, and labourers. To amuse ourselves with contemplating the superior claims to regard enjoyed by this or that class is ridiculous. If a worthy tenantry sustains the centre stone of the arch, the labouring classes give him the power which executes, while the landed proprietor has been encouraged to save a capital for him to work upon. Were it not that the labouring classes are urged to industry by reward, the tenant from a desire to save a movable capital for the management of land, and the landlord to invest a capital in the soil from similar motives, the arch would loosen from its centre, and soon crumble into dust."

The publication of his work cost upwards of £50, and it is doubtful if he had fifty readers throughout England! The book was the result of many years' labour—the foundation of it being laid as far back as 1812, when his mind was first directed to the subject of political economy. It was based on extensive

years, the writer's memory is refreshed as to the grand passage-at-arms (intellectual weapons only) at Glasgow between his friends Drs Alison and Chalmers—the most noted men of their epoch in Scotland—by the perusal of the plain matter-of-fact views of the Cumbrian yeoman.

reading, and a large and continuous consideration of both theories and facts; moreover, the facts were collated from every available source. Twelve years of hard thought were comprised within five hundred pages of printed record; and these pages were not consulted by the English public for whose benefit the work had been in a great measure undertaken. All this probationary labour—his brain being used like a winnowing machine to separate the profuse chaff from the little corn—his extensive and varied reading, his daily excerpts, his tabulated forms of statistics, were meant for this large effort, the publication of a volume that was to embrace a full exposition of his politico-economical doctrines. But the general and ignorant public could see nothing but dry-as-dust details of a "dismal science" in Rooke's work, and therefore gave no heed to its philosophy. A few able men recognised the true character of the book, as one of great research and careful reflection; and, amongst this discriminating class, was a Cumbrian, educated and wary, though then a young politician — Sir James Graham of Netherby Hall. The full approval of his researches, and in great part of his doctrines, by a person so distinguished, happily made Rooke forget a deal of the general neglect to which his views were subjected.

The disadvantages of position in social life were manifest in Rooke's instance; he was a plain countryman, odd in manners, blunt in expression, timid with strangers, and in every way unobtrusive, and therefore unnoticeable. He sought no patron to his book, and was ill adapted to court the smiles, or to seek to bask in the sunshine of the more pretentious squirearchy in his county. He wrote for the country at large, and even there he found the public mind uneducated to the point of comprehending political science in its application to trade, and commerce, and the general prosperity of the nation.

A review of the book, with suitable quotations, would occupy a large amount of space, and moreover, any abstract that could be furnished would labour under the disadvantage of being but a crude exposition of a theme as devoid of general interest as any other abstract proposition in science. The object sought in these pages is to offer the men of Cumberland a general notion of Rooke's labours as a political economist, rather than attempt an analysis of his voluminous writings, or to show their relative position in the science that only a few great men have entered upon.

FREE TRADE IN CORN.

Mr Rooke's pen did not remain long idle after issuing his large work on the "Principles of National Wealth;" and though he had advocated the importance of Free Trade as part of his general scheme of political economy, he felt that something more was necessary to open the eyes of the public to the true state of affairs. It was about this period of his life that he had frequent communication with Sir James Graham (see Appendix for Graham's letters). Before Sir James issued his pamphlet on "Corn and Currency," he had carefully gone over the ground with his quaint old friend of Akehead, and benefited no little by the extent of his information; nor would he fail to seize the salient points in Mr Rooke's theories and arguments. Whether influenced by Sir James, or, more probably, actuated by a wish to make another effort to enlighten the statesmen of George IV.'s time on one of the most pressing questions of the day, Mr Rooke issued, in 1828,* a pamphlet of eighty pages octavo, entitled "Free Trade in Corn the real Interest of the Landlord and the true Policy of the State." His name did not appear on the title-page; he wished to be unknown apparently, and styled himself a "Cumberland Landowner."

This "Free Trade in Corn" pamphlet gained great notoriety in the political circles of Great Britain; and this fact must have gladdened the author's heart after the poor luck that attended the sale of his large work, and the little estimation in which it appeared to be held, except by the "renowned few" who understood it. Had the public become more discriminative, or had the question of free-trade grown in interest, as it became more and more evident that the various panaceas of Parliament failed to satisfy the English mind? It was pretty obvious that the whole subject demanded thorough ventilation; and for at least fifteen years subsequently to the issue of Rooke's *brochure*, the Anti-Corn-law League of 1845 would have had no *locus standi* if the practical views of the Cumberland laird had taken deeper root and got more fair play at the hands of the press in 1825.

The first words of the essay prove the author to be

* Colonel Thompson's "Free-Trade Catechism" appeared a year later than Mr Rooke's publication. The Colonel's book made thousands of converts, and was daily utilised by the Anti-Corn-law League in their public discussions.

in earnest, and assured as to the honesty of the ground upon which he treads. He boldly says:—"Experimental evidence, the safest test of what is practically true, proves that this country has been most prosperous, and the medium price of corn highest, in a series of years, whenever the most unrestricted and largest importations of foreign corn have been made."

He shows that from 1765 till 1795, when the importation of corn was virtually free, corn attained higher prices, and the same state of things held good till 1819. He also cites an "unbroken chain of evidence" to prove that between 1702 and 1824, the price of corn during peace had, on the average of years, been higher than during war. Both of these views seemed highly paradoxical, nay, outrageously wrong, to the majority of readers. The prohibitory system was introduced in 1819, and writing in 1824, he remarks:—"In the last fifteen years, when an artificial scarcity of corn has been enforced (that is, by prohibitory duties), the price of wheat has fallen 18s. 7½d. per quarter below the average of the last eight years of the period in which a free trade in corn was virtually admitted." Again, on another page, he writes:—"Neither an extraordinary increase in the supply of labour nor of corn has been followed by a fall of prices; on the contrary, they have nearly doubled; and were more than doubled between the years 1780 and 1806, when the trade in foreign corn was most free, and our foreign commerce most prosperous." These and similar facts set forth by Mr Rooke formed part of the famous Catechism of Colonel Perronet Thompson, and were the staple or materials out of which Messrs Cobden and Bright wove many a speech twenty years later. No difficulty presented itself with greater force in the controversies on free-trade than the question of wages, or the value of labour, amongst the uneducated politicians. The Protectionists preached many an awful sermon to the working-classes on the danger of cheapening corn; and how much it would destroy their wages and comfort; and their preachments, like some pulpit utterances, were unfortunately believed.

In another section of his work he quotes additional proofs in favour of his views, and shows the absurdity which England for centuries practised of selling corn in opposition to Poland, when she should have attended to her marine affairs and commerce and her own workshops, allowing Poland to be our customer rather than a forsaken friend in barter. He concluded this chapter by a serious string of evils as the consequence of a scarcity of corn;—the embarrassment of our shipping, mercantile, and manufacturing interests; want of employment; increase of crime; a tendency to emigration; a loss of our currency; and a fall of the prices of labour and of corn; and, more than all, the certain ruin of the agricultural interest itself.

The third section embraces a consideration of "Peel's Currency Bill," in relation to the prohibitory duties on corn, and is perhaps the most telling of the four divisions of the pamphlet. He tries to soothe the fears of the agricultural body, and to calm their special fear of England becoming a land of pasturage from the free importation of corn. He called this a groundless bugbear, and thus writes:—"The danger is that pasturage will not prevail to a sufficient extent; for this is the evil at the present moment (1828).

Pasturage, in succession to good culture, is the most certain sinking-fund by which the rent of land can be raised; for rest alone augments the natural fertility of the soil, without expense to the owner. . . . The soil of England is at this moment outploughed, and must remain so, to the great injury of its possessors, whilst the corn-law system stands unredressed. Over-cropping by the tenant is the sure impoverishment of the landlord, a deterioration of the fee-simple value of his estate, in effect more ruinous than mortgage at annuity interest."

This section of Rooke's book, as the above quotation proves, teems with sound clear views of the position of England in respect to this great question of free-trade; and the quotation in a previous paragraph reminds the writer of Sir James Graham's emphatic declaration, at one of the greatest agricultural meetings ever held at Carlisle, of—" Graze more and plough less!" The prophetic bearing of Rooke's opinions is quite remarkable; and so is the general structure of his theories and doctrines.

Though free-trade has long been established in this country, the circumstance of Mr Rooke being little understood by his county-folk will justify a few more remarks on his pamphlet; each page of which contains political maxims laid down with terseness, or stated with the breadth and freedom of a well-discussed philosophical argument.

He shows how closely interwoven are the national interests with the peace and comfort of mankind; and that nations deriving mutual advantages from the reciprocity of trade are bound in heavy recognizances to preserve the general peace; that the current of trade, once suffered to flow freely, never fails to deepen its own channel; and that neither despot nor governments can change the natural wants of a people. He is particularly strong in the belief that free-trade was the firmest basis on which the tranquillity of the world can rest, and cites the folly committed by Napoleon I. in his Berlin and Milan decrees, by which he hoped to shut England out of the commerce of Europe, and to ruin her interests for ever. The exclusion of our trade from the Continent the French despot accomplished for a time, having a *particeps criminis* in the Emperor of Russia; but as the raft upon which the two Emperors met at Tilsit to divide the world between them rested on unstable water, and was of itself liable to be torn asunder by natural force, so were their pledges of amity, and their concerted measures to ruin English commerce, transient, mutable, and fruitless; for no imperial edicts could resist for long the sweeping current of public opinion and the natural force of outraged humanity. The grand scheme of Napoleon, by which England or its shopocracy were to be ruined, proved the first step to his own ruin. He had long usurped dominion, and believed he could usurp nature also; but nature rebelled, and cast him down from his pedestal of ambition. Though many of the nations subjected to Napoleon's rule had taken to French *ragouts* and bureaucracy, they felt the pinching process that attended the exclusion of English commerce most keenly; and in course of time their wants became a greater force in deciding the destiny of affairs than the heavy battalions of their great enemy.

Mr Rooke dwells on this warning example, and

writes of Napoleon :—" He whom armies could not vanquish, or rival monarchs overthrow, fell at last a sacrifice to the indignation of combined multitudes, whom the interdiction of commerce had roused to a struggle in defence of national rights." He asks what have we to fear from the open competition of free-trade, when nature and art have fitted up our native land with the means of carrying on production and barter beyond any other nation in the world, while its civil institutions and the spirit of its people are every way qualified to bear out these great advantages?

Rising with the grandeur of his theme, he becomes eloquent and impressive :—" Look at our roads, our canals, our docks, and our public works; arms of the sea traversed by bridges; hills, and even rivers, undermined by tunnels; our steamboats covering every navigable water. Then consider our natural advantages: our sea-girt islands, intersected by mighty rivers worthy of a continent, our meadows fertilised by living streams, our verdant pastures, our climate favourable to the growth of corn, our sheep and cattle on a thousand hills. Look at our smiling land, where nature has been prodigal, and where art has supplied what nature refused;—then say whether we need fear competition with any foreign state? whether we have not the start of a century in the career of commercial rivalry? and whether, with seaports and trade unfettered, the half-cultivated sands of Poland, or even the vine-clad hills of France, need excite the envy or the fears of Great Britain—of Britain, the seat of wealth, of freedom, and of arts?"

In the history of free-trade Rooke's name should

be incorporated with that of Adam Smith.* Their views of political economy were alike; they maintained them against the current opinions of the times; and during life they were both laughed at for their pains. Rooke was a consistent advocate of freedom of commerce throughout life, and he never deviated a hair-breadth from the principles that he had learned to believe in from his early manhood.

Had the essay on free trade in corn appeared with the name of a noted politician or writer on public affairs, it would have fared better, if not been lauded for its merits and arguments; but coming from a "Cumberland Landowner" gave it no significance among "the upper ten." The first edition might have lain on the shelves of the publisher had it not been rumoured that Sir James Graham was its author; it forthwith reached a second edition. In Cumberland it was universally attributed to the Netherby Baronet—the author of "Corn and Currency"—and that belief reached the House of Commons. Cumbrian readers never dreamt of such arguments arising

* John Rooke was laughed at by his neighbours now and then, but at no time was he made the subject of greater ridicule than fell to his more famed prototype, Adam Smith, whose "Wealth of Nations" ranks with the golden works of the past, made so applicable to the present age. Adam Smith was a native of Kirkcaldy, in Fifeshire, one of the small royal burghs of the last century. The "Lang Toun," as it was called, had its Provost and Council. One of the worthies of this corporation, just before the meeting of Council, was seen laughing, nay, almost convulsed with laughter; and some time elapsed before he could restrain himself to explain the cause. At last he said—" I'll tell you the reason : It's a grand joke as e'er you heard. Addy (Adam) Smith, our Addy, is gaun ta write a buik ! Ah ! ah !" in which the rest of the Kirkcaldy corporates joined very freely. No doubt the lang toun of Kirkcaldy felt, with the tickled town councillor, that if "Addy Smith" had taken to buik-making, it was a' ower wi' him, and that he "maun be fairly daft."

from such a Nazareth as Akehead; and if any one had ventured to suggest John Rooke's name, he would have been laughed at for his pains. It was a great compliment to the author to find that so renowned a statesman as Sir James Graham should be credited with its paternity. In March 1834, it may be remembered that Mr Poulett Thompson, in his advocacy of free-trade in the House of Commons, quoted largely from Rooke's pamphlet, believing all the while that he was hitting the Netherby Baronet's tergiversation on this path of political economy. (See "Life of Sir James Graham," p. 117.)

FREE AND SAFE GOVERNMENT.

Seven years elapsed after the publication of his celebrated pamphlet before he again ventured to address the public; and this time he complained of the landed interest being unconvinced by his "Free Trade in Corn." In 1835, he issued an octavo volume of upwards of 300 pages, entitled, "Free and Safe Government traced from the Origin and Principles of the British Constitution," which he dedicated to King William the Fourth. In his dedication he disclaims all party feeling, and professes to act on straightforward principles for his king, his country, and the supremacy of her free laws.

He first adverts to the proper aim of freedom, and then traces the source of the British constitution and the leading principles on which it is framed; now and then basing some of his arguments on ethnographical data, and dwelling with special interest on the influences of Germanic blood, at an early date in history, on the institutions and liberties of England. He then surveys the "refined wisdom" of Alfred, the great king who introduced free government, and laid the basis of the British constitution—a constitution possessing within itself the principles of renovation, and that has survived the disasters and violence of the most troubled times, and has passed through the fiery ordeals of popular commotion, not only unscathed, but with increased lustre and beauty, and with increased capabilities of diffusing and securing public contentment. He condemned the feudal system, and then proceeded to explain the causes and incidents which have led to the re-establishment of freedom in England. He discusses the principles and form, or the theory of the constitution in a long chapter, and shows the organization of the Government, the completeness of its several parts as a system —not omitting, however, to note the imperfections of some of its details, and the need of improvement. Whilst praising the mode in which the public service is watched over by so many national trustees, he is "constrained to acknowledge the fact that the sacred duties of the ministers of the Church, which call for the highest official purity, cannot claim comparative excellence with those offices immediately under the control of the unpaid trustees of the people."

He approved of the Poor-law Amendment Act, and gave some striking facts in favour of the system of local government. "Reasonable poor-laws," says Mr Rooke, "wisely and discreetly administered, are a national blessing; a vicious application thereof, a terrible evil." As exemplifying the difference between good and bad management of the laws affecting the poor, he cites Wigton, in Cumberland, with 4985 inhabitants (at that period) in full profitable employment, with poor relief at the rate of 2s. 4d. a head on the whole, as having less actual indigence and crime than prevails among 684 inhabitants in the parish of C—— in Northamptonshire, at the rate of £1, 15s. 1d. to each person yearly! He was fully of opinion that, by good local management, aided by a sound commercial policy in the State, the poor-rates of England and Wales might be reduced to two millions a year. He was calculating more largely on emigration removing a surplus of labour from those parts of the kingdom in which it exceeded the demand, than really occurred; and he was not in a condition to anticipate the growing centralisation of poor-law affairs in London and the ever-increasing number of officials, with higher rate of pay than existed thirty years ago. He pointed out the danger likely to arise from an unrestrained executive, and, like all writers of his class on political economy, deduced arguments from Ireland.

He approved of the Parliamentary Bill, and, amongst other reforms which he thought could not be stifled, that of the Church, and the continued payments of its revenues in tithes. Though a good Christian, he saw the great abuses in the Establishment, and wished it would "take the lead in the furtherance of Christian principles, having clean hands and pure conduct, lest it should lose its hold on the affections of the people, suffer desertion, and subject itself to castigation in another form than correcting abuses within itself." His remark on the furtherance of Christian principles by the Church implied, that, in his day, these principles had been ignored by the clergy in their greater attachment to the anise and cummin. When writing on this subject of tithes, Rooke little dreamt of the near approach of the Tithe Commutation Act,—the work of a Cumberland farmer, his neighbour and friend, William Blamire of Thackwood.

When writing of the causes of Parliamentary Reform, he endeavours to typify the Whigs and Tories. The former he associates with freedom and constitutional government; the latter with commerce, industry, and safe government. His distinction is a curious one, and far from correct. Mr Rooke's antipathy to the Whigs arose from his aversion to the corn-laws, which he considered the great fortress of Whiggery up to 1765. Though a good Tory, he saw the virtues and vices of both parties, and dwelt with emphasis on the corruptions of Toryism; but whenever he reverted to the favourite political dogma of free and unrestricted commerce, he placed the Whigs lower in the scale than his own friends. Thus, he says, "a free distribution of bread satisfies the people. Want is sure to urge them to acts of turbulence; hence the corruptions of Toryism by bread are more grateful to industry than Whig freedom and famine."

His ninth chapter, "On Commerce and Corn-Laws," is the longest in the book, and is a careful *resumé* of all his cogitations on the subject, very temperately argued,—his views resting on data obtained from statistical records and other trustworthy sources. There is a large fund of useful information throughout the whole of his writings, and naturally more or less repetition in his statements; but he writes with the earnestness of conviction, and with a steady adherence to the truths of political economy. Occasionally he speaks fearlessly and openly, as thus, he says, " The Corn Bill, the Gold Standard Bill, and Sir Robert Peel's Currency Bill, working conjunctively, are the last stronghold of feudal despotism, barbarism, and lawless oppression. Let the landed interest trust to delusion no longer. Their arts are seen through; their folly is manifest. The Reform Bill has shattered their ultra domination in pieces, like some potter's vessel broken into fragments. Commercial justice alone can secure the inviolability of property, the supremacy of free laws, and the ready submission of the people."

He devotes a chapter to currency and the national debt, and another to the refutation of Mr Malthus on the principles of population. Mr Rooke had no difficulty in showing the Malthusian principle to be indefensible, and he did not fail to notice the errors into which Mr Ricardo, Colonel Torrens, and Lord Brougham fell on the same subject in mistaking the rise of the rent of land to the principles of population, instead of greater efficiency in production, which a multiplying state of commerce originates.

How imperfectly the English mind must have been informed on matters of history, as well as geography, to entertain any fears of redundance of population in a country that could boast of more colonies than all the world besides! Malthus wrote, it is true, in 1798, when America was not so tempting a field for our emigrants; but future editions of his work showed no correction of his closet-developed economy. It was to the last degree improbable that men of English blood and enterprise, who, as the song says, " love to roam o'er the wide sea's foam," and whose boast it is that the sun never sets on the dominions under the sceptre of Britannia, would starve whilst continents remained unexplored, and the richest lands of the world were still in their virgin condition. Mr Rooke showed that population depended much on moral as well as industrial causes ; and that " commerce, which accelerates both the production and distribution of wealth, involves every object and law of political economy most intimately, deciding the principles of population on the physical, intellectual, industrial, and moral state of man."

Writing " On the Advancement of Agriculture by Commercial Progression," he traced the great progress made by England, and believed there was nothing to dread from incapacity in her soil; and that the sixteen millions of population of his day were better fed than the four, eight, or twelve millions of the past. He showed from the county of Cumberland, that, though the population had more than doubled, the real reward of labour had risen, that clothing was cheaper, potatoes abundant, and corn not dearer; and that this increase of population did not necessarily imply a deterioration in the means of subsistence. Proportionately as commerce multiplies, so do the means of subsistence become more plentiful. Knowing the value of labour to mankind, he pointedly says, " There is no Eden in nature." " Providence having made the earth a rude uncultivated wilderness, and endowed man with reason and forethought, continually endeavouring to subdue this wilderness, a path to endless happiness is prepared for him through the medium of social and commercial progression, which adds to the more effective productiveness of labour." He was hearty and hopeful of social happiness; all that he sought was commercial freedom, and free and safe government.

The writer is not able to speak of the attention given to this elaborate work of Rooke's by the community in general, nor of any special allusions made to it by political authorities, either within or without the walls of Parliament. Sir James Graham no doubt studied the work, were it only for the high respect he entertained towards his Akehead friend. It is, however, reasonable to infer that more cogent reasons would induce him, namely, the hope of acquiring information and instruction. Rooke's theory of the constitution, its workings and defects, its capacities and worth, deserved profound consideration, as the study of a political economist who had occupied himself for upwards of twenty years in endeavouring to unravel and assort the threads of the constitutional web of England.

GEOLOGY: ITS PRACTICAL APPLICATIONS.

The English mind has found in geology a science of great and pleasurable interest. The science, though comparatively modern and theoretical, affords sufficient inducement, along with its natural history relations, to make its study a highly popular pursuit. Practical or applied geology in guiding the operations of the miner, and in contributing to the daily comforts of life, comes home to every man's hearth. It was this view that influenced the utilitarian spirit of John Rooke, who cared less for the niceties than he did for the useful applications of the science. When he could spare time from his political economy, he launched out in various directions of inquiry, and was probably amongst the first in Cumberland to be drawn towards geology, which he studied as a connoisseur for a time, but aftewards with special regard to a scheme that long engaged him—"the silting up and reclamation of estuaries from the dominion of the sea." It will be observed that with geology, as with every other study that suited him, Rooke always aimed at practical results, and the promotion of the public interests. As a geologist he was probably as theoretical as his predecessors, and perhaps more abstruse and high-flown in his writings; but he atoned for his fanciful theories (if such they were) more than any other man of the age by showing the advantages of "applied geology" to the successful carrying out of the great commercial undertakings in which England became engaged after the completion of the Liverpool and Manchester Railway.

Mr Rooke could not pass a quarry or open pit without exploring it, and much questioning of the quarrymen. He knew every exposed rock in Cumberland; and in his remarkable tours throughout England he adopted the same practice, so that in time he became familiar with the geology of his own country. In visiting his brother Thomas in Northamptonshire, he was led to maintain that no coal would be found south of the Rutlandshire oolite; but, as Mr Thomas Rooke informs the writer, local geologists and miners, viewing the matter differently, sought for coal near Northampton, and expended fearfully large sums in doing so, but with no successful results.

For many years Rooke had been an observer; the railway interests made him an author on geology. Mr Hyde Clarke, the projector of a railway across Morecambe Bay, had induced Rooke to survey and report on the practicability of effecting that object; and this circumstance gave rise to a long discussion on the nature and influence of tidal action in sedimentary deposition. Imbued with a desire for more knowledge than the study of isolated districts like Morecambe Bay was likely to confer, he commenced a survey of the whole range of the science, and gathered the opinions of other observers. Having framed his notes, he was induced to publish them in an octavo volume, under the comprehensive title of "Geology as a Science applied to the Reclamation of Land from the Sea, the construction of Harbours, the formation of Railroads, and the discovery of Coal; with an assumed Map of the Granite Formation of the Earth." The first edition of this book was issued in August 1838, and a second followed in April 1840, containing an additional chapter, entitled a "Dissertation on Geology."

Rooke was not a closet philosopher in geology, but spent several summers in making excursions in England, Ireland, Isle of Wight, and in France, &c., and in observing carefully for himself an extent of country of not less than 2500 miles. This was done specially for the purpose of testing his theory of oceanic deposition. He attended the Birmingham meeting of the British Association in 1839, and learned much concerning the grounds of difference among geologists, and was shocked to find how little attention was given to the views entertained by himself on tidal currents, and how little faith was attached to the Mosaic geology, "even by the high ones in science." The first chapters of Rooke's volume have not had many readers; indeed it is no easy task to go through his "primary formations," "depositions of diluvial beds," and the discursive topics he introduced in explanation; all which display too much cosmogony and vastly too much biblical Mosaic. To construct the earth, he assumes a granite formation as a kind of irregular skeleton, with numerous granite arms, extending across each continent; and these are made to represent the leading outlines of the primary formation which eventually decided the figure of the earth. Having got unbroken chains of granite as primary breakwaters, he strengthens them by sedimentary depositions of newer formation, the abutments of the granite wall have their asperities rounded off by softer materials derived from fluid action; and thus the orb called Earth is fashioned in the rough by the Akehead cosmogonist. Granite he considered to be a primeval sandstone, composed of crystalline grains, and that igneous action, combined with pressure and chemical influences, caused "its induration and compact cementation." The Rooke structure, or construction of the earth, may appear fanciful; but keeping in view that the subject is one admitting of the widest possible scope for hypothesis, it is as ingenious and plausible as many others that have been offered on the formation of our globe.

When a doubt arises as to the validity of his argument, or he wishes to anticipate possible objections, Rooke has the happy art of sheltering himself under the first chapter of Genesis, which he held to be a helmet of proof against all attacks. He attributed something to electric magnetism and chemical affinities in the arrangement of the earth's crust; and assigned to the same forces that happy combination of elements which constitute the respirable atmosphere around us. He dwells with particular interest on the coalfields of Cumberland, and is exceedingly ingenious in his explanations of the presence or absence of these along the coast line.

Rooke was an advocate of the Neptunian theory, and remained as immovably fixed to it, as the granite dyke upon which he made his Neptunian forces to rest in the construction of the earth's formation. Still he was obliged to admit igneous or Plutonic action as a cementing process to his sand, as well as being the great upheaving force of his breakwaters. He gladly availed himself of any new doctrines in this allied science to sanction his geological views. Thus he laid hold of the atomic theory of Dalton in the hope of strengthening his " oceanic power,"—apparently overlooking the fact that the physics of chemistry with which Dalton's name is associated pertain to the arrangement of simple elementary gases or ultimate atoms, whilst the action of the grand upheaving forces affecting geological masses can only be interpreted by the laws of general physics or natural philosophy.

His chapter on the deposition of diluvial beds and alluvial plains, in its passing references to local geology, should be of interest to the people of Cumberland. Taking the heights of mountains, he considers that a primeval tide-wave pervaded the earth at least 3000 feet above the present level of the sea. He marks diluvial beds overlying the red sandstone, on a right line twenty-one miles in length, from Cummersdale, near Carlisle, to Mealow, on the shores of the Solway Frith, and looks with pleasure on the orderly character of these ridges, as if coming fresh from the hands of Neptune,—from north to south from one to three hundred yards in breadth, and elevated from thirty to fifty feet above the gentle vales which separate one line of ridges from another. His own freehold occupied one of these ridges, and from it he could see these elevations extending east and west, and rising to higher and higher elevations as they extended from north to south; and there seems great reason to believe that they gave the first bias to his geological theories. On tracing the land from the level of the Solway on to Akehead, and southwards to Brocklebank Fells, these parallel ridges are visible enough, and the only explanation that Mr Rooke could offer of their formation was a tidal wave. Indeed this tidal wave became unfairly associated with Mr Rooke's name, as much so indeed as if all his geological theories rested on it.

The fifth chapter of his book refers to the improvement of navigation, the construction of better harbours, and the reclamation of land from the sea in reference to the British isles.

He estimated the estuaries on the coasts of Lancashire and Cheshire at 200,000 acres in extent, and in reference to the Mersey, he believed that the formation of a marine dike, like that of the Low Holme on the shore of the Solway Frith, projected on Formby Point, and continued eastwards to Liverpool, would augment the scour of the Mersey, deepen its sea channel, and sweep off those sandbanks which impede and endanger its navigation.

In reference to Morecambe Bay he is more special and descriptive, and had no doubt that the tide-wave in the bay, by a little assistance, would effectively embank itself; and that these half-formed embankments would in course of time become the basis of a railway; that much land would be reclaimed, and converted into a highly fertile soil, with the navigation improved. "Viewed in a proper light," adds Rooke, "the speedy silting up and crossing Morecambe Bay by railway is unquestionable." For this last statement Rooke was taken severely to task by the would-be critics of railway schemes, and the local prints were especially facetious at his expense; the reader can readily fill up the epithets applied to his scheme by the self-constituted oracles, and they are always prolific enough in Cumberland. Nevertheless, all that Rooke predicted has come to pass at Morecambe Bay!

A more daring venture upon the credulity of the public than the crossing of Morecambe Bay speedily emanated from the same brain, as if Mr Rooke were regardless of the derision of the press, and, if he knew it, the laugh of his countrymen. In seeking to carry out his general survey of railways from the South into Scotland by the Cumberland coast, Rooke talked not only of reclaiming land, and improving the navigation of the Solway, but actually of crossing it by a railroad. This opinion made people stare, as the crossing of the Solway by a railway, and the limiting of its powerful tidal current, seemed as hopeless a scheme as the removal of "Robin Rigg"—a very formidable sandbank in the Solway, upon which so many vessels have been wrecked. A still more remarkable proposition, though but part of his greater scheme—the navigation of the Solway—was made by Rooke, and that was to render Robin Rigg itself nearly innocuous to vessels sailing up the Frith. He boldly stated his views thus:—"The reclamation of land and the improvement of navigation in the Solway Frith, as well as crossing it by a railroad in an available form, are plain and comprehensive." He showed that, with the configuration of the valley of the Solway, deposits have a tendency to accumulate on the side of Cumberland, owing to the large bend northwards of the Eden, and the influence of other streams which fall into the estuary of the Solway between Burgh and Maryport—the principal being the Waver and the Wampool. These two streams, he suggested, should be carried into the channel of the Eden, the Esk, and the Sark, at or about Port Carlisle, where they would have been joined shortly by the Annan, and lower down by the Nith; so that all the tributaries of the Solway would have been directed into one channel on the Scottish side. This would have been a great achievement, and the benefits resulting from its accomplishment would have outweighed all the costs attending its execution. The levels and sections proved the practicability of his scheme; and had it been carried out, twenty thousand acres might have been reclaimed, and the channel of the Frith would have assumed a regular curved line from Maryport to Rockliffe, abutting on Newby and Tordiff Points. The expense of taking the Waver and Wampool towards Port Carlisle, calculated at £10,000, would have been met by the gain of four thousand five hundred acres of fertile marsh. There would have been a gain also on Burgh Marsh, particularly if Rooke's plan of cutting a fresh bed for the Eden, about a mile in length, towards the river Esk, had been carried out. He calculated, and reasonably too, that if these engineering views had been adopted, a powerful scour around Bowness would take place, deepening the channel of the Solway, compressing its tideway, fixing its streams within narrower limits and on a surer ground. The land reclaimed by his scheme, its acreage and probable rental, were also duly estimated. He thought that Allonby Bay could in part be reclaimed, and Robin Rigg lessened of its horrors by carrying out the same diversion of streamlets, and by the adoption of artificial means to aid in the natural embankments.

Mr Rooke believed that a great harbour could have been formed at Port Carlisle, or in the triangular space which lies within the lines of Bowness, Tordiff Point, and Raven Bank; and that a railway could be carried from Raven Bank to Tordiff Point. He speaks of a scar of red sandstone from Tordiff Point on the Scottish side, extending four hundred yards, upon which could be built a viaduct of at least three hundred yards—leaving the rest of the scar for a new channel through which the tideway might flow; thus he calculated upon a silting up of the English side, so that an embankment of ten or twelve feet high from Raven Bank to the projected viaduct might complete the formation of a railroad across the Solway Frith. Everything he said or wrote on the Solway was ridiculed, and the mention of a railway made some charitable folk point significantly to the forehead as an indication of Rooke's whereabouts.*

Though Rooke made a general survey of the English coast, he returns with increasing interest to his own county and the Solway seaboard. He pointed out the deficiencies of Whitehaven harbour, and made valuable suggestions regarding it. He formed a higher estimate of Workington as a harbour of refuge than any other to be found in the Solway Frith, provided a bold projecting breakwater was rightly placed to the southward of the embouchure of the Derwent. As Mr Rooke was a county man, he was not consulted by any local authorities in the West; and his having no claims to engineering skill excluded him from all consideration. This might

* If the promoters of the Solway Junction Railway had consulted Rooke's Geology before launching their scheme, they would have done wisely for themselves, and still better for the unfortunate shareholders in the concern. By adopting his plan of crossing the Frith, they would have saved themselves thousands of pounds of outlay upon the viaduct, and avoided all litigation with the Trustees of the Port Carlisle Navigation Company. Between Raven Bank and Tordiff Point is a good bottom for stone-work, so that the foundation of their viaduct would have been easily obtained; the passage across the estuary would have been shorter and much safer, owing to less tidal action and currents; and being south of the Port Carlisle harbour, the railway would have met with no hindrance from the navigation interests of this part of the Solway.

Had the greater scheme proposed by Rooke been carried into effect, namely, that of draining "Bowness Flow," by carrying the rivers Wampool and Waver through it to Port Carlisle to join the Eden, the Solway scheme would have been highly feasible. It is painful to see the waste of money arising from ignorant engineering skill: the directors of the Carlisle Canal & Steam Navigation Company committed lots of blunders; the Silloth scheme has also been unlucky, for want of due consideration; and lastly, the Solway Junction Railway has rashly formed a railway likely to be equally unproductive. John Rooke's counsel could have saved all three from their bad management.

have been expected, or the old adage regarding prophets would have been reversed. Cumberland has always shown great partiality for strangers in every walk of life. An ordinary man, from a distance, if he only have assurance, is looked upon as worth two good men at home. Distance seems to have an enchanting power when the merits of individuals come to be balanced. There was no belief in Rooke, he was "one of ourselves," a yeoman who wrote in the newspapers and talked very fast. What could he know about estuaries? and had not his Morecambe Bay scheme been discountenanced by his friends? So Mr Rooke shared the fate of the prophets—he was stoned with the hardest epithets, and left outside the gates; whereas, had he been called in to the council boards of railways and harbour trusts, he would have proved himself an important coadjutor, if not a pioneer, in carrying out schemes of great commercial import.

RAILWAYS.

Looking to population as a basis of traffic, and a criterion of the extent of intercommunication, Rooke divided England, Scotland, and Ireland into commercial sections, each section embracing a population of two and a quarter millions of people in round numbers. Thus Scotland, with its 2,365,000 (census of 1831), was to have a section of its own; Liverpool and the large district immediately adjacent, and bound to it by shipping interests, with its 2,558,000 people, he formed into another section, and called it the north-western section; and so on. He made the five great seaports of England the respective *termini* to and from which railways ought to run —London, Bristol, Hull, Liverpool, and Newcastle being looked upon as commercial entrepôts or great marts to sections of populations — each of them equal to the whole kingdom of Scotland in point of numbers. These different sections would also have to be in communication with each other. Thus Hull should be connected with Bristol by a direct line, also Liverpool with Hull, London with Liverpool, &c., and these great trunk lines again would have had their local branches all through the country. In respect to Ireland, he advised that Belfast should be in communication with Glasgow by Greenock and Ayr, and also Newcastle-on-Tyne by way of Carlisle and Dumfries; and he took Stranraer as the natural pivot on which these respective lines should converge, and as the best place for constructing a port in the northern Irish Channel.

The above scheme was not less original in conception than comprehensive in plan. It deserved the attention of Parliament as well as of the monied interests of England; for be it remembered that Mr Rooke launched his ideas in the earliest days, when there was time to have stayed so many worthless projects, and to have saved so much English capital.

Having made his sectional areas of England— Scotland and Wales having each one of their own— he returned to his geology proper, and showed the applications of the science to the construction of the said railroads. He wished the railway engineers to follow the lines of continuous geological currents, and not to cross the Pennine chain of hills in the north, but to mark the series of plains which stretch from the basin of London and Bristol to the Solway Frith, and again along the eastern borders of the kingdom. Keeping this plan in view, it would be comparatively easy to form a line "from London to Cheltenham by the valley of the Thames, with a lateral branch to Bristol and the south-west counties generally. From Cheltenham a plain also runs directly northwards, as far as Dumfries and Carlisle, by the valley of the Severn and the Weaver, along the vast levels of the red sandstone group, and by the diluvial and alluvial depositions on the west of Lancashire, across Morecambe Bay, the estuary of the Duddon, and by the western shores of Cumberland, across the Solway Frith to Dumfries, and laterally to Carlisle.

Mr Rooke considered it a vital error to carry railways across geological ribs of iron, and cautioned the public against the fearful expense about to be incurred by their leaving the plains. In reference to his north-west route he says, "Here the question arises of crossing Morecambe Bay, on the one hand, or scaling the vast and continuous primary Isle of Cumberland and Westmoreland (Shap Fells), on the other;" and of course his opinion was decisive in favour of the former. The project of crossing Morecambe Bay was not a matter of doubt, but of certainty and success; and whatever might be the prejudice raised against it, Mr Rooke felt sure that truth and national interests would prevail in the end; nay, more, and, in a prophetic tone, he says, "a railroad is certain to be completed on the line here marked out," regardless of the *previous follies of any company whatever.* His opinions on the Shap line that had been meditated were not less full of augury as to the expense of constructing the road and maintaining it in order, and the propelling powers needed to overcome its steep gradients. He knew his principles to be sound, therefore he had no hesitation in propounding them; and asking "capitalists to pause ere they rashly clutch at shadows, and forego the substance more easily secured." However, nothing would serve but straight lines "uphill and down brae," and at all hazards. Engineers soon found the ways and means in the pockets of the capitalists, and with money as a *vis a tergo*, they cared not for mountain heights and mountain ruggedness. They could climb the one and tunnel the other; and, in short, seemed desirous to rest their claims for fame and patronage more on the boldness of their schemes than the exercise of economy in constructing their works. To-day the public pay for all this rash and unnecessary outlay of money. Had Rooke's views been listened to, and his general plan adopted for linking the great commercial marts of England by cheap lines of railroad along the vales, it is reasonable to infer that instead of the parliamentary train costing a penny a mile, the first-class passengers, with all, if not more than the present amount of comfort, would have travelled for that sum, and with more safety and general security. Englishmen are liable to epidemics of folly, and the railway mania of 1845 * was one of

---

* The small voice of Akehead, however, was not to be heard in the storm of clashing interests, when the furor of the day was rather to decide who should be the first to get a railway bill, than temperately to consider what line of route would be best for the general interests of the country. The Government issued a commission to relieve the official brain at headquarters, but nothing good came of it. Here was a highly feasible scheme of John Rooke's claiming to be heard on reliable

those acute financial attacks, marked by engineering at all costs and a wasteful expenditure—nay, an expenditure so great that it would have been looked upon, only a few years previously, as incredible, both as to the fact and as to the means of sustentation.

Page after page of the book shows how carefully Rooke had considered the whole subject, and how much he interpreted the history of the next twenty-five years of commercial England. Thus (p. 250), speaking of the proposed line across Shap, and the double expense of constructing and working it, he adds, " Higher chances of accidents and delays, and passing over a mountain wild, can never be a competing line with that which proposes to turn those mountains, without undulations, without curves, and without the boring of monstrous tunnels, on almost as short a line of railroad, providing for the wants of considerable towns of a wealthy agricultural district over and above." Again, " Confirming our geological theory with the utmost exactness. The very channels along which the pine forests of a diluvial age have floated, now form obvious tracks which invite, and cannot invite in vain, the construction of railways; profitable investments for capital at the same time, which may not offer a substance and yield a shadow, but remain for ever secure against competition. First, they traverse the most easy ground; they may be worked at exceedingly high speed; they may be

grounds, of which the geological, the populational, and the economical relations were patent to all men. But Rooke was not one of the "collective wisdom" of St Stephen's, not a town's oracle, or meddling politician, not even a member of any Government circumlocution office; as he had no *locus standi*, his advocacy remained as *nil!*

cheaply propelled; they at once open out those industrial energies of England which are seated on and within the borders of the coal measures; they bring into direct and speedy intercommunication the ports of the Bristol Channel, which open the way to the Western World with those possessing a speedy access to the North of Europe; they concentrate the commerce of England on natural and fixed points, and they at the same time open out the vast agricultural mining wealth of England." He thought, and wisely too (before 1840), that a national survey and an enlarged scheme of railway ramification were exceedingly urgent, and could no longer be delayed. "Comprehensive systems can never spring up incidentally; they must be trained by intelligence. It is supremely ridiculous to trust the laying out of national railroads to disjointed and isolated bodies of men. An organic system of our national railroads is called for at the present juncture (1840), and it behoves Her Majesty's ministers to repair defects in a discreet and statesmanlike manner."

APPLICATION OF GEOLOGY TO AGRICULTURE.

Rooke wrote a chapter "On the Application of Geology to the Quality of the Land." Though containing frequent allusions to his favourite tidal-wave, and occasionally diverging into the more theoretical paths, he keeps the goal pretty fairly in view, and his farming experience comes timely to his aid. Climate, rainfall, drainage, are touched upon, along with the "diluvial clays" and "alluvial soils;" also natural history and other facts of a more practical nature, by which he hoped to see agriculture moulded into a regular science. Knowing as he did that works on agriculture are not read on account of their "unmeaning generalizations," or "commonplace details indifferently described," he longed to change all this by the introduction of natural history and other aids to a true agriculture. His concluding paragraph may be quoted. "British agriculture, viewed through the medium of plain and enlightened science, would seem but in its dawn, rising to a state of vigorous maturity, active industry carried on in better forms, and a liberal advancement of capital in the careful cultivation of more fruitful fields. The soil of our sea-girt isle is by no means wearing out, as closet-philosophers would infer; but, under the direction of liberal landlords, and in the hands of skilful tenants, its annual fruitfulness is multiplied and multiplying."

Not content with the relations of geology to the land and the waters around him, he soared, with the spirit of a philosopher, to a higher region,—"the laws of the universe,"—where he attempted to grapple with "the gravitation" of Newton and the atomic theory of Dalton. This was a bold step of Rooke's, and can hardly be considered a successful one. He admired the generalizations of Sir Isaac Newton, but he differed from his rigid explanation, and instead of the apple falling to the earth by the attraction of gravitation, Rooke considered that *it* was forced down by the active agency of some opposing force. The *atoms* of Dalton were more in his way than the "*Principia*" of Newton. Atoms appeared as tangible things with form, surface, density, elasticity, and the like; and their affinities and non-affinities he could work according to his own fashion. They were the very things for a theoretical philosopher to handle, and Rooke was not sparing of his use of them. He arranged the atoms on a Rooke pattern, not always in accordance with the laws of combination; and then appealed to Infinite Wisdom in corroboration of his views of organic forces!

Mr Rooke's "Dissertation on Geology" is the last and probably the least worthy chapter of the volume. He takes his cue from Moses, attaching import to the education and learning of the wily Egyptian, and, as may be inferred, making his geology square with the Biblical Genesis or Jewish cosmogony. He also calls in the aid of Job and David to his theories, neither of whom had hitherto been associated with scientific truth, but rather as gifted with Eastern imagery,— the one being known to the world for his patience and long-suffering; the other for his scandalous impatience and readiness to make others suffer. Mr Rooke's argument throughout is to reconcile geology with Scripture. He admits of no compromise, but remains staunch and orthodox by the first chapter of Genesis. His Neptunian proclivities find a strong utterance when he asks, " Shall we then believe in the testimony of Holy Writ, or in the theories of Pyrogenian philosophers?" Yet in another place he makes a half admission in favour of the said philosophers; thus, " If the scornful Pluto" (head-centre of Pyrogenians) "appeared, and placed the granite formation in the way of his rival god, it prepared a foundation for Neptune to rest his fabric upon—disburthen his waters of mere gross matter, slacken the pace of his rage, and go down into the cavities founded for him." Pluto may go down, but unfortunately for the stability of Rooke's hypothesis, science will stand up, and refuse to recognise the Mosaic description of the creation of this globe. Science puts her faith in the book of Nature, and the full exercise of the brain-power allotted to man as the superior entity on earth. Mr Rooke had been present at one of the British Association meetings, and observed, with indignation, that the leaders of science passed his friend Moses the Israelite by on the other side; but he did not live to see the greater inroads made upon the lines of orthodoxy by the "Essays and Reviews," Bishop Colenso and Dean Stanley; so he died happy in his own simple faith. But whilst he lived he should have borne in mind that Sir Isaac Newton and Galileo, the greatest of thinkers, had been led by their philosophical discoveries to run counter to churches, infallibilities, and trinities, yet were of blameless life, and the most eminent on the side of real and demonstrable truth. Moreover, Baron Cuvier, Professors Owen, Falconer, Lyell, and others, have, in their explanations of nature's arcana, destroyed all faith in "*the Book*" as a guide to a true cosmogony; and each year reveals abundant data tending to annihilate all trust in Jewish chronology,—the presumed six thousand years being looked upon as a mere mark in time, even in the life of man himself, viewed as he is, or as he was, in prehistoric times.

Mr Rooke's geology is that of a painstaking observer, who made himself familiar with the whole of the British isles, its coasts, bays, estuaries, rivers, and mountain ridges. All his views are backed up by an appeal to some district where the grounds of his theory can be tested. No closet study and no geological maps, plain or *alto relievo*, could have given him a tithe of his knowledge. It is much to be regretted that his book was so little known, seeing that the highly valuable suggestions contained in its pages could have been turned to special account, and earned for him the distinction of being a public benefactor. He had done good service to the State by his dissertations on political economy, but his "applied geology," fairly construed to the requirements of railways and navigation, should have added greater lustre to his reputation. Like many gifted men who have had the misfortune to live before their time, or to pass their lives amid bucolic society, jealous of other men's superiority, Rooke went to the grave but little honoured for his geological knowledge.

PERSONALITY—HOME—ILLNESS AND DEATH.

Mr Rooke was a tall, spare man, rather gaunt-looking, with shoulders considerably bent. His head was more lofty than broad, and his temples rather flattened; his eyebrows shaggy and marked; his eyes were sunk, and somewhat peering. He had a Roman nose; his thin lips, though subdued in character, were voluble enough in action. His complexion was rural and fresh, and his expression simply honest. He always dressed in black, and appeared tidy and gentlemanlike. He could talk or walk with any man in Cumberland. His long legs were not burdened with the carriage of fat and viscera, so that his pedal strides enabled him to get over a great amount of ground in the day. The man who, in his fifties, could walk from Akehead to the top of Skiddaw, 3200 feet above the level of the sea, on one day; and next morning walk to the shores of the Solway at Skinburness, cross its tidal stream, ascend Criffel, and stand on its highest peak (2000 feet above the sea), and then return home to sleep, was worthy of the name of pedestrian. This effort was prompted by his geological fervour, a wish to compare the formation of his own county, on the south side of the Solway, with that of Dumfriesshire on the north; to survey from Skiddaw's heights the lake country, the grand chain of mountains and widespreading plains of Cumberland, and, when his mind was freshly impressed with the geological arrangement, to view from Criffel the vale of the Nith and the rocky masses of southern Scotland bordering the Solway.

Mention has been made (p. 222) of the draining of his father's meadow, and the good results attending it, not overlooking the higher purpose it served of making John Rooke personally known to the leading minds of Cumberland. This meadow was prolific of advantages to him; for, some years subsequent to the draining operations, he was led to adopt a mode of irrigation; and watching the effect of crossing currents of water through his tiny meadow, oddly enough, created in him a passion for geology. The poet might well say, that "great events from small beginnings flow;" for the miniature currents in his meadow, viewed by the light of a true generalization, led him in course of years to develop a system of railroads—nay, a truly organic scheme—not unworthy of the highest engineering faculties and foresight. In maturing his plan, he gave great attention to his native county, and how he could best serve its commercial interests; and though his views were as patent as the light of day, he could obtain no hearing among the clashing of engineers and the soap-bubble blowings of financial schemers, and their ready dupes.

Every year he made pedestrian excursions to gratify his geological views. For several weeks he would be absent from home, and with the aid of railways and coaches, got over a considerable portion of the United Kingdom, also Normandy and Brittany. If the little meadow was his *alpha*, the many years he spent in exploring the earth's crust in England and France, afforded the grounds and the big *omega* of his geological theories.

Many stories could be told of his odd experiences and misadventures on the road of his geological inquiries; for as his enthusiasm led him at times to forget both daylight and distance, he wandered far from turnpikes and hostelries, and had to put up with odd quarters, and to become acquainted with strange bedfellows.

On one of his excursions he took the rail from Carlisle to Gilsland; but before leaving the Border city was tempted to buy a fine salmon trout, which he carried in his pocket, possibly anticipating the wants of his journey. Getting upon the wild moors beyond Gilsland, night set in; and it was one o'clock in the morning when he reached a lone house in Liddesdale, and craved admission. He was answered out of an upper-floor window, and informed that there was only one bed in the house, which the gudeman and the gudewife were then occupying. Most men would have yielded to such a *contretemps;* John Rooke, however, shared not in the connubial feeling that kept him at the door at midnight, a tired and wearied traveller. After much parleying between the geologist and the cottager, it was arranged—and probably with more appropriateness than in the case of Yorick and the *fille de chambre*—that the goodwife should seek repose in some other part of the house, and that Rooke should share her portion of the bed. In the morning the salmon-trout was cooked for the trio, and the philosopher went on his way rejoicing.

Mr Rooke and his favourite nephew, Mr Richard Rigg, one night found themselves in a small public at Flamborough Head, and at least twelve miles from a suitable hostelry. Mine hostess reminded them of Meg Dodd; but there was nothing for them but to sleep in a room in the roof containing three beds, to which access was had by a ladder and very low door. About two in the morning, Mr Rooke was out of bed, and looking after his coat and purse, being surprised to find four strapping lads taking possession of the only unoccupied bed; they were the sons of the landlady just come home from a fair. Having gone to bed in fear of damp sheets, and alarmed by such an accession of numbers, made his night in Flamborough anything but agreeable.

He was temperate in eating and drinking, and apparently temperate in love affairs, as he remained a bachelor. In politics a Tory, in religion an English Churchman, he placed great confidence in the British constitution, and believed it capable of meeting any emergency either at home or abroad. He took great interest in the town of Wigton, and aided it in various social and intellectual schemes, *e.g.*, schools and Mechanics' Institute. He was a trustee, and took great part in road and also in parochial affairs. He supported the Druids, Oddfellows' societies, &c., wherever good feeling was cherished and benevolence upheld. He was the first president of the Wigton Mechanics' Institute.

He saw little of society, but when he joined a circle of friends he made himself agreeable. In card-playing his mind was as much absorbed as if engaged in abstruse philosophy. When discussing his favourite theories, his tongue was exceedingly fluent. The Cumbrians compared his tongue to the clack of a mill-hopper; it went on and on, steadily, fervently, and uninterruptedly. The writer has listened to Mr Rooke for two or three hours consecutively in a long country walk, and with scarcely a break in the dissertation. A nod from his listener, whilst he himself took breath at the end of a proposition, sufficed; on he went; fresh illustration, fresh comparison, and fresh emphasis were brought into play to carry conviction, and to make it doubly sure. Given a listener, Rooke could talk and descant on everything; and if that listener showed appreciation, Rooke was off at full canter till he reached the goal of a fixed hypothesis in his political and scientific creed. He laboured under the great disadvantage of not being understood by an agricultural and trading community. His talk, it must be admitted, was not at all times easy of comprehension. He was deemed clever by a select few, queer and eccentric by the majority of folk. What with the laws of electricity, caloric, and the other imponderables, the atomic theory and organic forms and molecular forces crowding the programme of his reasoning, to be a correct interpreter of the Rooke generalizations required you to be unusually well versed in both the physical and natural sciences. He wandered over a wide domain of chemistry and physics; but for want of a clear enunciation of his principles, the structures he built appeared to others rather as a huge conglomerate of styles than a piece of simple architecture. The mingling of postulates and premises, of data and suppositions, and, when hard driven, citing biblical authority on his behalf, with other divergences more plausible than logical, rendered the cognizance of his views difficult even to the well-educated, whilst to the bucolic class they appeared a jargon or a Babel of words. "Thus, you see," was a great phrase of Rooke's; and his argument was generally clenched by, "Thus, you see," followed by a pause, then a fresh start and long-continued display of energetic action. Whilst vastly too credulous in some directions, he was proud of his own opinions, naturally dogmatic, and difficult to contravene. At times he seemed to merit the appellation his neighbours gave him of being eccentric, by asking unusual questions, and in an abrupt manner. He would break off the everlasting weather topic by a brusque comment on things most incongruous, as if his mind got impetuously away from its common moorings.

Assiduous in his application, he mastered whatever was compatible with his nerve power; his walk was as varied as the best of men—including surveying, engineering, geology, and, above all others, political economy. He seemed to ferret out everything pertaining to the subject on hand; and whatever he gathered he gave utterance to among his compeers; the more discussion he provoked, the better he liked it for his own enjoyment.

Though little more than a stone's-throw from a public road, John Rooke's residence was shut out from view by rising ground and trees. Being his own forester, he was slow to use the axe or the saw; and it might have been well if he had always denied himself the use of these implements. One morning his nephew Richard found him sitting in his arm-chair, exceedingly silent, if not gloomy and disappointed. After repeated inquiries as to the cause of this, it came out that a favourite ash-tree wanted a branch lopped off, and the master-forester, finding a difficulty in getting at it from a ladder, seated himself on the branch itself, but unfortunately at the wrong end, so that he sawed himself down to the ground along with his work. His fall of twenty feet might have been a serious affair, had he not fallen into the little brook, unusually flooded on that day.

The old clay bield of the family and a modern brick structure, in which John spent the greatest part of his life, occupy the margin of a small watercourse running between two eminences of land. No house could well be more retired; yet what an odd fancy of the first yeoman Rooke to locate himself in the lowest and narrowest of places, when he had fine sites on every knoll of his estate! If shelter and privacy guided his choice, he was surely the prototype of our John Rooke, who liked seclusion, and specially enjoyed his little sitting-room, hidden from everybody's gaze by the old fruit-trees with unpruned and straggling branches hanging down in front of the window. Nor was he less partial to the shelved recesses in his den, containing all his books and stock of lore, from the many-volumed Gibbon and Rollins to the last brochure on political economy. His books, it may be here observed, were more select than numerous; he was more prone to record his own thoughts than to read and be guided by authorities.

He lived in an atmosphere of political economy all day long and far into the night; and this mode of life could not escape both attention and comment. It was thought that if he lived long enough he might become like a hard-dried flitch of bacon that had hung for years in the open chimney of an old-fashioned farmhouse, and blackened and withered beyond "kenning." Rooke, however, was in his proper sphere sitting in his little parlour in company with Hume, Adam Smith, Paley, and Ricardo, and amid big tomes, half-bindings, pamphlets, reviews of the corn trade, agricultural magazines, parliamentary blue-books and debates, and even more dry-as-dust and recondite histories. There he conned over figures and statistics, with special regard to fractions and decimals, and tabular statements, or whatever else could help his argument or illustrate his theories.

When tired of work—and the brains of the hardest-headed men get muddled with too long study—John sought air and exercise along a walk of greensward by the side of the diminutive stream, and sheltered by a high thorn-hedge. Here he gave his limbs full play by rapid walking or running, and his brain more or less relaxation. The adjacent meadow was the chief aim of his cultivation in his riper years, and when political economy pressed too much, he left his foolscap and folios, put on his clogs, and, with spade in hand, attended most assiduously to its irrigation. Long after farming had lost part of its charms, he still clung to his meadow, and no one was allowed to interfere with that special hobby of the master. Sir James Graham made happy allusion to this meadow in one of his letters to Mr Rooke. Ten years after his death, the writer rejoiced to see the meadow in luxuriant herbage, and that the management so largely bestowed by his old friend was marked as ever. The little lawn of his garden and his favourite walk were also profusely decorated with snowdrops; each tiny white flower, with all its delicacy and green fringe, made nature's simple casket a bed of magnificence, in no small degree heightened by the damp morning giving rise to beads of aqueous prisms on every leaf. How these natural gems would have gladdened the eye of the old philosopher!

Born too soon for his times, he was misunderstood, or found fault with for entertaining doctrines incompatible with the landed interests and his own prosperity. The opinions which he worked out fifty years ago, and for the entertaining of which he was laughed at, pitied, and blamed, are now the opinions, not of parties, not of sects, and not of mercantile companies only, but of the people of Great Britain, and of the best-informed minds of Europe and America. Free trade, for which he fought for thirty years at least, when almost alone as an English writer, and entirely alone as a Cumbrian (men's minds began to awaken after 1834);—free trade, for which he incurred the censure of his agricultural friends, and not less of his political (Tory) party, is now the great fact of all our financial relations. Well might Sir James Graham write to Mr Rooke, praising, in no measured terms, his steady, consistent advocacy of free trade doctrines throughout his whole life, when not one of a hundred thousand persons could see the import of the principles, and the grand consummation of England's commercial glory.

His works brought him, in course of time, a large correspondence. On his list, and chief among statesmen, was Sir James Graham, who thoroughly appreciated the retired philosopher of Akehead, some of whose letters are quoted in an Appendix. Mr Attwood of Birmingham, who wrote so much on currency questions, often interrogated Rooke on his views of political economy; and Mr Crosse of Norwich, and many others, both greater and lesser in fame, addressed him on electricity and geology. He liked letter-writing, and indulged his hobby in filling every corner of the biggest sheet allowed by law before the days of penny postage came to his relief. His sofa was literally crammed with letters both above and below the cushions, and every bit of space not occupied by the more ponderous volumes was made the receptacle of his correspondence.

He was a member of the London Archæological Society, but there is no evidence of his having contributed any essays to the Society, or to any other Society, metropolitan or provincial.

He had no sympathy with Dissent or Nonconformity; his belief in Episcopacy was paramount to all other things; hence his anxiety in 1849 to see the

Wigton Mechanics' Institute "placed on a sound Christian basis."

On being apprised (March 2, 1850) by the Clerk of the Peace that his name was placed on the Commission of the Peace for the county of Cumberland, he immediately wrote for the requisite books—"Burns' Justice," &c.—to qualify him for the new duties. He wrote to his nephew Richard Rigg on this subject:—
"Honest and straightforward intentions temperately acted upon must be my strongholds. However, mere ambition would have failed to lead me into this, had not public services to those around me called me forward." He was then in his seventieth year, but not afraid to put on fresh armour in the service of his county. If he had expected the office, he had waited long and patiently. Whilst he was approaching the end of man's natural career, mere striplings in age, with no knowledge of social life or equity or justice, but born to acreage, and too often to yellow political colours, were perched on the magisterial bench— serving no better use than convenient black-boards upon which the officiating clerk might chalk his attorneyship's decision! Could Shakespeare but return to life, and visit certain counties on the banks of Lowther, how readily he might verify his Justices Shallow and Slender,—without wigs, it is true, but also without pates!

In visiting his friend Francis Bennoch of London, he met Haydon, the historical painter, who invited him to his studio, at the very time he was painting the "Banishment of Aristides." The economist and painter discussed the historical group on the canvas; at length Haydon remarked that he had long been in search of a suitable face to aid his representation of the "Just Athenian;" and, after a slight pause, then fixing his eyes on Rooke's physiognomy, he tapped him on the shoulder, and said—"As Nathan said unto David, 'Thou art the man'—for my Aristides." Mr Rooke consented, probably thinking that as his studies resembled those which in part engaged Aristophanes,* he might not be so ill suited to the type of Aristides. Haydon got a sufficient likeness of the Akehead philosopher to enable his friends to recognise him. This picture was exhibited at Carlisle in 1846. Mr Rooke sat for his portrait to Cocken—a Wigton artist—now in the possession of Mr Thomas Rooke of Gretton; from it the photograph in this volume was taken.

In his latter years Mr Rooke enjoyed very indifferent health. It seems paradoxical to state that when in good health he used to vomit part of his food every day, and when he was really ill, and confined to bed, his vomiting ceased. No wonder he was thin and gaunt-looking; his dyspepsia robbed him of the usual supplies of food; and in time an enlargement

* Nicole Oresme, a schoolman, and Bishop of Lisieux, in France, wrote a treatise on Money, a few years after the battle of Poictiers, five hundred years ago; and his theory as to the origin and use of money seems to be in wonderful conformity with the views of Adam Smith and John Rooke of these latter days. This would show that political economy had not slept after Aristophanes, and that the dark mediæval ages contained some traces of light, which historians have been apt to overlook. Thanks to Monsieur Wolowski, the learned Nicole Oresme, whose mortality lies in the choir of Lisieux Cathedral for five hundred years, has got his share of immortality in the year of grace 1864. Another illustration is thus furnished in corroboration of the old adage that there is nothing new under the sun. Even the dismal science had its votaries, ay, and in churches too of the fourteenth century.

His Death and Burial.

of the great artery (aneurism) leading from the heart tried his powers of life very much. On the 24th April 1856, he had a paralytic seizure, by which he was deprived of the use of his right side; and two days subsequently he died very peaceably. As he had expressed a wish to be buried in sight of Akehead, his remains were interred in the Wigton cemetery, that had been just completed, but not consecrated. As Bishop Percy would not consecrate the Church of England division of "God's acre" till a wall separated the portion allotted to Dissenters, no clergyman dared to officiate at the funeral of a man who had defended Episcopacy with his last breath! Mr Rigg, banker, and brother-in-law of Mr Rooke, felt it his duty to conduct the burial service, and this he did with becoming solemnity. A plain pillar marks the grave, and is inscribed:—"John Rooke, born Aug. 29, 1780; died April 26, 1856."

APPENDIX.

LETTERS FROM SIR JAMES GRAHAM TO MR ROOKE.

THE first letter bears very much upon Mr Rooke's publication of his essay on "Free Trade in Corn," discussed in pages 240-248 of this volume; it also lays claim to the soundness of their views (Graham and Rooke) respecting the Currency Bill of 1819.

No. I.

"GROSVENOR PLACE, LONDON,
29th June 1827.

"DEAR SIR,—My time has really been so occupied by my duties in Parliament, and by my attendance on the Emigration Committee, and other important inquiries in which I have been engaged, that I have not answered your letters with the punctuality which my respect for your character dictates, and which the importance of your communications merits.

"I hear from you, however, at all times with pleasure; and I frequently derive very useful suggestions from the train of thought to which your speculations lead.

"I shall have the greatest pleasure in assisting you to publish the little treatise which you have prepared; the present moment is peculiarly well adapted for such a disquisition; and if you will send it to me by the coach with the least possible delay, I will endeavour to come to an arrangement with Ridgway for printing and publishing it on the terms which you specify. I shall not abuse the liberty which you give me of revising it before it goes to press; I shall not, of course, violate even principles from which I may dissent, but I shall confine myself to verbal alterations, and to any abbreviations which may occur to me as improvements.

"The recent struggle of parties has been highly injurious to the public interests; and never was a session less productive of solid advantage to the community. I am not pleased with the present position of affairs; and I fear that for some time the Government will be disorganized, and public attention dedicated to the character and conduct of men without much reference to measures.

"Every day's additional experience convinces me more and more of the soundness of our views respecting the currency; the bill of 1819 lies at the foundation of all our difficulties: corn laws, custom regulations, emigration reports, and relief to the manufacturers, all are but the fringes of *this one* great first cause, on which our difficulties and our fate depend. We must come to the discussion of it at last; it will be forced on us; but the

Legislature is not yet ripe for it; and the ignorance still prevalent on the subject exceeds your belief of possibility.—Yours, very truly,

"J. R. G. GRAHAM."

Sir James wished Mr Rooke to be made more fully acquainted with his opinions respecting the currency, and his letter No. II. concludes with expressions of regret at the apathy of the people. Letter No. III. sufficiently speaks for itself.

No. II.

"NETHERBY, 5th January 1830.

"DEAR SIR,—I have been dangerously ill, but am now recovering, and hope to be able to resume my habits of active life. I shall attend the Sessions, and dine and stay all night with Mr Matthews on Saturday next. I have a book or two which I wish you to see, and I will leave them for you at Mr Taylor's inn.

"You well know my fixed opinions respecting the currency. Ministers intend to adhere to their insane policy, which tends directly to convulsion; and all the efforts of some few representatives will be vain, unless the *constituent* body come forward, and the nation raise its voice in a tone which will shake the nerve of any Minister, however bold. This is no time to recollect even past party differences; a new question has arisen involving the existence of our establishments and of our country; the war is between the taxpayers and the tax-receivers, the landowners and the stock-jobbers; every honest man must take his part; and those who hesitate are lost, for the crisis is at hand; it can only be arrested by decisive measures; the Ministers seek to temporize; the country must demand a change of policy; but the Duke [Wellington] will not yield easily; and if the yeomen remain silent, the voice of a few members in the House of Commons will be found to avail little; the worst symptom of the times is the apparent apathy of the people.—Very faithfully yours,

"J. R. G. GRAHAM."

No. III.

"HOUSE OF COMMONS, 21*st June* 1830.

"DEAR SIR,—The Government and Parliament are both equally determined not to touch the currency, and to try the experiment of a high gold standard and of a pure metallic circulation for another year; they are confident that the country can bear it, and that a revisal of the whole measure will not be necessary. I hope these are right; but I think them wrong; and I do not believe we can go to war again without touching our currency or debasing our standard; and corn laws will prove the ruin of our manufactures and commerce; yet a landed aristocracy cannot be preserved without them, unless prices be raised through the medium of an operation on our money.

"Nothing, however, can be done at this juncture, when the fate of parties, and the fortunes of Kings and Ministers are in the balance.

"I shall soon have to appear before the bar of my constituents. I shall appeal to them with hope and not with fear; for I have endeavoured to serve them honestly and boldly.—With sincere esteem, yours very faithfully,

"J. R. G. GRAHAM."

There had been some political sparring and hard hitting on the part of the Lowthers, which Sir James could not help noticing to his Tory friend Rooke. Sir James was a dangerous person to attack, as no man was more cunning of fence, or more apt to deal heavy blows upon an antagonist.

No. IV.

"NETHERBY, 28*th August* 1830.

"DEAR SIR,—Mr Yule will be happy to meet you and Mr Parkin on the Burnfoot Farm either on Wednesday or on Friday next, at half-past ten o'clock; and if you will inform me which of these two days you choose, I will let Mr Yule know, so that he may be ready on the ground to meet you. If I am at home on that day I also will meet you, that I may have the pleasure of conversing with you.

"As for myself, you well know that angry violence forms no part of my natural character; I never wish to be the aggressor; when attacked, I always endeavour so to defend myself as to make the assailant more cautious for the future. I think that Colonel Lushington at Carlisle, and Colonel Lowther at Whitehaven, both used language which was intemperate and indiscreet, and provoked in great measure what took place at Cockermouth. I, however, am induced to take my stand on my own character, and to defend my own seat, equally avoiding compromise and coalition, and quite satisfied with *my single seat*, while on public grounds I can command the confidence of the freeholders. I hope and think that this tower of strength is now on my side, and I hope I shall never either abandon it or be driven from it.

"You do wisely to rest on your oars at the present moment, for we know not what an hour may bring forth; in the meantime clouds and thick darkness hang over the future; but great events, I am persuaded, are about to happen. Steady principles and firm resolution will be required to shape a course in the midst of the coming storm.—Yours very faithfully,

"J. R. G. GRAHAM."

Mr Rooke, looking upon the conduct of the *Carlisle Patriot* as unfair towards Sir James, had kindly interfered with the editor on his behalf. This service is noted in Letter No. 5, and after expressing his wish to pursue a course most conducive to the public good, and independently of the zealots of all parties, Sir James writes:—

No. V.

"NETHERBY, *October* 15, 1830.

"But I am content to submit to this inconvenience [a crossfire from the Tory press of the county] in preference to a compromise of my own opinions; and I put my trust in the honesty of my intentions, and in the sound judgment and good sense of those whom I endeavour to represent, and whose favour and approbation I value; for although I have no hired journal at my command, yet justice in the long run is sure to be rendered to faithful service; and however misrepresented, in the end I shall not be undervalued.

" Your observations on the character of the Duke of Wellington, I fear, are just, but the days of his power are numbered, unless he be prepared to satisfy the reasonable expectations of that middle class which is the life and marrow of the State; and this he cannot effect without the concession of great reforms, and a new adjustment of the entire scheme of our taxation and commerce.

" The crisis is awful, and I hope the peace of this country will be preserved.

" I go to London immediately after the Quarter Sessions, and am always glad to hear your sentiments.—Very faithfully yours,

"J. R. G. GRAHAM."

No. VI.

"ADMIRALTY, 7th January 1834.

" DEAR SIR,—I always hear from you with pleasure, and am disposed to receive your lucubrations with the respect due to your private worth. My opinion of the fatal error committed in 1819 very much coincides with yours, and remains unchanged; yet all the relations of social life, however disturbed by the bill of 1819, have in some sort settled down in conformity to its measure of value; and the risk of fresh alterations are to be weighed against the dangers of adherence to the present standard. Your view of the future is gloomy; my consolation is, that it is in wiser and in better hands than ours; and in the meantime you are happy on your farm, and I am earnest in my endeavours to be useful to the public, whom I serve. Civil liberty may still last our lives; and I hope yours may be long, yet never doomed to witness the ill which you forebode.—I am, with sincere esteem, dear sir, very faithfully yours,

."J. R. G. GRAHAM."

"John Rooke, Esq."

Though attacked in 1834 by the Free-traders for his tergiversation, based on the supposition of his being the author of "Free Trade in Corn," he never attempted to put the public right; but having taken office as Home Secretary in Sir R. Peel's Ministry, Sir James seems to have come to the conclusion that he must clear up the mystery attached to Mr Rooke's pamphlet.

No. VII.

"GROSVENOR PLACE, LONDON,
June 30, 1841.

"MY DEAR SIR,—You will have observed that the attempt has been renewed to father on me the authorship of your pamphlet, entitled, 'A Free Trade in Corn the Real Interest of the Landlord and the True Policy of the State,' which was published in the name of a 'Cumberland Yeoman.' Now, my recollection is distinct, that, though I saw that pamphlet in manuscript, and made some verbal corrections in it, and assisted in inducing Mr Ridgway to publish it, acting as your friend, the composition is your own; you alone are responsible for the principles it advocates, and for the opinions therein expressed; and moreover, that at the time of the publication you were aware of the opposite opinions entertained by me, which were favourable to a protecting duty on corn, adjusted on the principle of Mr Huskisson's self-acting scale. I am confident that your recollection on these points will agree with mine; if so, I should be obliged by a short letter from you, stating these facts, which letter I may be at liberty to use and to publish, if I am again charged with inconsistency on account of my conduct on the corn question being at variance with certain passages in a pamphlet written by you eleven or twelve years ago.

"I will thank you to direct your answer to me here; and, begging you will excuse the trouble which I give you, I remain, always yours very faithfully,

"J. R. G. GRAHAM."

Considering his able and long-continued advocacy of the doctrines of free trade, Mr Rooke must have felt unusually elated, after the final blow to restrictive duties on corn, in the autumn of 1846, to have the following high tribute paid him by Sir James Graham :—

"NETHERBY, 4th September 1846.

"DEAR SIR,—I am sincerely glad that the course which my sense of public duty has compelled me to adopt with respect to the corn laws meets with your entire approbation. Your views on this subject have been consistent and uniform; and the necessity of no longer treating the trade in corn as an exception to general principles was obvious to you long before it had forced itself on my conviction. I give you full credit for your foresight, and disinterested boldness and honesty in the early avowal and steady maintenance of these opinions. . . . .—I am, dear sir, yours very faithfully,

"J. R. G. GRAHAM."

The reader is again referred to Sir James Graham's Life for other letters addressed to Mr Rooke on questions of great public interest.

CAPTAIN JOSEPH HUDDART.

"Upholding Britain's fame and Britain's weal."

THE shores of the Solway Frith, the sea-boundary between England and Scotland, can lay claim to no small share of classical repute, derived from the noble Roman; a mediæval history reflecting the struggles of monarchy with monachism; and a more modern yet no less exciting participation in the feuds of Border warfare. Here, on the English side of the Frith, were the standards of the Roman cohorts last seen in defensive attitude against the Caledonians; here, too, favoured by sea communication with Hibernia and Mona, came roving ecclesiastics, whose instinctive sagacity led them to the rich alluvial soil and salmon streams of Cumberland; here encamped, on a large grassy plain, the most numerous army that ever responded to the call of an English monarch—he who threatened to make Scotland a waste, and died on Burgh Marsh with a breath of revenge on his lips; here also, but more westerly, landed a Scottish Queen, whose beauty and passions had created a deep interest in Western

Europe, taking refuge from the snares of her own subjects, to fall into the greater mesh of her rival, the last of the barbarous Tudors. These associations are of the past. To-day, the Solway Frith reveals numerous safe harbours, and the busiest of commercial enterprise, invested in coal-mines and iron-fields of the most promising kind.

About midway between Bowness Point and St Bees' Head, the Solway tide has formed a bay, upon the banks of which stands the village of Allonby. Of the traditional foundation of Allonby by Alan, Lord of Allendale, in the twelfth century; of the unsuccessful attempt made by Thomas Richardson to renovate the village in our own day, and rob it of its stagnation; of the dilapidated boats on its beach, and "its dirty beck,"* no record need be made here. Quakerism had a strong hold upon the two or three hundred population of Allonby last century, and preferring for itself a four-walled room and silent worship to "steeple-houses" and surpliced priests, showed its usual tenacity of opinion by opposing the interests of a minority seeking to erect an Episcopal chapel; and for long its opposition prevailed. Whilst this bickering for the salvation of the souls of the Allonbites was going on between the keen "regiments of drab" and the psalm-singing, tithe-exacting Tudor Episcopacy, Mr Huddart, the shoemaker of Allonby, took to himself a wife, who bore him a son on January 11, 1740-41, o.s., and this son was named Joseph. With

* Charles Dickens and his friend Wilkie Collins, as "two idle apprentices," visited Allonby some years ago, and narrated their travels in "All the Year Round;" in which periodical the dull aspects of the place were brought out in strong relief.

the doings of this Joseph Huddart in his way through the world this narrative is specially concerned.

In 1745, a "chapel of ease" got built at Allonby, by Dr Thomlinson, prebendary of St Paul's, London, and the first clergyman ordained to the incumbency was a Mr Wilson, who commenced a school to eke out his bare living. Young Huddart became his pupil, and a favoured one, as the lad showed a partiality for mechanics, astronomy, and other branches of learning. The parson's son and Joseph Huddart were companions in play as well as in study; and something might have arisen out of this, had not Huddart senior wanted his only son and child for his own avocation. Joseph did not like shoemaking and sedentary life, but preferred boating and star-gazing; and, on discovering this, his father yielded to the circumstances that deprived him of a trade successor. Shoemakers have done great things in their day, and risen to eminence as algebraists, poets, painters, and politicians, nay, founders of religious sects; nevertheless, there is no reason to regret that young Huddart's seat in his father's shop became vacant. The Church was thought of as worthy of a lad of promise; but seafaring and engineering tendencies carried the day, so that the stall of St Crispin *in esse*, as well as the stall canonical *in posse*, were thrown up as fruitless objects in the life of Joseph Huddart.

Joseph had his eyes open to everything passing, "a sharp lad and no mistake;" and if his vision was acute, and his mind inquisitive, his ears were not less alive to harmony. In his early teens he could play on the violin, and exceedingly well on the flute, and no doubt sing a song with any lad in Allonby.

Judging from the holes or stops in his flute, he must have had uncommonly long fingers. Whilst sitting in his father's shop, a Scottish bagpiper came to the door, and delighted him greatly. After watching the Highlander's performance, he asked for a trial of the pipes, and soon proved his aptitude for playing on the new instrument. His mechanical turn, love of music and drawing, were hardly suited to the obscurity of Allonby, where there was so little to cheer his mind but the scenery of his native mountains and the fine marine views extending from Rayberry Head to Criffel's base. This scenery, indeed, was likely to create a love of travel and voyaging; but another faculty predominated in young Huddart's mind—constructiveness. Stories are told of the boy's early partiality for mechanics; of his propelling a little boat without oars, by means of some machinery within it impelled by a spring; and of his imitating to a great nicety the mechanism of a flour-mill in the course of erection near to his father's door. Very opportunely a "Treatise on Shipbuilding and Navigation," by Munro Murray, fell into his hands, and this had much to do with his future career. He laboured assiduously to construct a model of a seventy-four gun-ship with all its details, though he had never seen any vessel larger than a coast schooner. He succeeded in his object, and this great effort of juvenile life, the miniature "man-of-war," is said to be still prized as an heirloom by the family.

In the year 1756, when Joseph was sixteen years of age, Allonby was awakened from its dull life by great shoals of herrings running up the Frith, filling the nets of the fishermen beyond all precedent. This unexpected prosperity induced the more enterprising inhabitants, among whom was Huddart senior, to form a company for the purpose of extending the fisheries and curing the fish. This was a golden opportunity for Joseph's acquiring the art of boating and fishing, and a larger experience of the sea. His father died in 1762, and he succeeded to his fishing interests, and was thereby enabled to take command of a small brig, for the purpose of conveying fish to Ireland. In the same year, as prosperity continued to fill his sails, he took to himself a wife in Miss Johnston of Cowper in Holme-Cultram, the daughter of a small landed proprietor, and had by her five sons, two of whom died in their infancy.

In the year 1763, the herrings disappeared from the Frith, and Allonby drooped. Huddart now took to the coasting trade, and as his shipbuilding ideas were revived, he went to Maryport, five miles farther west, and had a ship built on his own plan, and partly by his own hands, in 1768. This ship of Huddart's has got the credit of being the first constructed in Cumberland from "draft," or drawings, and working by scale. As master of his own ship, and about to extend his navigation beyond the coasts of Britain, Joseph now seems entitled to the name of Captain Huddart. A voyage to America being determined upon by Huddart, his friends suggested that a sailor who had frequently crossed the Atlantic should form one of his crew; the advice was adopted, but, curious to relate, the sailor of many passages' experience was no match for the Captain, who only made it for the first time. The Captain's observations and reckonings were so accurate, that he was enabled to point to the land first seen on the American coast as the very port he was bound to; and though his sailor judged very differently, he steered for the river, and found the wished-for haven. Here was a triumph of science over uneducated experience; and it is but one of the thousands of proofs daily occurring to show the accuracy of astronomical data, and the glorious privileges possessed by modern navigators.

Captain Huddart continued in the American trade till Christmas 1773, when, by the pressing request of Sir Richard Hotham, to whom he was allied by marriage, he entered the East India Company's service, and made a highly successful voyage, to his employers at least; it was not so to himself pecuniarily. He resumed charge of his own ship, and confined himself to the coal trade between Maryport and Ireland. During his nearly two years' engagement in the Indian voyages, he employed his leisure time in scientific inquiries and in surveys of the coasts. These surveys, especially that of Sumatra, came to the knowledge of Mr Sayer, a chart-seller in Fleet Street, London, and so pleased him, that he solicited Captain Huddart to undertake a survey of St George's Channel. This was the first recognition of Huddart as something more than the ordinary sea-captain—a man of science. He laboured to prove his fitness for a post that required energy and the full exercise of his mental powers. Though the pecuniary reward derived from this survey (completed in 1777) was small, the fame he acquired was great; and he had the pleasant reflection of knowing that he had done nautical men a real service. It seems odd that so important a channel as St George's should have been without a reliable survey till the year 1777.

Again he is prevailed upon by his London friends to enter the East India Company's service, and is so satisfied with the offers made to him, that he returns to Cumberland to sell his own sailing vessel, and dispose of other business at Allonby. At Deptford he superintended the building of a ship, and then sailed from the Downs, in April 1778, for Bombay. His eldest son, William, accompanied him as midshipman, and both had a narrow escape from a watery grave. The loss of a fine ship upon an unknown rock off the Cape of Good Hope induced Huddart to ascertain the true situation of the rock, and in his laudable endeavour to accomplish this task, the pinnace was upset, containing himself, his son, and other officers. He threw himself into the sea, his son followed, and got upon his back; after swimming sixty yards they reached the land, and, thanks to the Captain's efforts, the rest were saved. On his third voyage to Bombay, in June 1780, he was under the orders of Admiral Sir Edward Hughes, and was engaged in the reduction of Jagginault-poram and Negapatam, two Dutch settlements, and otherwise actively employed in the King's service.

Accustomed to hear of great riches amassed by all in the employment of the East India Company in the last century, it is curious to note that Huddart, after ten years' service, benefited but little pecuniarily. It was only when he obtained the chance of one of the Bombay and China voyages, through the kindness of Sir Henry Fletcher, that the tide was turned in his favour. This success was overpowered by losses of a different kind; for on his return, he received the painful news of his wife's death, which took place at Allonby on February 12, 1786. In the following year his eldest son William, a naval commander of great promise, died in China on the 30th March 1787. Captain Huddart felt the death of his son most deeply, and said to a friend, "that it was the first and only time in a life of hardships and vicissitudes in which he had repined at the dispensations of Providence, but that he hoped the Almighty in His infinite mercy would forgive him."

With his last voyage to India, Huddart completed twenty-five years of a sailor's life, and, with the exception of the dangerous expedition off the Cape of Good Hope already mentioned, experienced no disaster. It might have been otherwise on his return voyage from Bombay, had he not exercised his usual vigilance in noting the meteorological changes. He set sail from Bombay with seven other vessels, and with the wind and weather most promising. Seeing the approach of bad weather, he returned in two or three days to Bombay, to the great dissatisfaction of the Governor, who threatened to report his conduct to the Board of Directors. A violent storm had overtaken the other ships, and nothing was ever seen of them but the wreck of broken timbers strewed along the coast. When the storm had fairly subsided, Captain Huddart called at the Government House to take leave, and accosting the Governor, jocularly said, "Governor, I am ready to sail, I only wait for your letter to the Court of Directors."

It should be stated, in connection with his India experiences and numerous surveys, that he completed a survey of the whole peninsula from Bombay to Coringo; also one of the river Tigris from Canton to the island of Sankeet, for which service he received the thanks of the Directors in October 1786. In January 1795, his son Johnston, who had also been in the seafaring line, died at Leghorn—another trying affliction to Captain Huddart.

He now settled down in Highbury Terrace, London, and erected an observatory and workshop, with lathe, forge, &c., to enable him to pursue his mechanical and astronomical labours. Like the famous George Stephenson of our day, he took great pleasure in the mechanism of clocks.

Looking to the character of his nautical engagements, it might be supposed that Captain Huddart had enough on hand; but with the eye of an observer, and the mind that sought light from every source, he had been struck with some curious phenomena exhibited by a family of the name of Harris in Maryport. John Harris, a shoemaker, could not distinguish colours, and when people talked of a stocking being red, he could speak of its form only—a stocking. The same peculiarity existed in two of his brothers. Captain Huddart gathered what facts he could from the Harris family, and sent them to the famous Dr Priestley; and under the title, "An Account of Persons who could not distinguish Colours," a paper was communicated to the Royal Society of London, on February 13, 1777. This "colour-blindness," as it has been called, will be discussed in a future biography, namely, that of Dr John Dalton, who laboured under a similar disease. This essay on the Harris family, and probably his nautical services, obtained for him the high privilege of being elected a Fellow of the Royal Society in 1791. In the same year he was made an " Elder Brother" of the Trinity Corporation, and became one of the most active of its members. He directed his attention to the improvement and security of the coasting navigation, and the erection of lighthouses. On October 8, 1795, at a General Court of the Corporation of Trinity House, he received a most flattering vote of thanks for his important services to the Court and navigation in general, by establishing a light on the rocks called the Longships, at the Land's End, and other nautical improvements.

As his engineering abilities became better known, he was consulted on some of the great works in London and elsewhere. He took an active part in the plan and execution of the London Docks, and soon afterwards became engaged in the construction of the East India Docks; indeed, so high was his position as Director of this Company, that, in the absence of the Right Honourable William Pitt, the great statesman and Premier, the honour of laying the first stone was delegated to him.

Though the busiest of men with engineering, astronomy, and other kindred pursuits, Captain Huddart felt no lack of energy in his sixtieth year. With him, as with all well-trained minds, rest was but *ennui*, and highly irksome whilst there was anything to accomplish that was worth the doing. His long nautical experience had too often proved imperfections in the manufacture of cordage, especially in the cable and larger ropes, and the heavy loss of life and property resulting from these imperfections, and he longed to effect a change. After much consideration, and many experiments, his inventive genius enabled him to establish a most valuable improvement in the manufacture of cordage. He described his plan to Mr Barnes of Maryport, and assisted in the first operation himself. The trials made of the new ropes in the neighbouring collieries were so satisfactory, that he offered his invention to the East India Company, in the hope that, through their influence, it would be made to benefit the maritime interests of Britain. The Company declined it, and "on the absurd and illiberal principle of not altering what had been long practised." Woe betide discoverers, when the richest Company in the world could not be induced to adopt a great improvement! Woe betide humanity, when the proprietors of the "wealth of the Indies" would hold by an imperfect cordage when a good article was offered, the use of which was calculated to save life and a thousand valued interests!

Thwarted where he least expected, Huddart seems to have allowed his discovery to remain in abeyance for six years, till some gentlemen in London offered to carry out his plans, provided he would undertake the erection of suitable works. Instead of accepting their offer to remunerate him as an inventor, to which he was fully entitled, he joined in the scheme as a proprietor, ready to sink or swim with his copartners in the business of cord-making. Early in 1800, the machinery at Limehouse was completed, and the first cordage manufactured was a cable of large dimensions. Everything prospered well; the machinery was his own invention, and all was done according to his plans. The works continued udner his own superintendence; and it must have been highly gratifying to him to know, that after sixteen years' experience of the new cordage, "no one reasonable instance had occurred of complaint or defectiveness in the cordage manufactured by the machinery of his own constructing."

As early as April 1793, he took out a patent for certain improvements in the formation of ropes; and on August 20, 1799, another patent for an improvement on his apparatus of 1793. On July 1, 1800, he obtained a patent for further improvements. Four years only elapsed, when he made a machine for manufacturing hemp and flax into yarn, which he patented; and on October 30 of the following year (1805) he obtained a patent for an improvement in the manufacture of large cables and cordage in general.

Looking back to his first effort in shipbuilding, he fancied that many improvements might still be made, and, in 1797, constructed another ship at Maryport, for the purpose of trying further experiments; and in connection with this subject, he followed out a series of observations bearing upon the motion and resistance of bodies in fluids. In this inquiry Huddart showed himself the true philosopher. To ascertain how, and to what extent, ships were impeded in their course, not from the natural obstacles of winds and waves and changing currents of the sea only, but from their own inherent shape or size, or general construction, was a problem worthy of the highest intellect; and no doubt it occurred to Huddart that by ascertaining the mode in which bodies are resisted in their progress through the waters, he would throw considerable light on the art of shipbuilding. The solution of the problem required familiarity with the laws of physics, and an ability to apply these laws to the furtherance of his designs. No one could be expected to succeed without a knowledge of the higher mathematics, a large inventive faculty, an aptitude for making and varying experiments, and, above all, a power to found upon these a correct generalization.

He saw the importance of his inquiries to British interests, inasmuch as our maritime superiority rested on our naval architecture; and that fast sailing and a staunch build must carry the day. He anticipated by forty years the Scott-Russels and Brunels, and may be said to have opened the path of inquiry which Russel made his own in the middle of this century. There were not the extensive canals in that day to facilitate Huddart's inquiries, nor many other circumstances favouring later experimentalists. Huddart, however, laboured with his usual perseverance, and had a vessel constructed at the shipyard of his friend Sir Robert Wigram, according to his own plans throughout; and such was the accuracy with which his experiments had been made, and the lines laid down, aided by mathematical calculations, that the ship realised everything he had expected from her in speed and draft of water. Like a true patriot, he wished to promote English interests by hiding from foreigners his shipbuilding plans; and the last years of his life were much occupied on this very subject—the reconstruction of our navy—by which he hoped to secure a build of ships possessing a larger stowage and greater speed, with equal powers of defence or resistance. It is much to be regretted that his plans were never so matured on paper as to be understood or carried out by his successors; and still more that his life had not been prolonged to accomplish his great desideratum, that of making the British "man-of-war" the first of its kind in the world.

In the capacity of engineer, he was consulted as to the formation and improvement of harbours in various parts of the kingdom. Thus Whitehaven, Boston, Hull, Portsmouth, Swansea, Leith, and Dublin had the benefit of his labours. The Government also employed him, along with Mr Rennie, to survey and report on the situation of Howth, in Ireland, for the accommodation of packets; also on the improvements of his Majesty's dockyards at Woolwich, Sheerness, &c.

In 1791, he made a survey and chart of the islands and coasts of Scotland. Wherever he was engaged, he pleased his employers, received their thanks, and occasionally more lasting tokens as an acknowledgment of his services. Works of this kind crowded upon him so, that, with all his industry and readiness to oblige, he was unable to undertake the commissions offered. A moiety of the surveying and planning he was called upon to do for corporate bodies, shipping interests, &c., would have sufficed to engage some men entirely, and to the exclusion of other work; but Huddart never lost sight of the higher walks of his calling as an astronomer and navigator. Thus, in November 1796, he read a paper to the Royal Society:—" Observations on Horizontal Refractions which affect the Appearances of Terrestrial Objects, and the Dip or Depression of the Horizon of the Sea." These observations were chiefly made at Allonby.

His name is associated with numbers of lighthouses

and floating-lights, both on the east and west coasts of the island; and allusion has already been made to his surveys in far distant countries, *e.g.*, Sumatra, China, the coast of Malabar, &c. He is said to have ascertained the longitudes of sixteen places on the Indian coast.

It was fairly stated by his son, that his works have "invariably been the results of arduous exertion, most *skilfully applied*, in situations and circumstances of peculiar danger and difficulty; for who but he would *voluntarily* have selected the extremity of Africa, or the rugged cliffs of Western Scotland, for the display of those talents which might have been exhibited in circumstances of comparative safety, with more benefit to himself in point of emolument, though proportionably with less advantage to others. . . . Thousands have reason to bless his name for that safety which has been derived from his labours; and the navigators of all nations may consider it as synonymous with benefactor" (Memoir, pp. 58, 59).

Money having flowed in from these multifarious employments, he purchased, in 1809, the ancient demesne of Brynkir, in Caernarvonshire, and shortly afterwards the neighbouring estate of Wern. These properties were placed under the direction of his son Joseph. By himself they were never seen, therefore could not be enjoyed. The pressure of business must have been great when he never could find rest from his avocations to visit his newly-acquired property, in the purchase of which, in all probability, he had looked forward to enjoy the *otium cum dignitate* of a well-spent life. His public and private labours seem to have been more attractive than a country-seat, and so he continued in the metropolis till 1815, when his health began to suffer, and travelling, even so far as Wales, could not be attempted. Confined to the house, and having a mind that, if not engaged, would feed on itself, he turned his attention to the study of the anatomy of the human body, for the purpose of tracing his disease, and aiding the doctors in attendance. It was a curious study for a man to take up in his seventy-fifth year, but one that had its charms to a philosophic mind. He had his body weighed, also the food he took, and noted what he lost; in other words, marked the progressive decay of his body. He appears to have died of abdominal dropsy. It was no wonder that he surprised his medical advisers, and elicited from the famous Dr Babington the remark, that had Huddart originally turned his attention to medicine, he would have reached the top of the profession. The disease wore him out, and on the 19th August 1816, he died calmly. His remains were interred in a vault in St Martin's Church, Westminster, on the 28th August.

Captain Huddart was tall and muscular, and in his full-grown corpulency weighed about sixteen stones. In speaking of his flute, allusion has been made to the great length of his fingers and breadth of hands; these hands he could thoroughly well apply to any purpose of life. He was evidently a man of great vigour both physically and mentally. The medallion on the tablet to his memory in Allonby Church shows the profile of a fine head, with what the phrenologists would call large perceptive and reasoning faculties; the eyebrows are marked and elevated, the eyes partly sunken, a well-developed handsome nose, with short upper-lip and large chin. The expression of Huddart's face, as shown by Petrus Fontana's chisel, is that of a man of energetic character and powers. The portrait taken by Hoffner when Huddart was sixty-one years of age, displays a mild, benign countenance, more philanthropic than philosophic in bearing. In his nature he was most humane, and ever ready to do acts of kindness and benevolence, whilst his public labours everywhere showed that the principles daily guiding him tended to the advancement of man's material interests and the safety of life. Hoffner's portrait had the advantage of being taken from the living individual, whilst the Carrara sculptor Fontana had to work from less valuable aid; both are, however, consistent with each other, and from them the personality of Huddart may be adequately recalled.

He was a thoroughly conscientious person, of high moral rectitude, and great benevolence. He was temperate and abstemious, but frequently smoked tobacco, the quantity consumed being greatly dependent on the depth of his mental calculations. His labours were heavy, and he worked whilst the day lasted, retiring to bed at ten o'clock. He cared little for dress, and as little for his bodily wants. Though much too occupied for partaking of the pleasures of society, he was cheerful and communicative to his friends, and most pleasant in relating the anecdotes and incidents of his laborious life. He had a strange partiality for cats, which he kept in great numbers in a special part of his establishment. He seems to have petted them like children, and is credited with having had the finest specimens in England.

Of his loss to science, hydrography, navigation, engineering, and shipbuilding, it is unnecessary to speak, and of the regrets felt and expressed by those who reaped his bounties, and revered his name in Cumberland, the words of the writer would be but a faint echo. The monument erected by his son in Allonby Church is very good of its kind as a sculptorial work; and every reader of his life will join in the encomium inscribed on the tablet:—"He has left a memorial of his fame far more lasting than this monument, in those numerous works of science by which he has done honour to his country, benefited commerce, and improved navigation;" and of him it may truly be said, that "the pre-eminent powers of his mind and his superior acquirements in mathematics, mechanics, and astronomy were unceasingly devoted to the services of humanity, by pointing out a more secure path in the trackless deep."

Captain Huddart may be ranked in history with Rennie and Watt,* and that class of men who have contributed to the exaltation of the national interests, and the enlargement of the boundary of civilization. Like these men, too, he went to the grave unhonoured by the State. Whilst Huddart, who had constructed docks, and harbours, and lighthouses, and surveyed dangerous coasts under tropical skies, and done great service to the maritime interests of his country, was

* Huddart was on happy terms with Watt and Rennie and other scientific men of the period. So great was James Watt's esteem for Captain Huddart, and "so anxious was he to evince it, that at a very advanced period of life, and without solicitation on the part of Huddart, he presented himself in London purposely to attend as evidence in support of a patent which had been infringed, and which was at the time under litigation."

passed by among the obscurities,—the soldier and sailor, and promoters of war, the artful diplomatist, and gold and silver sticks in waiting, had titles and orders, ribbons and pensions, showered upon them broadcast. How differently he would have fared in France, in Prussia, and Russia, where meritorious labours invariably meet with honourable acknowledgment. Pursuing science for its own sake, and its application to the exigencies of the State, it is probable that Huddart never gave courtly honours a moment's consideration. His independency of character, however, offers no ground for palliation for the official neglect of his highly valuable services. It is said that he was offered a knighthood, but if this had been so, his son would surely have mentioned it in his biography.

Milton Keynes UK
Ingram Content Group UK Ltd.
UKHW022248080124
435706UK00005B/348